A BROAD CHURCH

*This book is dedicated to my late grandfather,
Michael, for his never-ending support,
encouragement and generosity.*

Gearóid Ó Faoleán was awarded a PhD in Modern Irish History
from the University of Limerick in 2014 and currently works
in scholarly publishing in London. He is a member of the
Oral History Network of Ireland and The Irish Association
of Professional Historians.

A BROAD CHURCH

THE PROVISIONAL IRA IN THE REPUBLIC OF IRELAND, 1969–1980

Gearóid Ó Faoleán

MERRION
PRESS

First published in 2019 by
Merrion Press
An imprint of Irish Academic Press
10 George's Street
Newbridge
Co. Kildare
Ireland
www.merrionpress.ie

9781785372452 (Paper)
9781785372469 (Kindle)
9781785372476 (Epub)
9781785372483 (PDF)

British Library Cataloguing in Publication Data
An entry can be found on request

Library of Congress Cataloging in Publication Data
An entry can be found on request

Typeset in Minion Pro 11/15 pt

Cover front: Photo by PL Gould/Images/Getty Images.
Cover back: Benbulbin, Co. Sligo, 1977
(photo courtesy of An Phoblacht).

CONTENTS

Introduction   vii

1. The Split and Emergence of the Provisional Republican
   Movement, 1962–9   1

2. The Formation and Nature of Southern Provisional
   Republicanism, 1970   21

3. Campaign Escalation and Internment, 1970–1   46

4. Explosion, 1972   73

5. Stalemate and Peace Overtures, 1973–4   91

6. The Truce and Restructure, 1975–7   116

7. Assassination. Escalation? 1978–80   147

Overview   168

Acknowledgements   174

Bibliography   175

Endnotes   187

Index   228

INTRODUCTION

The 'Troubles' arose primarily out of the Northern Irish state's hostile reaction to the civil rights campaign. Secondary to this was the Irish republican perspective of 'unfinished business' with regard to the partition of the island. Accepting 1998 as the principal cessation of this period of violence, the number of deaths during the preceding thirty years stands at over 3,500.[1] This figure fails to adequately convey the intensity and extent of the conflict. Online resources such as Conflict Archive Northern Ireland (CAIN) and printed works such as *Lost Lives* personalise individual deaths. Even then, the greater number of those physically affected remains unrecorded. Twice as many civilians were shot in Derry city on Bloody Sunday as actually died, while nearly four times as many British soldiers were wounded as were killed in the 1988 IRA attack at Ballygawley, County Tyrone.[2] The effects of the violence continue to the present day. Since the signing of the Belfast or Good Friday Agreement in 1998, the number of euphemistically termed 'peace walls' has increased in the towns and cities of Northern Ireland.[3] Attempts to promote equality and the notion of a shared future have fallen disappointingly short of original intentions. The Stormont administration has not yet passed an official languages act pertaining to Irish or initiated significant reform leading to integrated education.[4] All the major unionist parties in the state legislature have consistently opposed a truth and reconciliation commission along the much-vaunted South African-model lines.[5] The legacy of the human cost is stark. Thirty-five million tranquilisers were being consumed annually at the height of the violence in a state with a population of just one and a half million. Twice as many women as men were dependant on these sedative drugs.[6] While the conflict proper may have receded, the psychological and emotional damage engendered by it did not simply disappear on 10 April 1998.

Most actions during the thirty-odd years of the 'Troubles' occurred within the Northern state. However, international actors played a crucial role which all protagonists were party to. Republican, and to a lesser extent, pro-British paramilitaries sourced armaments from abroad. British Army and IRA operations were conducted across mainland Europe. Groups and individuals in North America played a crucial role in supplying Irish republicans with money and weapons. Many of these people later helped to further the cause of peace. A great number of the ancillary events of the conflict occurred in Britain. Beginning in late 1971, England was the target of an increasing number of IRA bombings, robberies, armed robberies and gun attacks. Neither Scotland nor Wales were considered legitimate targets by the Provisional or indeed the Official republican movement.[7]

The Provisional IRA was a principal party to the conflict. Their origins lie primarily in the aftermath of sectarian pogroms in Northern Ireland during 1969, attacks which were themselves a response to the campaign of the Northern Ireland Civil Rights Association. As the largest and most active militant republican organisation, the Provisional IRA maintained a campaign against the British state for three decades. As a result of that campaign, they were responsible for over 1,500 deaths; many hundreds of these were the deaths of civilians. Their political wing, Sinn Féin, was party to the eventual peace talks in the 1990s and is now the largest nationalist party in Northern Ireland. The Provisionals drew considerable support from areas such as west Belfast, south Armagh, east Tyrone and the Catholic areas of Derry city. Their support base also stretched across the entirety of the Republic of Ireland. Irredentist sentiment in that state persevered from the time of partition. For most of its citizens, reunification remained a considered aspiration. It was embodied in the state's constitution. For republicans, militant and constitutional alike, the North represented 'unfinished business'. The escalation of events from 1968 allowed for the galvanising of public opinion in that respect. Indeed, many of the founders of the Provisional IRA were from the South. For them and others, there was undisputed continuity to the Provisionals with respect to the separatist republican tradition in Ireland.

The Republic of Ireland is perhaps the most overlooked of all the theatres of the conflict during the 'Troubles'. The largest single loss of life in one day during the conflict occurred there in May 1974, when pro-British paramilitaries exploded no-warning bombs in Dublin city and Monaghan town. Thirty-three people were killed and scores more injured.[8] The Garda investigation was haphazard and unusually inert. Files went missing, witnesses were ignored, and seemingly crucial leads were not followed up.[9] Relatives of the victims have dubbed it the 'forgotten massacre'.[10] Numerous other incidents occurred in the South over the course of the conflict. The largest ever IRA arms importation took place in Leinster, while one of the most infamous IRA attacks, the killing of Louis Mountbatten and several other civilians in 1979, occurred in Connacht. The shooting of a Special Branch detective in Munster in 1996 arguably signalled the beginning of the end of contemporary widespread IRA support.[11] The Southern state endured attacks or incursions from all parties to the conflict. Government fears that the Northern Catholic refugee crisis could lead to a Palestine–Lebanon type situation illustrates the consideration and awareness given to its effects on the state.[12] By the end of the 1970s, the Southern state had experienced bombings, kidnappings, shootings and assassinations, armed robberies, police brutality and state censorship. It was far from untouched by the 'Troubles'. Active republicans and much of the broader population in the South contributed to the Provisional IRA's campaign. Safe houses, training camps, arms supply routes and bomb factories existed in the Republic. Hundreds if not thousands of young men and women from that state joined the IRA as volunteers during the 1969–98 period. The state responded in a variety of ways to this. At the beginning of the conflict, an attitude and practice of toleration – even support – permeated official Ireland, whether the press, judiciary, security forces or elected representatives of mainstream political parties. After 1972, the bloodiest year of the conflict, this increasingly gave way to censorship, harsh legal measures and repression. Police brutality and forced confessions presented to juryless courts became part and parcel of the state's campaign to defeat the IRA. These tactics developed against a backdrop of increasing lawlessness in the Republic engendered by the Provisional IRA's actions. This included the killing of members of the state's security forces on occasion. As the 1970s progressed, militant republican support went underground. Nevertheless, emotive events such as the deaths of IRA hunger-strikers demonstrated that sympathy or support could be reactivated.

Numerous books have been published on various facets of the 'Troubles' and its organisations, though far more works exist on republican than pro-British paramilitaries. In terms of fiction, Patrick Magee identified some

480 novels directly dealing with the conflict, with over 200 more works of prose.[13] Specialist books address issues ranging from the IRA's bombing campaign in England to their links with organisations and émigrés in the USA.[14] Of the considerable body of academic literature on the IRA, much has an almost exclusively Northern focus. Only a small number of books focus on the South, and there are limitations to each. The authorised biography of Martin Ferris, for example, suffers from the subject's inability to discuss IRA activities which are not already in the public domain.[15] The book does not refrain from bluntly discussing several controversial issues, however, such as the ill-treatment of prisoners by Portlaoise prison warders. The late Sean O'Callaghan's biography suffers from the opposite issue to Ferris'. It is presented as an 'exposé' of the IRA written by a self-described former commanding officer of that organisation's Southern Command.[16] In a series of articles for *The Irish Times*, Vincent Browne exposed the lack of cohesion in O'Callaghan's accounts over the years. Some of his claims were magnified out of proportion while others simply disappeared or were eventually refuted by their own author. This includes an admission of murder.[17] Other, more revealing accounts tend to have a local focus, including histories of republicanism in Leitrim, Kildare and east Cork which also cover pre-'Troubles' periods.[18] In a study of the Republic of Ireland's internment of republicans during an earlier period, John Maguire noted that the issue represented 'an obvious research gap in the historiography of twentieth century Ireland'.[19]

This observation applies to many themes regarding militant republicanism. As noted, there are many works that focus on specific subjects. However, the history of the IRA – particularly in the Republic of Ireland – is far from definitively documented. No published study specifically details the role of the IRA in the South during the conflict. This is a major omission. One reason for this is the general lack of recognition about how integral the Southern state was to the longevity of the Provisional IRA's campaign. The island-wide organisation of the IRA ensured that the South would be exploited to the full to help prosecute the campaign in the North. Many IRA volunteers from the Republic served prison sentences in Northern Irish prisons during the conflict and vice versa.[20] To understand just how organised the Provisionals were as a cross-border organisation, the hunger-strikes in Portlaoise prison during the 1970s give some indication.

Of the dozens of participants who took part in those hunger-strikes, there were men from every province. Most of the counties on the island were represented.

In her people's history of the English Civil War, Diane Purkiss noted one historian's reference to that conflict as 'the war of the five peoples': English, Scots, Irish, Welsh and Cornish. The assertion was that each saw the war differently. Purkiss went further, arguing that one could as easily refer to it as a war of two million people, each with his or her own perspective shaped by 'national or regional identity or religious conviction or social and familial tradition or, simply, personality, luck and experience'.[21] The implication for the study of other conflicts or periods is obvious. But while Purkiss and her fellow early modern scholars are bound by written sources – albeit researching a period of increasing democratisation of the written word – those researchers who focus on the twentieth century are at a greater advantage. Historians seeking to construct a narrative 'from below' of more recent times have the benefit of being able to acquire new sources by interviewing witnesses or participants. The role of oral history in historiography remains contentious. Questions abound regarding its validity, reliability and relevance; yet the undue weight given to the written word as a reliable source is also being re-evaluated.[22] This is fed, in part, by the realisation that the written word and orality are not entirely at odds; the relationship between the two is less dichotomic than congruous. Rather than existing separately, many written sources stem from orality.[23] As this book will discuss, the enforcement of Section 31 of the Broadcasting Act in the Republic of Ireland in the early 1970s ensured that no member of Provisional Sinn Féin or the IRA could speak on television or the radio. Thus, they could not provide a counter-balance to the assertions and opinions of their opponents and detractors.[24]

As republican newspapers had a limited readership, there was a forced reliance on mainstream print media; those such as the *Irish Independent* which, in a 1983 editorial, called for Sinn Féin to be proscribed.[25] Due to decades of official and unofficial censorship, oral history must be utilised to gain a fuller understanding of the 'Troubles'. This does not mean that oral testimony should be accepted unquestioningly. As the noted social historian Alessandro Portelli warned, oral history is never objective.[26] Portelli did, however, add that non-objectivity 'of course applies to every source,

though the holiness of writing often leads us to forget it'.[27] The controversy
over Peter Hart's historiographical legacy is a reminder of how heated a
subject the role of oral sources can be regarding conflict in twentieth-
century Ireland.[28] Ideally, all transcripts and the identities of interviewees
are made public where academic research is concerned. Things are rarely
that simple, however. Many interviewees fear legal, professional or social
censure should their accounts be made public, yet these people do not
wish their experiences to pass unrecorded. Anonymity is often a necessity.
In such instances, limited access is better than no access at all.[29] The legal
implications of oral testimony for historical projects is a major concern
where the recent 'Troubles' are concerned. Much of the early research for
this book took place during the Boston College controversy.[30]

Ultimately, any work seeking to detail the 'Troubles' – or any particular
aspect of it – which does not rely to some extent on interviews with
participants, will have gaping holes in its narrative. Restrictions and caveats
may demand application and, truly, no history may ever be said to be
definitive. However, this work is not intended to be definitive, merely an
attempt to fill some of the many gaps – quite a few deliberate – in our
understanding of the 'Troubles'. In particular, it is intended to better our
understanding of the role and experiences of Southern republicanism.
These accounts are sorely lacking from nearly all published works on the
conflict.[31] The failure to sufficiently record the views of republicans has
led, for example, to largely unchallenged and erroneous assertions of their
pursuit of a romanticised Gaelic Ireland. Such misinterpretations betray
a failure to understand or acknowledge the realities in response to which
young men and women became involved in the IRA during the 1970s, or
indeed the 1990s. Academics who bought into this analysis were berated by
the US historian John Bowyer Bell in particular. As he succinctly put it, such
researchers found the empirical approach of gaining knowledge on 'terrorist'
groups to be too disconcerting, preferring instead to work from behind
the steel doors of the academy.[32] Employing Irish and British government
records, interviews and numerous other primary and secondary sources,
this book aims to provide as comprehensive a view as access currently
allows for. It documents the Provisional IRA in the Republic of Ireland
during the 1970s. It casts light on its structure and activities, its support
base and its impact on broader Southern society. This study provides the

first comprehensive historical analysis of the Provisional IRA in the context of the South. Both the history and historiography of conflict on this island during the twentieth century remain incomplete. A number of important under-researched themes are addressed here.

A Note on Terminology

Terminology is a political minefield where the politics of Ireland are concerned.[33] The local term for Derry city – 'stroke city' – is now likely to gain acceptance further afield given the appeasing title of 'Derry-Londonderry' during the 2013 UK City of Culture festivities.[34] Although recognising that specific terminology can indicate political sympathies to some, the following terms are used interchangeably throughout this work: 'the North', 'Northern Ireland' and the 'Six Counties'; 'the South', 'Republic of Ireland' and the 'Twenty-Six Counties'. Some other terms require explanation. Unless quoting from an interviewee or other source, 'murder' is not used to describe deaths that occurred during the conflict. No consensus exists on many of the deaths in this conflict. Emotive and subjective terms such as 'terrorist' are also avoided. 'IRA member', 'volunteer' and 'militant republican' are all used interchangeably for narrative purposes. The term 'republican' describes those who adhere to the 1916 Proclamation which asserted the indefeasibility of the republic and the legitimacy of using armed action to uphold it. 'Nationalists' are all those others who aspire to a united Ireland but do not necessarily support violence.

1

The Split and Emergence of the Provisional Republican Movement, 1962–9

It is widely accepted that 'Operation Harvest', the IRA's border campaign of 1956–62, was a strategic disaster. Politically as well as militarily, the republican movement offered little innovation or relevance to the realities of the period.[1] Following the campaign's abandonment, the reconstituted IRA leadership understood that a major re-evaluation was needed if the republican movement was to have any hope of survival.[2] Under new Chief-of-Staff, Cathal Goulding, this re-evaluation and concurrent reorganisation was nearly complete by the end of the 1960s. Tensions in Northern Ireland, which had been escalating throughout the decade, derailed any chance of a smooth internal revamping and presaged a split resulting in the formation of the Provisional and Official IRA and Sinn Féin. The subsequent conflict known as the 'Troubles' and several internecine republican feuds aggravated tensions, making consensus on the causes of the split unlikely. A broad generalisation is that the Provisional republican movement was a marriage of conservative or doctrinaire Southerners and militant, but apolitical, Northerners. A preponderance of media commentators sympathetic to the Official republican movement ensured that this interpretation remains popular to the present day.[3] The reality is far more nuanced. The Provisionals were a broad church, united by a common belief that military force was necessary to ensure a British withdrawal from Northern Ireland. Those who supported the Provisional IRA in the South would, in time, range from communists to orthodox militarists, cultural nationalists to apolitical young men. Shortly after their formation, Provisional Sinn Féin published a document outlining their reasons for the split entitled *Where Sinn Féin Stands*. The contents of this document offer an important insight into the motivations of Provisional Sinn Féin and can be used to test the veracity of its claims and determine who the Provisionals really were. This chapter examines the 1969–70 split with reference to this document, to help understand the motivations linked to the significant overlap in leadership of the two organisations – Sinn Féin and the IRA – and their common principles. The five headings under which the Provisionals outlined the incompatibility of recently adopted policies with orthodox republicanism were: (1) Recognition of parliaments (2) A formal alliance and extreme socialism (3) Let down of the North (4) Abolition of Stormont (5) Internal methods.[4] While the document is open to charges of self-serving bias, the Provisionals remained consistent in citing these causes.[5] For the sake of this study, an understanding of the formation of the Provisional republican movement contributes to an understanding of those who supported, assisted or joined the Provisional IRA in the Republic of Ireland during the 'Troubles'.

Quo Vadis Hibernia?

Of the reasons outlined for the split, those of 'a formal alliance' and 'extreme socialism' are perhaps the most misunderstood. In large part, this is due to subsequent black-and-white portrayals of the split. The Provisionals were painted as apolitical, sectarian and primarily fixated on militarism.[6] The formal alliance refers to the National Liberation Front (NLF). This concept was proposed in the Sinn Féin party document 'Ireland today', published in March 1969; this was a constructively intended critique of the republican movement up to that date.[7] The document chastised the republican movement for not building on the electoral victories of 1957 and noted that 'opportunities presented by mass unemployment in the fifties, and land agitation in the midlands, were passed over'.[8] A recurring theme was the need for political participation and the benefits of a leftward shift in that regard. The document recognised the republican movement as being in competition with the Southern state's Labour Party which was then attracting a 'steady trend of young radicals' that might otherwise have joined the republican movement 'were [we] more credible'.[9] In analysing political, class-based trends 'Ireland today' assigned numbers to sections of the population. Such calculated divisions represented a radical shift from Irish republican norms where support traditionally transcended class. In *Where Sinn Féin Stands*, the Provisional movement noted that the leadership of 1969 wished to cooperate with the small Dublin-based Irish Workers' Party, and subsequently with the wider labour movement. This cooperation was to be formalised into an alliance, the aforementioned NLF.[10] Concerns about this alliance were not simply or uniformly about left-wing politics, as will be discussed. For some republicans, the notion of a broad front with any organisation that did not subscribe to the fundamental principles of republicanism would inevitably lead to a dilution of the movement.[11] For others, grave concerns existed regarding the ideologues behind the push. *Where Sinn Féin Stands* claimed that a number of people joined the movement post-Operation Harvest who possessed distinctly left-wing views, but no militant republican tendency or inclination.[12] Though not actually naming individuals, subsequent accounts indicate that the document appears to direct particular ire at Anthony Coughlan and Roy Johnston, two returned émigrés who influenced the new direction.[13] That Johnston was chosen to lead the IRA's newly established Education Department – set up to deal with new recruits – was concerning, given his previous involvement in the Communist Party of Great Britain. *Where Sinn Féin Stands* says of the results of this placement that 'for four or five years many young people came into the republican movement without knowing many of the basic tenets of Irish republicanism'.[14]

Johnston's own account of the period is notable for the offhand disdain in which he held militancy.[15] Gearóid MacCárthaigh, an IRA volunteer since the 1930s, was a particular opponent of Johnston's new position. Johnston himself recalled 'a somewhat unfriendly encounter with him (MacCárthaigh) in Cork, which was set up by SmacS (Seán MacStiofáin – first Chief-of-Staff of the Provisionals), as a sort of verbal ambush'.[16] According to MacCárthaigh, the events surrounding this encounter were symptomatic of the concurrent secret machinations within the movement. Although MacCárthaigh was Commanding Officer (O/C) of the IRA in Cork city at the time, he had not been officially informed of the Army Council's decision to elect Johnston as Director of Education. Rather, he had been unofficially informed by a high-ranking dissenter.[17] According to MacCárthaigh, he and Seán MacStiofáin approached Johnston in a public house in Cork city shortly before the June 1966 Bodenstown commemoration. Producing a pistol, he gave Johnston an ultimatum to be out of the city by midnight. Following the Bodenstown commemoration, MacCárthaigh was summoned to a meeting by acting Chief-of-Staff, Seamus Costello, who demanded to know why he had threatened a member of General Headquarters (GHQ).[18] MacCárthaigh replied that he had no way of knowing Johnston was a member of GHQ as nobody had officially relayed that information to him. Following Costello's order that, in future, he was to obey any directive given to him by Johnston, MacCárthaigh resigned from the IRA.[19]

While advocates and opponents of a leftward shift in republican ideology often conflate socialism and communism, there is an important distinction to make regarding the IRA. The former had a long and fluid history in the organisation. Opposition to the latter was entirely in keeping with Irish republican ideology. Membership of the IRA was not open to members of communist organisations. This was a long-held policy that had nothing to do with opposition to leftism and everything to do with fundamentally conflicting ideologies. Communism was internationalist whereas Irish republicanism was about asserting the sovereignty of the Irish nation. Hostility to communism was therefore inevitably widespread within the movement. Despite this, Goulding did little to assuage fears among republicans regarding collaboration or potential alliances. That he reportedly travelled to Belfast several times as Chief-of-Staff to meet with Communist Party members without initiating any contact with the IRA leadership there caused real concern and anger.[20] Furthermore, leading Communist Party member Betty Sinclair was scheduled to deliver the Easter 1966 oration in Belfast until opposition to the prospect caused her to withdraw.[21] As a young man travelling to Bodenstown from Kerry in 1966, Sean O'Callaghan recalled older men muttering about the movement seemingly 'turning communist'.[22] Here, as in other circumstances, terminology and meaning can become blurred, making it difficult to discern the true motives behind various outward displays of opposition. For example, at the 1965 Sinn Féin ardfheis, there were motions from Kerry opposing support for strike action.[23] Whether this was anti-leftism or simply anti-Roy Johnstonism is difficult to determine. The previous year, Johnston had advocated for trade union infiltration by the republican movement.[24] Radical or leftist action was not un-welcome among IRA volunteers in the South during the 1960s. In 1968, for example, a large US-owned trawler was blown up by republicans while docked in Connemara. According to media reports there had been a long-running enmity between this trawler, its sister ship and the local small fishermen.[25] The IRA also became involved in an extended dispute at the Ei Electronics factory in Shannon, County Clare, burning out buses used to transport 'scab' workers from Limerick city, and reportedly issuing death threats to those who persisted in blacklegging.[26] Some social activism, such as involvement in the Dublin Housing Action Committee (DHAC) paid dividends in terms of later support while other campaigns proved more fleeting. One interviewee said of the Ei strike:

> There was a big strike. So, we started a cumann and some of the people who were on strike were in the cumann … But the Sinn Féin cumann kind of fell apart, because all the fellas that were in it during the strike, they went back to wherever they came from, and one or two of them joined the Labour Party, like [redacted]'s husband, he went and joined Labour. The rest of them, they all went off and joined something.[27]

The potential outcomes of such activity were not missed by the media. An editorial in *The Irish Times* some days after the Connemara incident warned that:

> A new force has arisen in Irish life. Hitherto the organisation confined itself to strictly political measures. Now it has entered the economic life of the country … [the state] must not allow any body to put itself above the law and to introduce the methods of old-time Chicago gangsterdom (or old-style American strike-breaking) into national economic affairs.[28]

An earlier article by the *Sunday Independent* had also warned of a 'communist revolution' within the republican movement.[29] Despite the sense of accomplishment that might accompany economic operations, unease persisted among many IRA volunteers. Ultimately, these were not actions directed at British military targets.[30] The attempted destruction of a republican monument in Cork city to be dedicated by Éamon de Valera in 1963, as well as the blowing up of Nelson's Pillar in Dublin three years later, are cited as two of the more extreme examples of expressed frustration.[31] The former of these, a protest against de Valera's presence, resulted in the death of one of those involved due to a premature explosion. The republican leadership closed Sinn Féin's Thomas Ashe hall in the city for two days to deny the use of band equipment and uniforms for the man's funeral and even dismissed several volunteers for attending the funeral.[32] By the latter half of the decade, there were undoubtedly many IRA volunteers who were disillusioned with the fruits of the movement's designated path. At issue for some rural republicans was the quality of the campaigns they were asked to partake in. Rural radicalism was traditionally tied up with land issues, specifically land-division and redistribution, a trend that continued in the South following British withdrawal.[33] It did not encompass or extend to industrial action as a result of more than just dearth of opportunities. One interviewee, a rural republican, said of it:

> They were also people who would have believed, an awful lot of people in rural Ireland believe, you know, don't hold for strikes. They're not radical in that sense even though they'd be very radical in other ways. They'd be physical force people, but they wouldn't be flying the red flag sort of people.[34]

An article sympathetic to the Goulding leadership shortly after the 1969–70 split conceded the shortcomings of the movement's rural campaigns. It noted that physical force republicanism 'has always been strongest in the countryside' and that 'it was traditionally strong amongst the small farmers and rural semi-proletariat'.[35] The article concluded that the republican movement failed to adequately tap into this potential source of support despite their own critique in 'Ireland today' and in contrast to the more successful urban campaigns: 'it provides for its rural militants only a revamped "Land League" … and a "National Water Restoration League" … Although there is a place for the small farmers in the Irish anti-imperialist struggle, Sinn Féin has yet to find any way of involving them during its present uncertain transition.'[36] The potential for channelling rural discontent into a popular struggle was a source of consternation for the Southern establishment. Allegedly, Taoiseach Jack Lynch asked newspaper editors to refrain from publishing IRA statements regarding attacks on foreign-owned ranches for fear that it would increase their credibility in rural areas if they became associated with land redistribution.[37] By not addressing rural discontent adequately and simultaneously neglecting military matters, the republican leadership undoubtedly alienated considerable existing and potential support.

Personalities and Purges

The shift to the left, as directed by the republican leadership, should not be viewed as the deciding factor in the 1969–70 split. At a micro level, much of the involvement in housing committees and co-ops – such as at Glencolmcille in County Donegal – involved those who later sided with the Provisionals.[38] Similarly, the credit union movement, a socially radical concept for contemporary Ireland, had the strong support of many traditional republicans.[39] Additionally, much of the militant rural activism was initiated by men like Seán MacStiofáin while many Northerners who would gain prominence in the Provisionals were notable leftists prior to the split.[40] One cannot simply isolate the political direction of the republican movement during the 1960s as the source of discontent. Rather, how new ideas were advocated and the personalities who led the charge must be considered. Attempts to secularise the movement provide illuminating examples. In 1966, Roy Johnston wrote an article for the *United Irishman* referring to the reciting of the rosary at republican commemorations as a 'sectarian practise'.[41] It has been noted by Ruairí Ó Brádaigh among others that recitation of the rosary was specifically for dead volunteers who had been practising Catholics.[42] The article was unsurprisingly ill-received by many republicans. Whatever the validity of Johnston's arguments, no attempts were made to win over stakeholders within the movement or effect a compromise. Speaking of the period in question, one Sinn Féin member recalled: 'a lot of it was blackguardism, you know, *even though their motives might be ok* ... Now I remember people up in Donegal talking about him [Goulding] mocking people for going to Mass and religious duties. And that didn't go down very well, you know.'[43] MacStiofáin refused to distribute the rosary edition of the *United Irishman* in south Kerry and was suspended from the movement for six months as a result.[44] Those republicans who had concerns about the direction the movement was taking were particularly attuned to the displayed arrogance. Compounding this was an apparent attempt to take control of the National Graves Association. This is an independent republican organisation composed of volunteers who maintain the graves of republican dead.[45] The organisation is strongly protective of its independence from party and leadership squabbles.

> Goulding thought he could do what he liked. I was in the National Graves Association, up in Dublin. I was on the executive. It's only a small organisation, but pretty powerful at the same time. And I remember Goulding meeting Seán Fitzpatrick – Fitzpatricks were a very respectable family and ran the National Graves – and acting the blackguard, effing and blinding about the National Graves, and he was going to decide, you know. It was, a lot of that went on, you know. And it built up over a couple of years, and it built up a lot of sourness.[46]

Such conduct was not unique to Goulding, nor can the degree to which opposition to the new direction stemmed from personalities and behaviour be overstated.[47] Seamus Costello has faced particular criticism for his behaviour during this period. His impatience and abrasiveness were key factors in alienating many republicans who might have accepted the ending of abstentionism but wished to move at a slower pace.[48] Roy Johnston has claimed that, if Costello had had his way, those who formed the Provisionals in 1969–70 would have been out of the movement by 1967.[49] Indeed, Costello was censured following the 1967 ardfheis when he illegally substituted an agreed IRA bloc-voting list for one of his own which was skewed heavily towards anti-abstentionists and those of his own faction.[50] Such antics, coupled with a public persona of hostility towards dissenters, could only polarise, enhancing the expectation of a greater internal conflict in the future. This leads to the fifth reason for the split as detailed in *Where Sinn Féin Stands*: internal methods.

At the 1968 General Army Convention, the Army Council was expanded from seven to twenty members, membership being heavily skewed in favour of Goulding loyalists.[51] At the next convention in December 1969, this grouping approved participation in the NLF. It also dropped the policy of abstentionism with regard to Stormont, Leinster House and Westminster. Following this, the IRA split. The Provisional IRA was formally established in Athlone on 22 December 1969 and the following month, in a hall rented at a Birr hotel, MacStiofáin swore in all the new O/Cs and established a command.[52] The Sinn Féin split occurred in Dublin in January 1970. At the party's ardfheis that month, Goulding had failed to achieve the required two-thirds majority vote to drop abstentionism. At this point, a delegate proposed a motion of support for the IRA's policies which now included support for parliamentarianism. This required a simple majority, which passed. Those who opposed the motion, or some of them, left the ardfheis and proceeded to a pre-booked room in another venue to establish Provisional Sinn Féin.[53] The 'internal methods' referred to in *Where Sinn Féin Stands* include the practice of ensuring voting majorities within the movement through a stage-managed expansion of the Army Council or politically through the establishment of paper cumainn.

Cruder methods also occasionally took place, such as simply ensuring that delegates who opposed the new direction did not make it to conventions. It has long been alleged that certain supporters of MacStiofáin were deliberately not picked up from designated locations to be brought to the 1969 General Army Convention. MacStiofáin states in his autobiography: 'I noticed immediately that several delegates who were strongly against the proposed changes were missing, in particular a group from Munster I had confidently expected to see there.'[54] This was confirmed by one of those Munster delegates who was due to be picked up in Mullingar by Seamus Costello. Costello simply never showed up.[55] Roy Johnston appears to confirm that it was a long-term objective of the Goulding 'faction' to co-opt members of a similar mind onto the political leadership; at one point, he wrote: 'I suspect that Goulding would have discouraged me from going [to the 1965 ardfheis] before a credible support network had been built up among the army politicisers.'[56] Those in favour of transforming the republican movement, feeling their ideology was in the ascendant, occasionally revealed themselves quite brazenly. In his account of republican politics in Cork city during this period, Jim Lane wrote:

He [Sinn Féin member, Jim Savage] reminded Gerry Higgins that the Roy Johnston that he knew back in his Cork Socialist Party days was now an important person in republican circles … It would only be a matter of time before Johnston, and others who were coming into the movement, would be running it.[57]

Where Sinn Féin Stands documents several other incidents. These include the expulsion of the north Kerry comhairle ceantair in 1966, the expulsion of the entire Cumann na mBan organisation for their objections to communist groups taking part in the 1968 Bodenstown parade, as well as the disbandment of the Sligo town Sinn Féin cumann in 1969. Like Cumann na mBan, the Sligo expulsion was due to their objection to the participation of the Connolly Youth movement in the Easter commemoration parade.[58] Regarding the 1968 Bodenstown commemoration, at the muster field, Goulding had assured the President of Cumann na mBan, Susie Mulcahy, that no communist banners would be carried at the march. According to MacCárthaigh, whose wife was marching with na mBan, Goulding had that organisation marching near the head of the parade and allowed communist banners to be carried near the rear when most of the crowd had set off. On being informed of this, the women's contingent stepped off the road en route to the graveyard. The entire organisation was subsequently expelled from the republican movement. In attempting to continue activities independently, the Cork city branch of Cumann na mBan was forcibly ejected from its room in Thomas Ashe hall by the local IRA. An armed guard was posted at the door who refused them admittance to buildings owned or used by Sinn Féin.[59] Connolly Youth again marched with the republican movement at Bodenstown in the summer of 1969.[60] Although these incidents are cited as grievances, it is important to note, as Sean Swan has, that those who constituted the new Provisional movement were not entirely removed from such activities themselves. It was MacStiofáin who had proposed the disbandment of the north Kerry cumainn (seconded by Goulding) while Seán Ó Brádaigh seconded Costello's proposal of actually expelling the comhairle ceantair of that region.[61] MacStiofáin would become the first Chief-of-Staff of the Provisional IRA while Seán Ó Brádaigh would become Provisional Sinn Féin's first Director of Publicity.[62] Also noteworthy is the aftermath to the extraordinary General Army Convention in 1965 which advocated a number of policies later adopted by the Officials. Gearóid

MacCárthaigh attempted to organise a secret meeting of delegates from all the Munster IRA units to reject these proposals – a mutiny, in essence.[63]

Demilitarisation

All the issues previously discussed polarised the republican movement. Some led to expulsions or resignations. Some policy changes would also undoubtedly have instigated a split, as with the abandonment of abstentionism. However, the nature and extent of the split were primarily down to the issue of the future of the IRA. Demilitarisation, the perception that the military side of the republican movement had been deliberately run down during the 1960s, was the key concern for most of those who would side with or subsequently join the Provisionals at the outbreak of the 'Troubles'. In the document *Where Sinn Féin Stands*, the issue is not addressed proportionate to its influence. As a political party press release, the case of armed struggle or lack thereof had to be made to the public somewhat implicitly. Reference is made to 'the escalation of events throughout the 6 Counties all through the first half of 1969' and how this was 'not foreseen', nor was the 'terror' of August 1969 'considered or provided against'.[64] An indication of the weight of this issue was given in a short section entitled 'let down of the North' in which Provisional Sinn Féin stated that they 'will not dwell at length on this matter since it is self-evident to any observer of the Northern scene. *We might add that we feel particularly strongly on this point*'.[65] In the 1973 Provisional IRA booklet, *Freedom Struggle*, there is far more emphasis given to this grievance. Specifically, the Provisionals vowed that there would never again be a repeat of the August 1969 burnings.[66]

To understand the split in its entirety and the formation of the Provisional IRA, North and South, one must consider the IRA during the 1960s: where it stood in 1969 and what it did and didn't do during the turbulent month of August of that year. In his study on the origins of the 'Troubles', Thomas Hennessey noted the logistical and financial difficulties the IRA encountered during the 1960s. Sufficient funds were not forthcoming from the USA, specifically from Clan na Gael, due to a lack of militant activity in Ireland which was usually needed to rouse fund-raising and arms purchasing in Irish-American communities.[67] The inactivity was due to the failure of Operation Harvest – caused in large part by the lack of public support for the campaign – which the leadership was attempting to turn around through involvement in popular causes. The left-wing nature of some of those causes was concerning to the more conservative supporters in Clan na Gael, all of which led to a veritable catch-22 situation for the IRA. Of the shortages, Goulding himself later remarked: 'We were broke, we hadn't got the wherewithal to buy arms.'[68] Such remarks have contributed to the popular perception of a movement afflicted by a severe arms shortage and thus reluctant, as presently constituted, to participate in military activity.

In the years following Operation Harvest, IRA training camps continued to operate in the South. One of these, discovered by the Gardaí in the Knockmealdown mountains in 1963, included men from the North.[69] The almost routine nature of these camps was noted in a 1967 Royal Ulster Constabulary (RUC) report: 'At the present time, there is no immediate indication of the I.R.A. resuming militant action against Northern Ireland. Arrangements are being made to hold the usual I.R.A. summer training camps.'[70] These camps could be of considerable size. In the years prior to the split, the IRA's Cork brigade held an annual training camp near Clonakilty involving forty volunteers, four training officers and a camp O/C.[71] No encouragement from the IRA leadership in Dublin was forthcoming, however; quite the opposite. A request to Goulding from a Southern O/C for more intensive training was allegedly met with the response 'the time has passed for skulking around barns with a Thompson'.[72] There was genuine concern that the military side of the republican movement was being permanently run down. As one former activist remarked, 'the IRA were practically, from the fifties, were practically on ceasefire, and there was no weapons, t'was all going to be talking'.[73] In his study of the republican movement during the 1960s, Sean Swan noted that there were virtually no attempts to obtain arms from 1966 right up until the August 1969 burnings.[74] The Southern government's reaction to an IRA statement in late August 1969 following these burnings was muted given that their Special Branch sources believed the IRA to be 'very weak in numbers, equipment and in leadership' at the time.[75] In effect, the government dismissed the IRA as a military threat. How much of Special Branch intelligence was based on IRA weakness in the preceding years rather than restrained potential cannot be determined. In assessing this period, some historians have charged Goulding and his supporters with deliberately running down the IRA. Matt Treacy, for example, wrote of Goulding and Seán Garland's ultimate intentions for the army: the IRA was to be reduced to a small, elite military force whose role would be to support and consolidate legally initiated revolutionary action. The IRA would cease to be an army.[76] Considering the subsequent transformation of the Official IRA to the small, deniable 'Group B', this is not a wild conclusion. According to one interviewee, the plan was to 'unilaterally disarm the IRA' and reduce its numbers to just one hundred volunteers. These men would be used 'solely for fundraising and internal security'.[77] According to this interviewee, following the split in Cork city, the local O/C Jack Lynch and Martin O'Leary (killed on an Official IRA operation in 1971), sought to recruit him into this new force while explaining its intent.[78] In the late 1960s, Goulding also reportedly told a meeting of IRA officers his plans for a 'strike force' of 120 men, stating further that 'the army should see itself as a revolutionary body and cease seeing itself as a purely military force'.[79] As Treacy has understatedly remarked, 'obviously, this was changing the nature of the IRA somewhat'.[80]

In the lead-up to 1969, IRA volunteers were involved in limited training nationwide and the General Army Convention the previous year had pledged 'maximum effort' to secure modern equipment.[81] However, this may simply have been an attempt to placate the more military-minded volunteers rather than a declaration of genuine intent. The shortage of arms in Belfast and Derry at the outbreak of violence in August, at least as far as the proto-Provisionals were concerned, was an unforgivable oversight. Goulding later claimed to be unsure about whether and, if so, where violence was going to break out. His opponents decried this as wilful blindness. Goulding had also opposed the notion of establishing defence groups in May 1969, as suggested by Ruairí Ó Brádaigh.[82] That such a suggestion could come from a Southerner three months prior to the August burnings belies protestations that the IRA in the North 'were taken by surprise' that summer.[83] According to Billy McMillen, O/C of the Belfast Brigade at the time, the movement knew in May that the arms situation in the city was chronic, stating 'the meagre armaments at our disposal were hopelessly inadequate to meet the requirements of the situation'.[84] Despite this, no attempts were made to arm units in Belfast. According to one source, the IRA had just twenty-four weapons – mostly pistols – and 120 members in the city by August 1969.[85] Estimates of IRA numbers vary wildly, however. Kevin Kelley put the number at 'no more than 50 fully fledged volunteers … and many of them were older men who could not engage in street fighting', while O'Brien wrote that several years earlier, the Belfast brigade could not even fill a mini-bus for the Easter commemorations in Dublin.[86] As to the number of weapons available, other sources seem to generally confirm what McMillen claimed; Mallie and Bishop put it at two Thompsons, one Sten gun, one Lee-Enfield and nine pistols, though also citing other sources that place the figures lower still.[87] The widely accepted notion that the IRA as an organisation was materially at a low point in 1969 is not borne out when all the evidence is compiled. As early as 1966, there were instances of arms dumps being moved to new locations with their location being revealed only to those considered loyal to Goulding.[88] This forced many Southern republicans to act on their own initiative and in breach of the IRA's constitution when the August burnings erupted in the North: 'I remember going around with a few lads all around Clare, we picked up a hundred weapons that were left in storage for years, you know. They weren't great, but we cleaned them and sent them up.'[89] At the same time, the IRA's Limerick city unit posted ten men to the border area, each armed with a rifle or submachine gun and a sidearm. These men spent a fortnight in the area before returning home having passed their weapons to local republicans. In fact, IRA volunteers from several Munster counties were ordered to the border, armed and on standby, during this period.[90]

Dumps in the Limerick area were also opened, yielding 'one hundred and fifty-odd' .303 and .22 rifles. This was not an insignificant number given the standards one might expect of the IRA of the day. Crucially, the weapons were not simply delivered up after transportation to Kildare for the next leg of their journey. Goulding and those loyal to him were not to be trusted with the weapons and thus they were to go to 'sound people' only.[91] Suspicions of the leadership were extremely high by the time of the August burnings. Months earlier, they had promised the release of Thompson submachine guns for defence purposes in the North. These had yet to arrive by the time violence erupted.[92] The wisdom of adding weapons to the highly volatile situation in Northern Ireland at this time is certainly questionable. However, broken promises and dissembling about the weaponry available would be key considerations for many republicans in the aftermath of August 1969. Furthermore, IRA volunteers in Belfast had demonstrated a willingness to go on the offensive – albeit a limited one – to deflect attention away from Derry both during the 'Battle of the Bogside', and earlier in the year following the Burntollet march.[93] With the quantity of weapons subsequently made available to beleaguered nationalists following the August burnings, claims that the IRA was inadequately supplied on a nationwide basis do not stand up to scrutiny.[94] Compounding the failure to provide arms to beleaguered nationalist communities was a bizarre publicity stunt undertaken by Goulding in a Potemkin village-style training camp in the Dublin mountains, put on for the benefit of a visiting BBC film crew.[95] The perception of the IRA having been deliberately run down, coupled with the events of August 1969, now convinced many members and former members of the republican movement that drastic measures were needed. As Jim Lane noted, 'years of running down the IRA had left its mark'.[96]

Form of the Split

When the republican movement did finally split in the winter of 1969–70, abstentionism finalised the rift; but this only. A motion to abandon the policy was proposed as early as the General Army Convention of 1965. Despite the support of Goulding and Costello, it was defeated by a large majority of the delegates.[97] Even with hindsight, it is difficult to determine when certain leadership figures were converted to support for parliamentary engagement. Tomás MacGiolla, for example, was publicly and vocally opposed to the notion of dropping abstentionism for much of the 1960s:

> I was in Dublin in the Russell cumann. And I remember coming in one night and I forget who was with me on the thing, proposed that we take our seats in the Dáil, something like that … So, it was put to the cumann and Tomás MacGiolla was there, and he read the riot act over anyone that dared suggest that we take our seats in the Dáil. Oh, the other fellow with me, he was a fella from Enniscorthy called C---

... And I remember him [MacGiolla] asking me about C---. Now I didn't know anything about C--- except he was a civil servant working in Dublin. 'Was he a Redmondite or something like that?' See I got on OK with MacGiolla always, we could be very friendly and all that. But I remember him then, and then he goes off and takes up everything, lock stock and barrel.[98]

It is simply too difficult to determine rhetoric from principle during this period without firm admission or proof of a designated point of conversion for much of the contemporary leadership. In the wake of the split, commentators were themselves divided on the relevance of abstentionism to recent events. One informed newspaper ran an article shortly afterwards entitled 'What is a republican?' with the sub-heading 'abstentionism alone not the cause of Sinn Fein split'.[99] Similarly, *New Left Review* claimed that the split 'was *expressed* chiefly over the question of abstentionism' while *The Irish Times* similarly stated: 'the split developed *ostensibly* over the issue of abstentionism from parliament...'[100] This latter article cited the differing priorities between competing factions within the republican movement, some of whom favoured 'social, civic and economic tactics' with others in favour of 'a more immediate militaristic position'.[101] As regards Northern Ireland, while many nationalists viewed Stormont with hostility, abstentionism was not an overarching principle. The Nationalist Party, the largest nationalist party in the north prior to the 'Troubles', was only selectively abstentionist; and this as a tactic rather than a principle since 1925.[102] Attitudes towards the Southern parliament were a different matter. Northern republicans were often bemused and frustrated at the hard-line attitude taken by their Southern counterparts towards recognising this institution. As one historian remarked, Southern republicans might view the existing Dáil as a usurping legislature, but to the IRA in the North, it was not so bad as Stormont: 'in Dublin the tricolour flew, and the "Soldier's Song" was sung'.[103] Such frustration existed through the decades. Liam Kelly was a Tyrone republican who led an independent militant republican group, Saor Uladh, which carried out attacks on British forces and installations during the 1950s. Kelly viewed the Northern state as illegitimate but considered abstentionism from Leinster House to be illogical and counter-productive. One of Kelly's younger comrades, who would later become a leading Provisional, was Kevin Mallon. He said of the abstentionist issue:

> Most of the people in Tyrone thought that the abstentionist policy should go. That we were hitting our heads against a stone wall. It wasn't revolutionary, or a bit flexible. We were losing members rather than gaining. The people wanted a voice, so we spoke very strongly against abstention. In 1967, Cathal Goulding, afraid of a split in the movement, refused to speak on it. But we felt that abstention was not a principle, only a tradition. The I.R.A., really, was represented by Bernadette Devlin. They got their people to vote for her. Someone who we didn't have any control over, whatsoever, and it didn't make sense to me because we could have fielded our own candidate. As a result of that, six of us resigned from Sinn Féin and the I.R.A. Public resignation. And my men were first up to the barrier on the first civil rights march. Up until the time I rejoined, I had my own organisation that fought. I was a free agent. We were independent but composed of both Officials and Provisionals. In the part of the county where I come from, where you have Officials and Provisionals, we all work together. If I go into any part of Tyrone tonight, and I need ten men to go along, five of them might be Officials.[104]

Many founding Provisionals saw abstentionism in the context of the split as being nothing other than a proxy for larger disagreements.[105] However, by taking this as a fundamental principle and insisting on its intractability, an already inevitable split could perhaps come about in a cleaner fashion than if other principal disagreements were aired. As Joe Cahill remarked: 'I don't believe that the split that took place in '69, '70 was over abstentionism ... abstentionism was used as a vehicle for the split, if you like.'[106] It is difficult to square Brian Hanley's assertion of the Provisional's formation as being 'a coming together of people primarily concerned about abstentionism' with the reality. Certainly not in reference to the younger generation.[107] Speaking of the 1950s, one interviewee said:

> I remember one time we had a [IRA] meeting ... and they got to talking about Sinn Féin and I remember me saying they didn't

recognise the state and they didn't recognise the court. Now I was only seventeen or eighteen. And none of them seemed to know anything about it, and the rest of them, they were kind of amazed like 'what?' you know. And it didn't seem to matter to them anyway, you know, I mean there was the IRA and it was for fighting ... most of the fellas in the IRA with me couldn't give a sugar whether they recognised the state or not, that is the truth of the matter. I don't think any of them cared.[108]

For others from the South who joined the IRA at the outbreak of the 'Troubles', the case seems to have remained the same: 'It wasn't a huge issue for me at the time';[109] 'I didn't know what the split in sixty-nine was about';[110] 'I didn't have a problem with it, taking the seats and all that, like';[111] 'I don't think I ever really gave it any thought from a political perspective.'[112] Guns and the organisation most willing to obtain and use them seems to have been the key issue post-August 1969. Even Belfast Official IRA leader, Billy McMillen, summed up the conflict in these early years as 'simply a fight for survival'. Máire Drumm allegedly travelled from Belfast to Dundalk at the height of the attacks desperately seeking arms for defence purposes, only to find Northern IRA leaders sitting down to a steak dinner in a local hotel.[113] That this trip was made at the behest of beleaguered nationalists ensured that her return empty-handed would become common knowledge within these same communities.[114] Similarly, when Seán Keenan travelled from Derry to Dublin during the same period to seek weapons, he complained that the IRA there told him 'to go back to Belfast and raise a large sum of money and then they would go about buying the required arms'.[115] The efforts of Keenan, Drumm and others would later be remembered by Northern nationalist communities. In their study of the period, Prince and Warner allege that the Provisionals rewrote history to have their own men being proactive during the August burnings. This interpretation fails to address the fact that the scouring teams that travelled south desperately seeking arms for defensive purposes were, in fact, mostly middle-aged men who would go on to establish the Provisionals. Similarly, this judgement fails to address the reason why upwards of eleven of the thirteen IRA units in Belfast subsequently declared for the Provisionals rather than the Officials. This included nearly all the units from the areas most affected by the August violence.[116] It appears likely that locals knew who had at least attempted to defend them during the attacks. It is also worth noting that the inner-city nationalist area of the Markets, which was untouched by the summer violence, was one of the very few places that remained a stronghold of Official republicanism following the split.[117]

***

The Provisional IRA emerged from the position to which the 1960s rethink had brought the republican movement by August 1969. Politically, a split was inevitable over abstentionism, but the extent of that split was determined by the various factors discussed in this chapter, in particular, the IRA and the situation in the North. There did exist in the republican movement a number of people for whom abstentionism was an inviolable pillar and it is likely that the majority of these people were in the South. However, had the IRA not already split the previous month, or had it been seen to do more in August 1969, the numbers that left to form Provisional Sinn Féin may well have been minimal. One study of a north Belfast community noted that when the local IRA unit was deciding what to do in the aftermath of the split, the only discussion point was the military rundown and its effect on August 1969 – not abstentionism, not democratic centralism, not extreme socialism.[118] It is highly unlikely that this discussion was unique to the area. And, for all the emphasis put on the General Army Convention in December 1969, a local, informal but seismic shift had already occurred in Belfast some months previously when Billy McKee, Seamus Twomey, the Kelly brothers, Jimmy Steele and others stormed into an IRA meeting called by O/C Billy McMillen.[119] The men who broke up McMillen's meeting in September 1969 allied themselves with those in the South who shared their horror at how events had transpired. If a split was inevitable, a substantial split only came about due to the leadership's attitude towards the military side of the movement in the preceding years.

Crucial to understanding the Provisional IRA is accepting that those who were involved from its early days cannot be pigeonholed. Few were ultimately anti-left. For example, Ó Brádaigh – among many others – regarded Goulding's social re-examination of the movement as essentially positive.[120] Many founding Provisionals were openly Marxist or otherwise militantly leftist.[121] In the wake of the split, MacGiolla confirmed that some of those who left to form the Provisionals 'fully accepted left-wing policies'.[122] The Provisionals were also not simply the Catholic guerrillas of caricature. Several founding Provisionals were virulently and vocally opposed to clericalism.[123] Nor was the movement as a whole abstentionist, in spite of what representation among the contemporary leadership would indicate, while some prominent republicans who stayed with Goulding such as Malachy McGurran remained wedded to the principle of abstentionism, belying any neat ideological delineation.[124] The split was first, and foremost, over the future role of the IRA within the republican movement. Though this issue was bound to arise eventually, immediacy derived from the events of August 1969.[125] Those events ensured the numbers and support the Provisionals were to receive from the early years of its existence. Everything else was secondary to this. The new movement emerged at the beginning of 1970, borne out of the events of the previous August and buoyed up by new recruits North and South. Composed of many different groups, they shared one core belief: that military force was necessary to smash Stormont and end British occupation of Ireland.

The Formation and Nature of Southern Provisional Republicanism, 1970

Provisional republicanism was the culmination of a painful process of change within the republican movement married to the sudden acceleration of events in the North during the summer of 1969. From its inception, the Provisional IRA drew support from veteran republicans, North and South. Credibility deriving from prior involvement was a major asset for the nascent organisation, the significance of which will be discussed. So far as veterans and their supporters were concerned, the Provisional IRA was *the* IRA, the prefix being a mere working title which stuck among the media and, in time, the broader population. The role played by older republicans in the South during the organisation's formative months was crucial. These people established or re-activated support networks and activity streams in their respective areas. They served as lodestones for a new generation of IRA volunteers. Citizens of the Republic did not stand in isolation from the process of radicalisation taking place among a considerable section of the Northern population. The television broadcasting of civil rights demonstrations in the Northern state served to inform many people in the South who had, up to that point, been largely ignorant of the realities of society across the border. In charting events from 5 October 1968 onwards in terms of an arc of escalation, radicalisation of a large section of the Southern Irish population is discernible in parallel, though perhaps not in scale, to that of Northern nationalists.[1] Incidents clearly recognised as watersheds in the conflict's early years convinced many

Southerners that support for, or involvement in, IRA activity was necessary or justifiable. The basis of republican support is discussed in this chapter, both historical and as developed contemporaneously with the conflict. An introduction to the jolting realities of the Northern state's treatment of its Catholic minority is examined from a Southern perspective. The effects of the split in the republican movement – who went where and why – is considered. Insofar as is possible, a profile of the Provisional IRA in the South is also discussed.

Theories of Support: Ideology and Legacy

The sectarian nature of the Northern state's response to the civil rights campaign appalled popular public opinion in the South. Notwithstanding the low level of liberal Protestant involvement in the civil rights movement, it was viewed as a state attack on co-religionists as well as fellow countrymen and women. Within Irish republicanism, there was traditionally a position of non-belligerence towards the Catholic Church. The extent to which this was manifest occasionally left the republican movement open to charges of sectarianism. As Seán Cronin noted of the 1920s, while the big houses of the gentry were burned, no bishop's palace was, nor were bishops threatened with death for the excommunication of republicans during the Civil War.[2] Though accurate, this risks a misunderstanding without a broader context. English – and, later, British – colonisation and plantation ensured that the largely agrarian Ireland was majority Catholic and composed largely of subsistence-level peasantry for centuries. This historically allocated class broadly along religious lines and blurred class differences within each sect. Some commentators insist that the identification of Provisional republicanism with Catholicism acted in their favour and was, in fact, intentional. In other words, the Provisionals understood that their support depended on presenting themselves as a right of centre, non-dogmatic, apolitical (in terms of social policy) Catholic organisation.[3] The IRA's role in the North and particularly Belfast was traditionally viewed by the Catholic population there as community defenders. Máire Drumm conceded this in 1973, stating that despite the non-sectarian principles of the IRA, community defence historically played a central role for the Belfast Brigade.[4] This simply reflected the realities of Belfast, where the pro-

British community had engaged in sectarian pogroms against the Catholic minority on a regular basis since the 1800s.[5] Given the primacy of Belfast in the Provisional IRA's subsequent campaign, perceptions of urban Catholic Defenderism would inevitably arise.[6]

A further theory of support for Provisional republicanism during the 'Troubles' was the broader socio-political struggle in Ireland. Arguably, however, such a subscription to social improvement merely constituted a majority subsection of a broader nationalist movement erroneously referred to as 'republicanism'.[7] One historian claimed that an echo of 'whiteboyism' lingered on in the west of Ireland well into the 1930s, noting, 'before it finally died out it was linked with the cause of a group for whom the convulsion of 1922–3 formed another martyrogenic step in the pursuit of purity, and who were to find a sempiternal holy land in the north'.[8] Following this argument, it could be said that the semi-public re-emergence of militant republicanism in areas of the South from 1970 was merely the re-awakening of a dormant, class-based sectarianism similar to that of areas in Northern Ireland. Too many exceptions exist belying this interpretation. In every generation there existed republicans who were outright hostile to the Catholic Church and would follow a line of social radicalism through James Connolly and Peadar O'Donnell.[9] As noted in the previous chapter, in the North, some of the earliest leaders of the Provisional IRA fit this profile and yet cooperated with pious comrades such as Billy McKee.[10]

Nineteenth-century British Prime Minister W.E. Gladstone is said to have remarked that, whenever a solution to the Irish question was found, the Irish secretly changed the question.[11] This was a droll remark to which the British historian Piers Brendon rebutted: 'the trouble was not that, whenever Gladstone found an answer to the Irish question, the Irish changed the question. The trouble was that the Irish question remained the same – how to get rid of the Union?'[12] Though seemingly elusive to the British, the question remained clear to generations of Irish. While many Southerners joined the republican movement in direct emotive response to contemporary events in the North, at its root was the notion of 'unfinished business'.[13] This objective provided the Provisionals – even in their capacity as individuals – with the virtue of pristine simplicity.[14] A succession of British governments was as mistaken about the potential success of the 1921 Anglo-Irish Treaty as Gladstone had been about internal appeasement two generations earlier. What changed with partition was merely terminological. From that point on, the Irish question became the 'Ulster question' and the answer remained the same. As one interviewee remarked:

> It's just a continuation, you know: United Irishmen, jumping up to *Buachaillí Bán*, the Fenians, it's like Clarke going from the Fenians to the Volunteers, the Volunteers going to the IRA in the nineteen-twenties – which are now classed as the old IRA, like, you're going onto the IRA, the officials and the Provos. And now you have another phase of republicanism ...[15]

Indeed, following the establishment of the Provisional IRA, two dozen Northern republicans travelled to Cork to meet with veteran IRA commander, Tom Barry, and essentially receive his blessing.[16] The reassurance of continuity that this meeting provided is immeasurable. For many younger activists, the involvement of republicans from previous campaigns and generations served to assure them further of the righteousness of their cause. A real danger for successive governments was that a significant percentage of their citizens viewed the conflict in much the same way.

The previous chapter detailed events prior to the split and formation of the Provisionals. While focusing on Belfast, it should be noted that the extremity of events there was not mirrored across most of Northern Ireland. The relative lack of state-supported sectarian violence in Derry city partly explains why it remained an Official IRA stronghold until that organisation's ceasefire.[17] The paucity of sectarian interfaces when compared to Belfast arguably allowed for a more left-wing republican activism to emerge in the city. Also, in contrast to Belfast, there was much less bitterness in the split. In rural areas of the North, the tradition of militant republicanism was long connected to land issues, lending a socio-agrarian angle. As Tyrone republican Tommy McKearney said of the situation in his own area pre-split: 'The elders in the community would have a very acute sense of the agrarian problem and they hated landlords. Small farmers don't necessarily become leftists but shooting landlords is a fair start, and these people utterly despised the "big house" and the aristocracy.'[18] This attitude was shared by many small farmers in the South.[19] Official and Provisional republicans in County Tyrone closely co-operated for years after the split, indicating that high political issues such as abstentionism were of little consequence. Indeed, any 'split' as happened in that county was often down to the simple matter of which organisation could guarantee 'the supply and availability of arms', with the Provisionals eventually winning out.[20] Returning to McKearney's comments on Tyrone, arguably the areas of strongest Provisional support across rural Ireland were those where socio-agrarian agitation was traditionally a much stronger force advocating change than what turned out to be largely cosmetic political reform following the 1921 Anglo-Irish Treaty. In the South, this could be identified as bastions of Fianna Fáil support in that party's early years, before the temporary shift of allegiances to Clann na Poblachta following their emergence.[21] Many of these areas saw little military activity in the Anglo-Irish War. Instead, there was considerable land agitation followed by bitter fighting during the Civil War. These were often the same areas where the pro-Treaty side had promised and then backtracked on major land reform having attained power.[22] A connection arguably exists between those areas in the South that went anti-Treaty, had the greatest record of land agitation pre- and post-independence and that also transferred their allegiances to the Provisional leadership in 1969–70.[23] Ruairí Ó Brádaigh noted that the 'core of the Provisionals were southern republicans living in the west and in rural areas' and, in his biography of Ó Brádaigh, Robert White noted Kerry and Cork as having strong Provisional support.[24] County Clare, another rural and western county, also had a long history of land agitation. It was considered dangerous for government forces up to a decade after the formation of the Free State for that reason.[25] One can include historic socio-economic conflict as a base for republican support.

Pre-'Troubles' involvement in republicanism was also often strongly familial.[26] Both grandfathers of Sinn Féin TD and former IRA volunteer, Dessie Ellis, took part in the 1916 insurrection while Cathal Goulding traced a republican pedigree back to the Fenians of the nineteenth century.[27] Ruairí Ó Brádaigh's father was an IRA volunteer during the Anglo-Irish War, whereas others could trace family involvement back even further.[28] The father of an interviewee who took part in Operation Harvest had fought in the Civil War in Wexford. This man's father continued his involvement in the republican movement after that war, clashing with Blueshirts in the 1930s and being interned the following decade.[29] Another interviewee was arrested in 1961 and brought to the local Garda station for questioning. When he refused to answer any questions, the sergeant remarked to another Garda, 'He's like his auld fella.'[30] Prior to this, the interviewee had not been aware of his father's involvement in the IRA. Many villages and townlands in the South contained families that were known locally as Sinn Féin supporters.[31] According to Ó Brádaigh, it was the presence of such families that ensured the survival of the republican movement during lull periods.[32]

An Introduction to the North

The Civil War was within living memory for a substantial proportion of the Irish population during the 1950s and '60s. With such a polarised recent past, the South's history curriculum avoided contentious positions that might exacerbate division. It did not cover the Anglo-Irish War or beyond.[33] As a consequence, many people in the Republic (at least those who did not live in proximity to the border) were ignorant of the political situation in the North with regard to gerrymandering and other nationalist grievances. This resulted in a rude awakening when the civil rights demonstrations began to gain media coverage in the Republic. In their efforts to avoid any internal controversy, the education system had instead, inadvertently ensured a sudden and jolting introduction to the realities of Northern Ireland. Despite the reluctance to deal with the post-independence period in the Southern curriculum, the fiftieth anniversary of the 1916 insurrection was one of great official celebration. Prior to this, two films, *Mise Éire* and *Saoirse*, had been produced containing archive footage from the revolutionary period – 1916 and the subsequent years – with pupils being brought from schools to view it in local cinemas. This contributed in part to 'a new run of people in the late sixties, the seventies, people who were kind of radicalised'.[34] In a broader context, civil rights demonstrations in 1968 and early 1969 tied in with a zeitgeist emerging among the youth across western Europe and the USA.[35] Many Irish republicans cite the emergence of protests in Paris, Czechoslovakia and civil rights and anti-Vietnam demonstrations in the USA as contributing to their radicalisation. Pat Magee spoke of this education prior to the outbreak of violence in the North:

> We were politicised, I mean, before I became interested in what was happening in Belfast I'd have been reading up on Vietnam and civil

rights and all those issues – the civil rights in the States – moved by that. And so, these were your frame of reference, so you were politically aware and interested, and suddenly it's on your doorstep.[36]

Southern Irishmen and women who become involved in republicanism echo this politicisation: 'All over Europe you had Czechoslovakia declaring itself free from the Soviet Union, you had the students' uprising in Paris, you had the workers, you had the civil rights here in Ireland. A lot of these people … when things didn't happen they said "well, they're not listening to us."'[37] An awareness of the success of social and political initiatives elsewhere bred a certain obstinacy as the Northern Irish civil rights movement increasingly received nothing but state oppression: 'It was becoming clear in sixty-eight, sixty-nine when the civil rights marches were going on that nothing was going to be given easily in the North.'[38] With television still relatively novel in Ireland and the state broadcaster, RTÉ, free from the later burden of censorship, the civil rights demonstrations in Derry and elsewhere were a rude awakening for many Southern Irish people. One Munster interviewee recalled:

> I knew absolutely nothing about Northern Ireland, I just knew it was there, but I hadn't a clue about the system, anything about it. And the civil rights, and all the publicity that gained about people, you know, looking for basic rights, whatever t'was; housing, jobs, and, of course, the attacks on the civil rights marches by the B Specials and that, like … I'd say a lot of lads, especially in the South, it was definitely the civil rights – and the response by the orange state to the civil rights campaign – that would have made us aware what was actually happening up there.[39]

This is echoed by another interviewee from Munster:

> I remember, for example, in 1966 they had the fiftieth anniversary of 1916. And all the respectable parties like Fianna Fáil were out there commemorating and all that and it was a big occasion. But, you know, a couple of years later you had people demanding basic civil rights in the Six Counties. Obviously, I was always interested in Irish history,

broadly nationalist in my views. But this was a sort of an eye-opener, such basic things as one-man, one-vote and an end to gerrymandering. I didn't even know what gerrymandering meant at the time.[40]

Many Northern nationalists felt a strong sense of betrayal prior to and during the conflict which permeated their views of the Republic of Ireland, its citizenry and government. Brendan Hughes would later ascribe the expectation in Belfast of 'a lot more support from the South' to his and others 'naïveté'; while Anthony McIntyre as a young man in Belfast considered the people of the South 'pretty much as traitors who had abandoned the North'.[41] Taoiseach Jack Lynch's famous 'no longer stand by' speech in August 1969 was a major contributor to this expectation and disappointment.[42] The exasperation and frustration of this perceived betrayal was forcefully brought home to Southern viewers on RTÉ's *7 Days* programme at the beginning of the conflict. Footage showed a middle-aged Belfastman pleading to the camera, stating, 'We were the prodigals left out in the Six Counties, cut off from our brothers and sisters in the South. And we want the sisters and brothers of that South, "get into the North!" Never mind Jack Lynch, get your army here!'[43]

The presence of British troops on the streets in August 1969 following the sectarian clashes partially restored order. The subsequent months are commonly referred to as the 'honeymoon period', before significant sections of the nationalist community turned against the British Army. Ed Moloney attributes the sea change in Belfast to rioting in Ballymurphy between Easter and the end of the marching season in 1970, allegedly orchestrated by Gerry Adams.[44] Other incidents such as the British Army killing of a South Armagh man in Belfast when his truck backfired, and the subsequent attempt at a cover up, further alienated nationalists.[45] In Derry, the shooting of Seamus Cusack and Desmond Beattie, alleged petrol bombers, led to a surge in support for militant republicanism.[46] In Belfast, myriad factors contributed to disillusionment. One man, who later fled to the South, was living in a predominantly Protestant area of north Belfast at the beginning of the 'Troubles':

The UVF [Ulster Volunteer Force] used to come around on a Friday ... They used to have batons and masks ... and bang the door ...

'Subscription for the UVF ... no subscription from 258'... I remember one Friday night in particular there was a Brit patrol going up ... and they should have been arresting these animals, they were armed to the teeth, and the young second lieutenant shouting over to them, 'Everything alright, lads?', 'No problem now, no problem, away you go.' They gave them leave for to do it.[47]

The flow of Catholics over the border as the violence escalated, the accounts they brought, aroused considerable anger among Southerners. As noted, the relative broadcasting freedom of RTÉ in the initial period of the conflict enabled many people in the South to get a real sense of events there:

Television was new in Ireland – and able to see what was actually happening in the streets of the Six Counties; the pogroms against nationalists and Catholic people, *refugees* coming across the border, the terrible viciousness and brutality of the six-county state, the acquiescence of this government down here towards what was happening in the Six Counties.[48]

This term 'refugees' is politically loaded in the context of Northern Ireland. Republicans often use it to define those who fled across the border because of the violence. Statistically, it was, in fact, the largest refugee crisis in western Europe since the Second World War.[49] The crisis of displaced people fleeing the violence did not simply end in August 1969 with the arrival of British soldiers. It became a seasonal issue, paralleling the climax of the unionist marching season.[50] Among those who fled over the border, there are differences in terms of defining what occurred and each individual's place within this definition. When one Belfast woman fled South with her young family, she was told by a Fine Gael councillor: 'Never let them call you a refugee. You're an evacuee because you're living in your own country.'[51]

The Geography of Provisional IRA Support in the South

Supporters of militant republicanism were present in every county and among every class in the South long prior to the outbreak of the 'Troubles'. Less certain is the validity of classifying anywhere specific as a 'republican area'. Such areas would be defined by stronger, more public support for the IRA, perhaps for Sinn Féin also, though these are not mutually inclusive. Several interviewees note the border counties as areas of strong republican support.[52] Elsewhere, events during the Civil War are often cited to account for the enduring support for militant republicanism. County Clare, for example, was long considered a hotbed of dissent in the decades prior to the 'Troubles'. Eoin O'Duffy considered it particularly notorious for 'agrarian and political crime' and it was not until a decade after the Civil War that it reverted to the general stability of other counties.[53] When conflict erupted in Northern Ireland, republicans in Clare were to the fore in providing support and assistance. The northern-based *Republican News* stated in 1971, 'Would that every county in Ireland were up to the standard of Clare [they are organising regular meetings on the RUC, on inequality, keeping up the pressure] … People here are glad to see that some of our fellow-Irishmen are interested in us.'[54] Kerry is another obvious example, given the brutal conduct of government forces there during the Civil War. In north Kerry in particular, the IRA remained very strong throughout the middle of the twentieth century.[55] Visiting that county during research for his book, *Survivors*, Uinseann MacEoin was called to the window by a Cumann na mBan veteran he was interviewing: "'Look out", she said; "as far as the eye can see, every house there has put up our men."'[56] Gearóid MacCárthaigh also spoke of the huge support there during his time on active service during the 1970s, adding that, though 'there were many people in Kerry who assisted me that winter', they couldn't be thanked by name for security reasons.[57] This summarises the difficulties in authenticating any republican areas. West Limerick lies just north of County Kerry and witnessed considerable IRA activity during the 'Troubles'. As Sinn Féin TD Maurice Quinlivan said of this part of the country:

> There's a tradition around north Kerry, west Limerick that came from the Civil War where people – a certain section of people … never bought into the state. And to them it was always a republic, not a free state, and they would have seen the outbreak of hostilities in sixty-nine as just a continuation of the struggle for independence, you know, that started in the GPO shall we say, and they would see no difference in supporting that.[58]

Another area that experienced considerable turmoil during the Civil War and remained a hotbed of IRA activity long after was County Wexford.[59] As with Clare, that county received honourable mention in *Republican News* in 1971: 'Shoulder to shoulder with our Northern Brethren is the spirit now emanating in Enniscorthy ... We are glad to have you back, now get stuck into the struggle that has already started and God speed.'[60] It was a similar case for Sligo.[61] Conversely, there were areas of relative quiet during the Civil War which maintained reputations as strong republican areas. North and east Cork and north Tipperary are but a few examples. Finglas in County Dublin is another. According to Sinn Féin TD, Des Ellis: 'There was an awful lot of support in Finglas and an awful lot of families put people up and were involved in the republican struggle.'[62] For the IRA in Connacht during the 1930s and '40s, much of the area stretching between Roscommon and the coastal Mayo towns of Newport and Westport were considered 'good republican areas'.[63] When the Provisional IRA's campaign took off, these very same areas were to the fore in terms of providing land for arms dumps and training camps.[64] As noted, the extent of support is difficult to collate or verify due to the illegal activities of those involved. In discussing the matter, one interviewee was also wary of undue attribution:

I'm not sure now ... I mean, there would be some areas where you would get a little nest of republicans we'll say, or maybe, you know, Kerry was always a strongly republican county, say. I wouldn't go as far as to say that any parts of Limerick or Clare, hardly Kerry even or Cork were sort of that strong republican ... I suppose there was individuals and there was, maybe in some areas, *a cluster of individuals* maybe whose republicanism was strong and goes right back to the nineteen-twenties.[65]

The mention of an individual or collection of individuals is significant. As J.B. Bell noted, a solid man could make a solid area.[66] Former IRA volunteers have expressed similar sentiments.[67] The presence of strong-willed and experienced veterans from previous campaigns was critical in providing leadership and continuity when the Provisional IRA emerged, men like John Hartnett of east Cork, Frank Driver of Ballymore-Eustace and Mick Lynch in the Spa area of Kerry.[68]

The Split and Membership Levels in the South

Following the split, both Official and Provisional wings of the IRA actively recruited in the South. For those who joined the IRA at this time, the choice of organisation was not always based on ideology. Those who were involved pre-1969 and who had sided with the Provisionals tended to have a sense of which side was more willing to strike at the British. In rural areas, one's choice of organisation was sometimes determined by geography. One interviewee, who joined the Official IRA in 1970, explained: 'some of the lads, some of the guys wouldn't have been far from here like, would have been involved in the fifties and that, and they were in the Official IRA, and that's who I made contact with like'.[69] County Clare appears to have largely broken with the Goulding leadership, if not instantly at least by 1972, as noted by an interviewee from that county:

> I chose to take the Provisional side. Well they were the ones mainly who were about in Clare anyway, and they were the ones who were doing anything about the situation in the North … So, and a few people I would have known, we'll say, would have been with the Provisionals, so they would have been the only people I knew in the area.[70]

By the latter half of 1971, the Provisionals were objectively the organisation of choice when it came to militarism.[71] Martin Ferris and another interviewee were two Southerners who joined the IRA in 1970, Provisional and Official respectively. Both cited the belief that what was needed was to 'hit back': 'I suppose the response was to join the IRA, you know. I suppose you thought about it a bit, you thought this was the right, you know, you thought that this was the right road; this is the only thing that they're going to understand.'[72] Similarly, Ferris described the prevailing mentality among many at the time: 'T'was quite ok for the Brits to do what they done, but it was wrong for Irish men and women to retaliate and do back, to try and confront this militarily.'[73] In Belfast and elsewhere in the North, many republicans who had dropped out of the movement in previous years became more active as the political situation deteriorated. This renewal was mirrored in the South.[74] Veterans like Gearóid MacCárthaigh had already begun to reappear on the fringes of the movement in 1969, seeking to channel the increasing dissent. Writing of this period, Eoin Ó Broin noted a critical mass in the immediate pre-split period, a coalescing of older political nationalists and younger anti-Goulding modernisers.[75] This notion of a disparate but unified 'critical mass' was also used by an interviewee when explaining the split in the context of Southern volunteers.[76]

Writing of the aftermath of the split, Hanley and Millar identified strong support for the Goulding leadership in Dublin, Wicklow, Waterford, south Kilkenny, Mayo, Cork and south Kerry. Opposition, or Provisional IRA support, was allegedly concentrated in Louth, Meath, Longford, Roscommon and north Kerry.[77] White echoes much of this geographical analysis of the Provisionals, putting their main strength (outside of Belfast) in Louth, Meath and Monaghan. Furthermore, the Provisionals had strong support in Limerick, Kerry, Cork and Waterford, and western counties in general.[78] A newspaper report shortly after the 1970 Sinn Féin ardfheis, where the political aspect of the schism was finalised, noted that 'following a meeting of the I.R.A. of Roscommon and Galway, a statement was issued that these units … pledged allegiance to the Provisional Army Council'.[79] Writing of north Kerry and the expulsion of all sections of the republican movement there in 1969, Sean Swan noted that these people did not simply go away but rather formed the raw material which would soon be used in the construction of an alternative movement.[80] Swan quoted Tony Meade, who said: 'the IRA unit in north Kerry in the mid-1960s numbered around twenty-two, with many of them being veterans of the Civil War'.[81] The value of this statement in the context of the following years must be questioned, however, as Meade ceased to have any real insight into this area following the expulsions several years earlier. According to MacCárthaigh – who certainly did have an insight, having delivered the Easter oration there in 1969 – the north Kerry unit continued to train, arm and recruit during these years in the wilderness. Subsequently, the north Kerry IRA was the first full unit to declare allegiance to the Provisional Army Council in December 1969.[82]

Research on twentieth-century Irish republicanism stresses the importance of localism and local leaders in determining the impact of a split. Indeed, if no other consensus seems to exist on analysing Irish republicanism, there is this salient truism.[83] Jim Monaghan, who was close to both Seán Garland and Seán MacStiofáin, stated his belief that 'many republicans based their decision on personal contacts and loyalties', though his own decision was based more on his perception of who was more committed to armed struggle.[84] Research for this book indicates that Munster declared primarily for the Provisionals, either over time or very soon after the split in December 1969. Cork city was the principal exception. A month after the IRA split and formation of a Provisional Army Council, a rented hall in a Birr hotel was the setting for the formal establishment of a Provisional IRA command. All O/Cs in the country who had sworn their allegiance to the organisation by that time were in attendance.[85] This had been preceded by an IRA meeting at Ballinamore, County Leitrim, several weeks earlier which Jim Lane described as 'a sounding board for what would later become the Provo movement'.[86] The Provisionals maintained the structures that had existed in the IRA since 1925: a General Army Convention composed of delegates from across the country selected an Army Executive of twelve men. This group then selected from among their own number a seven-man Army Council which in turn elected a Chief-of-Staff.[87] The Chief-of-Staff appointed a General Headquarters (GHQ), made up of several departments: quartermaster, engineering, publicity, operations, finance, intelligence, security and training. This level of continuity cemented the Provisional IRA's legitimacy. The endorsement of the organisation by Tom Maguire, the last surviving anti-Treaty member of the second Dáil, made for good publicity if not any tangible benefit. The willingness to act, coupled with the continuity of title, deed and structure, are what arguably had the most impact in strengthening the notion of legitimacy as time went on.[88] At the initial meeting in Birr, it was decided that GHQ was to remain based in Dublin away from the 'war zone'; a pragmatic decision but with significant consequences in later years. During that same meeting, the establishment of Munster Command was agreed upon. This was to remain the only separate command area in the country for many years.[89]

Prior to the split, Limerick city possessed a strong IRA and Sinn Féin organisation. Except for one man, the entire IRA structure in the city declared for the Provisionals.[90] Shortly after the split, one of these volunteers threatened young Official Fianna members from Cork who were selling their organisation's newspaper in public houses on Limerick's O'Connell Street. One interviewee was so aggravated by this that he returned to the Officials.[91] Feuds between the Officials and Provisionals rarely affected the

South.[92] There was one incident in County Clare in 1971 when a Limerick-based member of the Officials was attacked outside a public house while selling that movement's newspaper. The attack was severe enough to require his hospitalisation. The victim's assailants were all from Belfast and only a meeting of senior republicans from both factions prevented further violence. In Limerick, an arbitration system was agreed so that, regardless of what happened elsewhere between the two organisations, nobody was ever to shoot anybody else in the city.[93] In a rare large-scale clash, a street brawl erupted in Bray between Officials and Provisionals in March 1971. Seamus Costello was personally involved. A British report of the event noted: 'This is the first mention we have seen of public street fighting between the groups. According to the Gouldingites, some of the Provisionals were imported from the north for the occasion. It seems clear that the Gouldingites came prepared to provoke and the Bradyites ready to retaliate.'[94]

In Cork, there was considerable debate among republicans following the split. Discontent had been rife among elements of the IRA in the city and county for years. A well-known republican in Carrigtwohill had even gone so far as to establish an independent unit in his own area. It seemed as though the movement was regressing into a position similar to that of the early 1950s of disparate elements with no overarching hierarchy. Some senior republicans in the city sought to keep a local unified movement following the split in the hope that the two factions would reconcile their differences and reunite. However, when a meeting was held on the matter, one of the delegates repeatedly and aggressively insisted on pushing forward a motion of loyalty to Goulding to be voted on by all present.[95] According to one account the O/C, Jack Lynch, was seriously considering transferring his allegiances to the Provisionals. At the time, his son was beginning a lengthy prison sentence in England for an unofficial arms raid along with another volunteer (a campaign for their release was soon to gain prominence in Ireland).[96] The Official republican movement had been financing his legal battle and, allegedly, Lynch was threatened with this finance being pulled if he did not remain committed to the Goulding leadership.[97] This charge is hinted at in Jim Lane's memoir of the period in which he wrote:

involvement in 'unofficial action' meant automatic dismissal. However, at a later date in 1970, following the split in the Republican Movement, at a stage when opposing sides were fiercely contesting for support, the 'Official' movement suddenly remembered the two in prison and claimed them as their prisoners. The fact that Conor Lynch's father, Jack ... aligned himself to Cathal Goulding in the republican split of late 1969 had a lot to do with their reinstatement in the 'Official' movement.[98]

Following a later split in the Officials, Jack Lynch departed from the Goulding faction to help form the Irish National Liberation Army (INLA) with Seamus Costello.[99] The Cork meeting concluded with a majority of delegates declaring for the Officials.[100] Although many of these men subsequently transferred their allegiances, the Provisionals in Cork had very little support initially. Gearóid MacCárthaigh, a former O/C of the city, approached all his former staff and those volunteers known to him asking them to report for duty: 'Not very many people did. I started off with about six volunteers in Cork.'[101] Passage West, formerly attached to the city brigade but now independent, was the first Cork IRA unit to declare for the Provisionals. This was soon joined by the aforementioned Carrigtwohill unit and the entire Midleton unit.[102] North Cork was a 'dead movement' at this time and had to be rebuilt.[103] Cork as a whole remained evenly divided between Official and Provisional IRAs for some time, with a noticeable Saor Éire presence also.[104]

It is not possible to give exact numbers of IRA membership, Provisional or Official, in the Republic of Ireland at any time. However, estimates and approximations based on particular areas give some indication of activity and alignment. According to one republican based in Cork city, the approximate ratio breakdown in the Twenty-Six Counties by mid-1970 was 3:2 in favour of the Provisionals.[105] Geoffrey Bell's article on Southern involvement puts Official IRA numbers at 'around 2,750 with about two thirds of this in the Republic'.[106] This would give a figure of over 1,800. It must be noted that this figure was provided by a member of Official Sinn Féin whose interest lay in talking up numbers. J.B. Bell stated that the Provisionals' presence in Dublin 'is probably less [than the Officials]' but, in border areas, 'it is the Provisionals who are dominant'.[107] A Garda report at the beginning of 1972 noted 'only a slight increase in active membership of the I.R.A. following recent events in the north and south', but qualified this by stating that 'there was a noticeable increase in passive sympathy'.[108] This report was compiled prior to Bloody Sunday. Furthermore, it is arguably indicative only of the dearth of Garda intelligence at a time when there was widespread sympathy for both wings of the IRA. The small County Limerick village of Castleconnell in the early 1970s is a case in point: 'at one time here … there could have been six, seven lads like, in the Official IRA'.[109] Considering the size of Castleconnell, this is a significant number. Shannon town had an active unit that generally numbered in the low-twenties in the early 1970s and Limerick city had dozens actively involved in the Provisional IRA.[110] As MacCárthaigh confirmed, north Kerry never ceased functioning as a viable branch of the republican movement during its years away from the mainstream. It escalated recruitment after aligning with the Provisionals. That many people contributed to a significant extent without formally joining the IRA must also be understood. Lastly, on numbers, tallies of republicans held in prison at this time are far from being a reliable indicator of membership levels. In April 1972, for example, a report on a protest by the Provisional republican movement at conditions in Mountjoy prison mentions only thirty republicans being held; up from twenty-two a few weeks earlier.[111]

Composition of the Provisional IRA in the South

There are obvious difficulties in accurately profiling IRA membership due to the necessarily secretive nature of the organisation. However, data can be generated through analysis of contemporary media records of court appearances and a picture emerges from which some trends can be identified. For this study, a system for identifying whether individuals in court were linked to Provisional republicanism was established based on several criteria. Firstly, court type: use of the Special Criminal Court in Dublin (from 1972 onwards) and arrests being made under Section 30 of the Offences against the State Act were almost exclusively reserved for republicans.[112] Secondly, court recognition: the Official IRA and, from December 1974, the INLA recognised the Southern courts. Reports of refusal to recognise courts likely come from Provisional IRA volunteers.[113] Thirdly, conduct in court: although denying the legitimacy of the courts, Provisional IRA volunteers often disrupted their own trials in the early

1970s with shouts such as 'up the Provos'. Also, non-sworn statements were occasionally entered into court submission where the defendant was on trial for possession of guns or explosives, typically, along the lines of said weapons not intended for 'use in this state' or being 'solely for use against the British Army'.[114] The fourth consideration is representation. Following the Provisional IRA Army Council's decision to allow volunteers to recognise the courts in 1976, ex-Army Council member Myles Shevlin was the counselman most associated with Provisional IRA defendants in the South.[115] Lastly, cases which involved gelignite and other explosive possession most likely indicate Provisional IRA involvement.[116] The Official IRA largely disapproved of bombing campaigns. Its volunteers were much less likely to be caught in possession of explosives. Furthermore, their ceasefire of May 1972 put an end to most of their limited bombings (though not gun attacks). The INLA rarely acquired significant explosives.

A survey of the court appearances of 414 defendants from 1970 to 1979 provides insight into the composition of the Provisional IRA in the Republic of Ireland during this period.[117] Research for this study shows that, over a ten-year period, the ages of republican defendants in court ranged from sixteen to seventy-one years of age. The average age was 28.2. This is somewhat higher than the results of a survey conducted by Gill and Horgan on IRA volunteers in the Republic, Northern Ireland and Britain. They found an average age (for first identifiable IRA activity) of 24.99 years old.[118] Age is a contentious issue in the context of involvement in IRA activity. Following the killing of three British soldiers in March 1971, one of whom was seventeen years old, the British Army removed all of their troops under eighteen years of age from combat zones.[119] The IRA continued to allow youths in combat situations, including members of Na Fianna and Cumann Na gCáilíní (youth organisations within the republican movement).[120] That young men and women could graduate to the ranks of the IRA proper before reaching eighteen was something which their detractors used to great propaganda effect. The sensitivity felt by the Provisionals at charges of youth exploitation can be seen in one of their booklets from 1974:

> Today, the British make great propaganda out of the 'ruthless exploitation' of youth by the I.R.A. This refers to the fact that some

I.R.A. volunteers are aged only 17; the minimum age for membership of the I.R.A. The minimum recruitment age for British troops is 18 years, so there is not a great difference. Despite this, it is a fact much played upon by British newspapers and government propaganda. The English have also alleged that youths under 17 are used by the I.R.A. but have never been able to prove this.[121]

This last statement is contentious. Patrick Quinn is now acknowledged as the youngest IRA volunteer to have been killed on active service during the 'Troubles'. He was just sixteen and one month old when a mortar exploded near Pomeroy, County Tyrone, in 1973, killing him instantly.[122] Cork volunteers, Dermot Crowley and Anthony Ahern, were still not legal adults when they were sent to Tyrone on active service; in the former's case, his seventeenth birthday was still days away.[123] Media reports often emphasised the youth of volunteers in order to imply that the composition of the IRA was predominantly that of youngsters seduced by notions of martyrdom and prestige or coerced and exploited by mafia-type godfathers.[124] A significant number of republicans surveyed were in the 17–21 age bracket, broadly in common with the age of national service in many European countries. However, 17- and 18-year-olds were a minority section of this group and it is worth noting that among the Dublin Brigade staff arrested during a raid in 1974 were two 21-year-olds, a 22- and a 23-year-old.[125] As with any organisation, the Provisionals talent-spotted youth and based promotion, at least in theory, on merit. MacCárthaigh referred to the Na Fianna Éireann

TABLE 1. Ages of defendants in court cases for Provisional
IRA-related crimes

Age of defendant	1970–2	1973–5	1976–9
16–21	10	62	12
22–9	21	94	40
30–45	12	55	29
45–72	4	9	5
Total (incl. %)	47 (13.31%)	220 (62.32%)	86 (24.36%)

teenage volunteers from his brigade, the abovementioned Dermot Crowley and Anthony Ahern, as 'two of the best recruits I ever met in the army'.[126] That nearly one-third of those surveyed were thirty and older is significant. Of the older men in his category, a number of them can be identified as having been interned during Operation Harvest.

Throughout the 1970s, IRA volunteers in the age range 22–29 years were most represented in Southern court cases, at 43.9 per cent. The age ranges 16–21 and 30–45 are roughly similar, at 23.7 and 27.7 per cent, respectively. This demonstrates a remarkable diversity of age and experience. Taking the youngest age range, they represent only 11.9 per cent of those charged in the early years of the conflict. This perhaps indicates the dearth of intelligence the Southern security forces possessed on the huge influx of young people into the IRA at this time. Conversely, the oldest age range has its highest representation during this same period. These were the local lodestones who helped re-establish networks and training at the outbreak of hostilities. They would have been well-known to Gardaí already. The various age ranges are relatively stable for the 1970–2 and 1973–5 periods. A significant shift occurs in the last period. This is at least partly due to an organisational restructure in the mid-1970s.

Of those surveyed, 175 (or 42.2 per cent of the total) had their occupation, or lack thereof, noted (see Table 2). In that table, 'Unskilled' includes building and farm labourers, general tradesmen and lorry-drivers. 'Skilled' refers to occupations that required an apprenticeship and acquired skill e.g. carpenter, mechanic and electrician. It is significant that this is the largest category of occupation. An internal British Army assessment in the late 1970s noted that rank-and-file republicans were not 'merely mindless hooligans drawn from the unemployed and unemployable' and were, in fact, often skilled and resourceful participants.[127] 'Professional' is a broad term, including Gardaí, teachers, post office workers and those working within ministerial departments of the government; as well as semi-state companies such as the Electricity Supply Board (ESB). It is remarkable that this group had the third-highest representation given the job security that such employment provided as well as the ostensible establishment loyalty it implied. Those listed as unemployed comprise a significant grouping also. One cannot definitively state whether those listed as such were actually unable or unwilling to find work and how many of them had left formal

TABLE 2. Employment status of defendants in court cases for Provisional IRA-related crimes

Years	Tradesman	Unskilled	Service	Unemployed	Professional	Farmer
1970–2	11	3	3	1	6	4
1973–5	30	40	4	11	15	7
1976–9	12	9	1	6	5	7
Total (incl. %)	53 (30.28%)	52 (29.71%)	8 (4.57%)	18 (10.28%)	26 (14.85%)	18 (10.28%)

employment in order to go on full-time IRA active service (as Gearóid MacCárthaigh did in 1973).[128] Thus, when MacCárthaigh was arrested the following summer at the aforementioned Dublin Brigade staff meeting, newspapers reported that he was unemployed. Along with the eight others arrested, any such media report must take into account the fact that these people were all on full-time active service.[129] Interestingly, the 'unemployed' category rises considerably over the three time periods. While the economy of the Twenty-Six Counties declined throughout the decade, one must also consider the increased professionalism and streamlining of the Provisional IRA following the 1975 ceasefire. This meant that those captured and convicted of republican activity from 1976 onwards were much more likely to be on full-time active service and thus not in any formal employment.

In considering the geography of Southern republican involvement, Leinster is disproportionately represented due to the appearance of Dublin city in many results. Kieran Conway noted in his memoir that the Dublin Brigade of the Provisional IRA received up to 200 applications in the aftermath of Bloody Sunday.[130] Of the 414 individuals profiled for this study, 39.8 per cent (n=165) of those were based in Dublin – city and county (see Table 3). This is more than six times the number of the next largest concentration (Donegal, n=25). Finglas and the working-class suburbs of Crumlin, Coolock, Ballymun and Ballyfermot-Clondalkin are highly represented.[131] Even removing Dublin from an assessment of Leinster, the province is still the highest represented, at 21.2 per cent. Mullingar, Portlaoise and Dundalk are most identified with Provisional activists.

Munster accounted for just over one quarter of all cases analysed. This can
be divided into urban (10.1 per cent), rural (10.5 per cent) and Cork city
(5.8 per cent). That city's northside, areas such as Mayfield and Farranree,
turned up in several cases as did the southside area around Ballyphehane.
Across the county, Midleton and Passage West seem to have had significant
Provisional activity as noted earlier in this chapter. The towns of south
Tipperary had relatively high numbers of people charged with activity
relating to the Provisional IRA, as did Tralee.[132]

Given the breadth of the survey of IRA volunteers conducted by
Gill and Horgan, some results are unusual. For example, they found that
a surprisingly small number of Provisional IRA volunteers came from
Munster.[133] Indeed, that survey found no cases involving defendants from
Carlow, Clare, Kildare, Kilkenny, Offaly or Roscommon. From the research
conducted for this book, all counties were represented; Carlow was the only
exception for Southern counties. In addition, a 1974 collection of signatures
from imprisoned IRA volunteers in Portlaoise prison also included men
from Kildare, Clare and Offaly (Table 4).[134] Lastly, results diverge when
examining an urban–rural delineation. Gill and Horgan's analysis found
that Southern IRA volunteers were more likely to be based in small villages
and towns, and far less likely to be based in large towns and cities.[135] As

TABLE 3. Defendants in court cases for Provisional IRA-related crimes

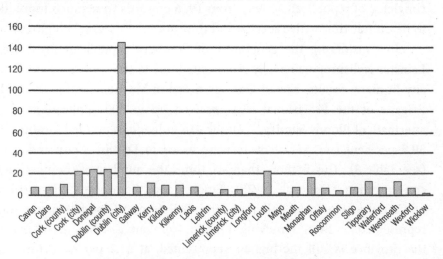

Defendants in court cases for Provisional IRA-related crimes

noted, research conducted for this book found that Dublin city accounted for 35 per cent of IRA defendants. Taken together with Limerick and Cork city, as well as Dundalk and Mullingar (two large Southern towns), the percentage rises to 47.3 per cent. Connacht had the lowest number of reported cases of Provisional IRA activity (4.8 per cent). The statistics for Connacht demonstrate the limits of court appearances as an indicator of the level of IRA activity. A significant number of IRA training camps went undiscovered in the province and a considerable support base existed in the province. While recognising such limits, the survey does serve to provide a partial profile of IRA activists; particularly the geographical spread. As one journalist remarked, it is noteworthy how much of an all-Ireland organisation the Provisionals represented during the 1970s.[136]

A British journalist in Derry city during the early 1970s was amazed to discover that the IRA in the area was 'as much a part of the community [they] lived in as the postman'.[137] In Belfast, similar popularity and sympathy existed: 'the whole community was part of it, you know, people have this idea that the IRA is something apart from the community, sort of external, parachuted in. And it wasn't, it was the community; the IRA was the community. It's not just the boys, it's not just the lads, it's the whole community'.[138] Episodes such as the Falls Curfew of July 1970, when the British Army saturated a residential area of Belfast with CS gas for several days and shot four civilians, shocked citizens of the Republic. For many, it spurred an immediate emotional response. This was galvanised by contemporary perceptions of the North as ultimately being an unresolved political situation. If the accounts of interviewees are taken as indicative of the general profile for involvement in militant republicanism, familial connections often played a significant part. Many IRA volunteers had no such historical links, however. As the 'Troubles' erupted, militant republicanism simply seemed an acceptable response to many in the South. A central theme of subsequent chapters is the degree of support the Provisional IRA benefited from during their campaign. Support and sympathy came in many forms. Collectively, it exceeded the level of overt support in the South during the 1956–62 campaign.[139] The period following August 1969 was, in a very real sense, fundamentally different from that of Operation Harvest, the latter being launched from the Republic during a dire economic crisis while the former was perceived

TABLE 4. Provisional IRA prisoners in Portlaoise prison, 1974

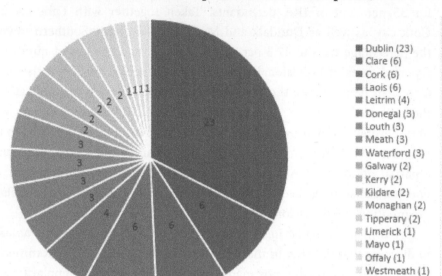

Dublin (23)
Clare (6)
Cork (6)
Laois (6)
Leitrim (4)
Donegal (3)
Louth (3)
Meath (3)
Waterford (3)
Galway (2)
Kerry (2)
Kildare (2)
Monaghan (2)
Tipperary (2)
Limerick (1)
Mayo (1)
Offaly (1)
Westmeath (1)

as a beleaguered nationalist community under attack from the forces of the state. As the situation escalated throughout 1970, republican supporters and sympathisers began to emerge or re-emerge in communities across the South.

> Obviously, there were people who you wouldn't have known were sort of republican, *they had no need to show they were republican till events kicked off again in the North* … some of them may well have been republican families, they were certainly republicans; I mean they were older and they were certainly republican before my time we'll say.[140]

These people may have had one or more motivations for their republicanism, drawn from a broad spectrum. Whether they were truly concentrated in certain areas of the Republic is open to question. The same question remains regarding their class origins. The Provisional IRA at the beginning of the 1970s appreciated and exploited the benefits of the Southern jurisdiction. The previous IRA campaign was fought predominantly along the border from bases in the Republic, with volunteers almost entirely drawn from that state. This new campaign was launched from within newly radicalised nationalist communities in Northern Ireland with volunteers drawn from local communities.[141] They were supported by Southerners. Operation Harvest-type strategies were a thing of the past. Indeed, no longer were they needed. Internment, Bloody Sunday and other British blunders ensured that support and sympathy for nationalist aspirations extended to militancy for many people. As the Provisional IRA's campaign gained momentum, the South was to serve primarily as a hinterland to the conflict, replete with training camps, bomb factories, 'fund-raising' and smuggling routes, dotted from the top of society to the bottom with sympathisers and supporters.

Campaign Escalation and Internment, 1970–1

The first British soldier killed on active service during the 'Troubles' was shot on a Belfast street by the Provisional IRA in February 1971. The weapon used to kill him was a submachine gun, almost certainly transported to Belfast from the Republic of Ireland the previous year. Following that shooting, Northern Premier Chichester-Clark declared: 'Northern Ireland is now at war with the Irish republican army Provisionals.'[1] The shooting itself came at a time of considerable Provisional IRA activity. This had been gradually escalating since the summer of 1970. Tim Pat Coogan wrote of how, during this period, an increasing number of British soldiers presented at hospitals for accidental discharge of their own weapons. He claims that a hospital orderly at the Musgrave military hospital in Lisburn revealed that there was a ward filled with gunshot victims, "'shotgun pellets, twenty-twos, everything"' – but the army was not issued with those types of guns and yet "'they were making out that it was accidental discharges that did it", said the orderly.'[2] The strategy of the Provisional IRA as determined at its foundation comprised three stages. Stage one was the recruiting and training of sufficient numbers of volunteers to defend nationalist areas of the Northern cities in time for the unionist marching season of 1970. This was to avoid a repeat of the previous summer's burnings. Stage two involved IRA volunteers being in a position to effectively retaliate against the British Army in the event of serious harassment of the nationalist population. The third and final stage of Provisional strategy was to bring the offensive to the British Army and establishment, to force them into a position where withdrawal was the only viable option. As far as the Provisional IRA was concerned, the third stage was not to be rushed. Time was needed to allow for effective training of volunteers, acquisition of arms and the winning over of local communities in the North. Republicans in the South were crucial to all three stages of this strategy. Financing, training, recruitment, arms and explosives acquisitions – all these activities were taking place from the beginning of 1970. Just how widespread such activities were is examined in this chapter. The methods and form by which the IRA reached stage three are documented. The widespread tolerance and growing governmental unease – which would take increasingly repressive forms in later years – in the South is also discussed. The introduction of internment in Northern Ireland in August 1971 was a response to the escalated IRA activity. Finally, the effects of this policy on the IRA and general population of the Republic are detailed.

Traditional Sources of Funding

The Provisional republican movement required significant funding to drive its political and military campaigns. Funding was also needed to support IRA members and their families who were affected by the conflict, through imprisonment, the necessity to go 'on the run' or death. Following the 1969/70 split, thoughts quickly turned to this issue. As a result of the burnings and population shifts of August 1969, the 'collection' re-emerged. This was largely an ad hoc practice: a table, placard and bucket on the side of a street, or even a box with a hole in the lid passed around a public house was usually enough. Supporters and sympathisers could donate as they saw fit. The sophistication varied from place to place and its informality allowed for there to be no more than an approach to a known republican and the handing over of money. Indeed, the Fianna Fáil government was criticising the illegal collection of 'defence' funds at church gates and public houses as early as August 1969.[3] An early formal initiative in this regard was Cabhair Uladh, an organisation which raised funds for families displaced by the Northern violence. This was an umbrella group comprised of Official and Provisional republicans as well as civil rights members and it was facilitated by the umbrella republican Wolfe Tone societies. Numerous local groups also sprang up such as Concern Ireland in the Shannon area of County Clare.[4] The establishment of such groups was down to the initiative of locals, usually but not always republicans. Ambiguity often existed regarding the destination of money collected. Officially, the Provisionals declared that funds were solely for 'relief', though this was itself a potentially ambiguous term.[5] Occasionally, the end point was stated explicitly, typically at times of great public anger over British Army outrages. *The Irish Times* reported on two collections, Provisional and Official, running in Cork city across the road from each other in the days immediately following the introduction of internment in 1971. Although not indicating which group garnered more money or a better reception, the report did note that the only attention either side received was positive. A Provisional spokesperson, when asked whether some of the money would go towards arms, replied: 'that's a difficult subject. People have come to us and given us money which they say they want to go towards defence purposes. In those cases, the money will be used for defence purposes.'[6] Another media report noted an incident in Dublin during this period when 'a group of men entered a public house and asked for money for "northern Provisionals". All the men were dressed in green combat jackets and behaved in a militaristic fashion.'[7] Seemingly such incidents were not uncommon. Given their overt intentions and the military paraphernalia used, the lack of any serious clampdown on the part of the authorities is quite remarkable. This is not to say that tolerance had no bounds. One interviewee served a brief sentence in prison linked to unlicensed money-collecting in the early 1970s.[8]

Another relatively small-scale method of raising funds was through newspaper sales. A journalist in late 1971 wrote that newspaper circulation for Official and Provisional wings of republicanism was 50,000 and 35,000 respectively, adding that sales of the Provisionals' *An Phoblacht* were on the rise.[9] To those interested in joining the IRA outside of Dublin, where the Sinn Féin headquarters was situated, the local paper-seller served as a useful entry point. As one Clare republican put it: 'there was some people selling papers or there was some bit of activity … there was people you could get in contact with who would have been involved or organising something and through that you'd get more and more involved, I suppose'.[10] Internally, a perception of ignominy often attached itself to newspaper selling. One interviewee recalled:

And it was stupid, going around selling papers and you'd show up and the only other one there would be [name withheld]. Myself and herself going around selling papers house to house. I didn't like that; it was a very humbling sort of a thing … Because selling papers was a very menial task and it was only, I don't want to call it the lower class, but it was only the worst kind of a job you could get, selling papers, you know.[11]

Another common source of fundraising was the sale of paper lilies at Easter time. This was a decades-old practice and often took place outside church gates. These annual campaigns traditionally had support across the political spectrum, as well as being promoted by non-political organisations such as Conradh na Gaeilge.[12] Following the cessation of Operation Harvest in 1962, and no doubt seizing upon the general weakening of overt republican sentiment in the state, Minister for Justice Charles Haughey had banned the unlicensed sale of the lily.[13] The following year a man was charged in Tralee district court with having sold lilies in defiance of the ban.[14] This signalled a concerted campaign by Southern authorities to stamp out the practice. In Waterford in 1964, two men were imprisoned for their part in a scuffle over the sale of Easter lilies where Gardaí sustained minor injuries. One subsequently went on hunger strike.[15] The previous year several men from Kildare, Meath and Laois also went on hunger strike in Mountjoy prison having been incarcerated for unlicensed selling of the lily.[16] Republican attempts to defy the ban led to violence on numerous occasions during the 1960s, including outside churches; as happened at Midleton and Aghada in County Cork in 1965 and 1966.[17] Matters came to a head on the fiftieth anniversary of the 1916 Rising with further court cases arising out of a clash in Birr, Offaly.[18] Incidents in Finglas and Cashel during these years point to a state-wide, if unofficial, republican campaign of resistance to the ban.[19] Even the Irish embassy in London was not safe. A petrol bomb attack on the building in 1966 was believed at the time to be linked to the dispute.[20] When the republican movement split in 1969/70, the Officials continued to sell lilies with an adhesive backing, a style that had been adopted some years before. The Provisionals reverted to the pin as a means of attaching the lily. From this arose the slang terms for members of the Official movement – 'sticks' or 'stickies' – and the less popular 'pinheads' for the Provisionals. Both sides continued to sell their respective lilies in the 1970s with the advantage for the customer of knowing who their money was supporting. Both sides also continued to experience Garda harassment.[21]

The Establishment of Provisional IRA Training Camps

In preparation for the launch of the IRA's Operation Harvest in 1956, the Republic of Ireland was used extensively as a training area. This training ranged from day-long drills and parades to camps which lasted up to a week.[22] Although that IRA campaign collapsed in 1962, arms training continued in the South on a much more restricted level throughout the decade. Following the formation of the Provisionals and the devising of their 'stages' strategy, IRA training was increased. Precisely where this occurred has hitherto received little attention. One reason is the lack of recorded sources due to the failure of Gardaí to discover all but a few such camps during the 'Troubles'. A 1971 article in *Fortnight* magazine briefly reported on IRA training, both Official and Provisional. In that piece, an Official IRA spokesman claimed that training was confined to each unit's own area.[23] Given most volunteers were from the North, this must be taken with a grain of salt. As one former volunteer noted, 'the South was used for that purpose because, when you think about it, it makes sense; rather than risking having a training camp in the occupied counties where you had British Army, RUC, every fucking thing on you, it made sense to bring people away to a quieter part of the country for that'.[24]

For security purposes, it is not surprising that an IRA spokesperson would seek to obfuscate the matter. Already by 1970, the Provisional IRA was organising training camps in the Republic of Ireland for volunteers from both states. One camp in County Laois risked exposure in the spring of the following year when a young man from Belfast died of a gunshot wound there; the result of an accidental discharge during a training exercise.[25] As *The Irish Times* reported: 'the government has been placed in a difficult position by the evidence, which was exposed at the weekend, of the existence of I.R.A. training bases in the Republic where Northern activists are being prepared for combat'.[26] That particular camp was established or overseen by a prominent local republican veteran who was then a member of the IRA Army Council.[27] It was never discovered. The extent of IRA training camps in the South becomes clear when one considers various accounts from volunteers. Brendan Hughes stated that 'all the training camps were across the border', while another veteran stated that hundreds of men and women travelled south in the early 1970s to receive arms training.[28] Unionist MP Herbert Whitten attacked the Dublin government later in 1971 for, as he put it, allowing their state to be used as a 'safe haven'.[29] There were more nuances at play than allowed for by Northern Irish unionists or their British counterparts. The previous year, Gardaí carried out two successful raids on training camps in north County Dublin and County Louth. At a secluded barn in Coolock, several men were arrested and firearms seized.[30] Another group of men were discovered that same day at a remote farm near Mullacrew, County Louth, where a 'significant haul of arms' was captured. *The Irish Times* noted that 'when detained they were all dressed in paramilitary uniforms'. Significantly, almost all the men were from Belfast.[31] Later, in 1972, Gardaí raided the uninhabited island of Gola off the coast of Donegal and found combat jackets and other kit. Although no arms were uncovered in the raid, it was widely believed that an IRA training camp had recently taken place there.[32]

Brian Hanley and Scott Millar have documented Official IRA intensification of training in 1971 with camps in Kerry, Louth, the Galtee Mountains, Wicklow and Galway.[33] A 1974 article on the Provisional IRA identified Monaghan, Donegal and the Dublin and Wicklow Mountains area as being the focus of their training.[34] The latter areas also catered for England-based volunteers including Frank Stagg, who travelled over for training in 1973.[35] These locations paint only a partial picture of Provisional IRA training camps in the South.[36] As Ruairí Ó Brádaigh stated, the core of the Provisionals was based in the west and in rural locations in general, being particularly strong in Cork, Kerry, Waterford and Limerick.[37] Training camps existed in all of these areas. Camps were also established in the early 1970s in counties Clare and Limerick, north and south Kerry, north and south Tipperary and County Cork. In the midlands, there were two large camps catering for Northern volunteers. The camp where Belfast volunteer Tony Henderson was killed catered principally for Derry volunteers while a camp in neighbouring Kilkenny was primarily for Belfast volunteers.[38] The likelihood of a hurried evacuation was usually a factor in decisions on establishing training camps.

As one Clare interviewee put it: 'Some counties had more than others. Clare was, up to a point, yeah, a few were held alright, but it wasn't isolated enough. There was very little done in west Clare and there's a reason for that: surrounded by water; there's only one way in or out.'[39] A camp discovered by the Gardaí at Crosshaven, County Cork, was somewhat atypical in terms of location, being situated near the coast.[40] Camps were also held in urban areas: 'Not everything is about running up and down a hill, you know, firing shots and all that. A lot of the modern warfare was about technology. So, a camp could be held right in the heart of a town and there was numbers of them held.'[41] Given the scale and regularity of IRA training during the conflict, it is remarkable how few locations were discovered by the Gardaí. The camp in Laois, for example, remained undiscovered despite a considerable Garda search of the area.[42] Often, sheer luck was a factor. For three successive years in the early 1970s, Gardaí launched raids in their search for poteen on the Clare–Limerick border. These raids netted over two thousand gallons of the spirit.[43] A nearby IRA training camp was never discovered.[44] This government campaign against illicit distillation also made Newport a high-risk area as the locals there were allegedly involved in producing poteen.[45]

Southerners primarily ran the camps. Many training officers had been talent-spotted for their knowledge of and proficiency with weapons. Others had experience from past campaigns. Volunteers who were involved in Operation Harvest often received their training from veterans of the Civil War. And many of these Harvest veterans imparted their knowledge to the Provisional IRA.[46] The continuity aspect helped solidify legitimacy among grassroots members.[47] Other training officers had received formal military training. One ex-Irish Defence Forces officer served as a long-time IRA training officer, while a former British Army paratrooper from Belfast provided specialist training in the Munster area during the 1970s and served briefly as Chief-of-Staff.[48] In an obituary for Derry republican, Phil O'Donnell, it was noted that he used his previous British Army training in his capacity as Training Officer for the IRA in Donegal. The obituary further stated that, upon his release from internment in late 1972, 'he reported back to the IRA and ran training camps across Ireland before being arrested and spending a number of years in Portlaoise jail'.[49]

Early Provisional IRA Explosives Acquisition

One result of the Provisional IRA's stages strategy was that increasing numbers of volunteers were returning to Northern Ireland newly trained but with no weapons to take up. At this early point, participation in riots was the principal outlet against the British Army. However, the Provisionals intended not simply to train recruits but also to arm them for an offensive campaign. From early 1970 onwards, Southern media reports of isolated cases of arms-related deviancy began emerging. A cache of stolen detonators recovered on wasteland, a midnight raid on an isolated gun dealer's premises, a miner arrested with several sticks of gelignite lifted from his workplace. Collating these reports reveals a concerted attempt by republicans, sympathisers and supporters to acquire arms, explosives and ammunition on a grand scale. In 1971, the Provisional IRA launched an economic bombing campaign in Northern Ireland. They were responsible for the vast majority of the more than 1,000 explosions that occurred in the North by the end of that year.[50] According to Brendan Hughes, the strategy at this early stage of the campaign 'was largely concerned with explosives' in order to wage an economic war in the towns and cities of the north.[51] To understand how the Provisional IRA was able to maintain this campaign logistically, the South as principal supplier must be acknowledged.

In March 1970, an explosion at a cottage in Carrigtwohill, County Cork, blew the kitchen door off its hinges, destroyed the kitchen itself and smashed the windows of the bedroom and nearby garage.[52] Remarkably, nobody was killed or seriously injured. While the explosion was believed to have been caused by a quantity of gelignite, it was difficult for Gardaí to confirm this as the owner of the cottage was reportedly 'reluctant to discuss the matter'.[53] Nor was he alone in his reluctance. A local man said to reporters: 'I know nothing about it – I heard no noise during the night.' This despite the fact that the blast was heard many miles away and many of the 200-odd villagers rushed to investigate that night.[54] The subsequent investigation illustrated the wide availability of commercial explosives and dearth of regulation in the state.[55] As the year progressed, a pattern emerged of Southern-manufactured gelignite being discovered in arms dumps and people's homes across Northern Ireland. In July of 1970, young boys playing in the grounds of Belfast Castle at Cavehill stumbled upon 20lbs of gelignite wrapped in plastic. According to a British Army spokesman, the explosives were hidden for further use and labelled 'Explosives, Dublin'.[56] Later that year, a Derry man linked to the Provisional IRA appeared in a Belfast court charged in connection with an explosion at an electrical transformer near the Malone Road. In the rear seat of the car linked to this operation was a 5lb gelignite bomb in a polythene packet. The label on the packet read 'Open cast gelignite, Irish Industrial Explosives Ltd., Dublin 4'.[57] There are limitations in using contemporary media reports to establish the extent to which Southern gelignite and explosive paraphernalia powered the IRA's bombing campaign. For every successful Garda, RUC or British Army seizure, much more was getting through. If the reported cases of public seizures give even a limited indication, however, the quantities involved are considerable. They range from the theft of 200lbs of gelignite from the Electricity Supply Board (ESB) construction at Turlough Hill in County Wicklow to individual cases of miners smuggling small quantities from their workplace after each shift.[58]

As well as the secondary explosive, gelignite, detonators and safety fuses were in great demand by the IRA. Mines and construction sites were exploited by Southern republicans familiar with their localities to obtain such equipment. In September 1971, 70lbs of gelignite, 100 detonators and 200 safety fuses were taken from a lime works near Kilmacow, County Kilkenny. This operation required considerable time and planning and local knowledge of the area to ensure a clean getaway. An oxy-acetylene welder was stolen from a truck repair garage nearby and used to open the steel door of the magazine.[59] For every major operation such as the above, there were numerous smaller hauls. In April 1970, for example, three men were arrested in Saggart, County Dublin, with six sticks of gelignite, six detonators and four feet of fuse wire.[60]

One man was in no doubt as to the South's contribution to the Provisional IRA's bombing campaign. Mr W. Stratton Mills, MP for Belfast North, declared in Westminster in late 1971 that the Republic of Ireland was a veritable 'holiday camp' for the IRA. He went on to claim, 'there is virtually a gelignite trail across the border', attempting to draw parallels with the famous Ho Chi Minh trail in south-east Asia.[61] The current affairs publication, *Fortnight*, also remarked on how it was a 'simple task' to obtain gelignite in Dublin.[62] Stung by such rebukes, some Southern politicians attempted to get a grip on the situation. In response to queries as to the number of gelignite raids that had taken place in the state between 1 January 1971 and 25 January 1972, Minister for Justice Des O'Malley replied that there were ten substantial raids between these dates.[63] Several months earlier, a similar question had been put to the minister, who declined to reveal the quantity of gelignite taken as this 'would only tend to reveal information regarding the disposition of stocks'.[64] In the nine cases cited between 1968 and the date of the question (4 November 1971), only one of the gelignite raids had resulted in any arrests, with cases for two men pending.[65] Antiquated civil laws undoubtedly contributed to the number of raids. As the *Irish Independent* reported, a loophole whereby any ratepayer was entitled to inspect registers and could 'demand to know the location of gelignite stocks and other explosives' was hurriedly amended by the government upon publication by that newspaper of the measure.[66] Poor security was another factor in the ease with which paramilitary organisations acquired commercial explosives. A report by Commandant McDevitt, Inspector of Explosives, following the review of a storage facility in Donegal is indicative of this laxity:

> I found the store to be insecure – the bottom hinge on the steel door was broken and only one lock was fitted. The lock was not a secure lock … old reels and fractions of explosives were lying around in the inside store and in the outer hallway … The detonators were kept in an untidy, unsafe manner – in fact when taking the explosives out, 2 detonators were found on the floor. The general condition of storage was most unsatisfactory.[67]

Following opposition outcries at the number of raids taking place, the Fianna Fáil government was compelled to take measures to control the possession of gelignite. In October 1971, following a two-week operation, gelignite which had been in farmers' and quarry owner's stores was transported to central depots. These were to be kept under army guard.[68] Approximately twelve tons of gelignite was collected during this operation, the bulk of it being brought to the premises of Irish Industrial Explosives at Enfield, County Meath, and the local magazines of Imperial Chemical Industries. This move was directly spurred by two more significant thefts of gelignite by unknown organisations. One of these raids netted one ton of the explosive, one hundred detonators and 200 safety fuses from a cement company in Drogheda.[69] Henceforth 'owners of magazines and explosives stores would be required to keep a daily record of the movement of explosives into and out of their property. Penalties for breach of the regulations would be a fine of up to £100 and/or six months imprisonment.[70] Although companies and businesses increased security for explosives storage during this period at their own expense, Commandant McDevitt did not renew licenses for many of these organisations. Even the semi-state Bord na Móna was refused a license renewal for one of their compounds in Donegal.[71]

The government went further still in January 1972 when revised arrangements were made for the storage of explosives. In this instance, all remaining gelignite was removed from existent stores nationwide.[72] These security arrangements came in the wake of two more raids by unknown men seeking explosives and assorted explosive paraphernalia. In the first instance, in Ballygawley, County Sligo, 750lbs of gelignite was taken. At a quarry near Carrickmacross, County Monaghan, 450lbs of the same along with 800 detonators were stolen. Alongside these two successful raids, Gardaí in Galway surprised several men in the early hours of 12 January trying to break into a gelignite magazine at the Irish Metal Industries in the city.[73] Shortly after the Sligo and Monaghan raids, Gardaí managed to recover what was most likely a quantity of the Ballygawley haul when they arrested two men in Sligo town. A search of the house where the men were arrested revealed 107 sticks of gelignite (about 23lbs).[74] Any government elation from that success soon soured. For the second time in less than a year, the ESB construction site at Turlough Hill, County Wicklow, was raided. This time with the loss of 1400lbs of gelignite – considerably more than the 200lbs stolen the previous year. More worryingly for the government, investigating Gardaí believed the raid to be an 'inside job'. A security guard who was tied up during the raid told how the intruders 'had a key to the heavily locked explosives' magazine ... knew exactly where to go and how to avoid [the] tight security'.[75] The theory that the raid was conducted with insider knowledge is strengthened when one considers its timing. The theft came just weeks before blasting operations were to be completed at the site, i.e. during a period when there was more explosives material on location than perhaps at any other time and immediately prior to the removal of said material.[76] Despite the efforts of the Gardaí, the gelignite was never recovered in any substantial form.

In a joint initiative in the summer of 1972, Northern and Southern explosives manufacturers introduced a means of stamping their gelignite with unique identification systems. This was to 'enable security forces on both sides of the border to trace the origin of explosives used by illegal organisations'.[77] Previously the cost of such measures was considered prohibitive. That they were introduced in the summer of 1972 indicates the ferocity of the Provisional IRA's bombing campaign and the pressure put on explosives manufacturers from British and Irish governments to address the issue.[78] Previous attempts to restrict or control commercial explosives at their source had failed. In late 1970 and early 1971, for example, government representatives had written to the two main suppliers in the Republic with suggestions on how to make their products more traceable. The first suggestion, to add 'perfume' – some kind of distinctive and strong odour – was rejected due to the inevitable objections of both production workers and users. Such 'perfumes' were both toxic and corrosive.[79] Sniffer dogs were considered ineffective, as were explosive-detection machines like those employed at Los Angeles airport (the cost of which was also prohibitive). Finally, the government suggested incorporating 'trace quantities of a radioactive material in the wrapping of the explosive. Explosives could then be detected and traced by a Geiger counter.' However, as Dr Bennett of the development division of Imperial Chemical Industries delicately pointed out, 'this could present more problems than it would solve'.[80]

Measures taken by the authorities undoubtedly impacted upon the Provisional IRA's supply capabilities. However, while gelignite was a crucial ingredient in their early bombing campaign, it was often intended only to serve as a primary explosive for a much larger concoction of homemade mixture. Gelignite and plastic explosives are considered secondary explosives in that they are not particularly sensitive to damage or heat for safety reasons and, thus, require a booster – a conventional detonator or blasting cap – to set them off. Anticipating the intensity of their forthcoming campaign, Provisional engineers had already been working on alternative sources of explosives. In particular, homemade explosives (HMEs) produced in what were rather grandiosely called by the media 'bomb factories'. Gardaí first became aware of this experimentation in late

1971 when IRA QMG, Jack McCabe, was fatally injured in a rented shed in Santry, County Dublin.[81] He had been mixing HMEs when a spark caused by the steel shovel striking the concrete floor ignited the mix. McCabe was able to impart a caution about HME preparation to his comrades before he died. IRA experimentation continued. Seán MacStiofáin wrote of how the following year, IRA engineers in the South were working very hard 'to develop alternative supplies of explosives following the crackdown on gelignite'.[82] By the spring of 1972, they were able to manufacture vast quantities of two types of explosives mix. Several months later, the British Army estimated that 90 per cent of recent bombings had involved HMEs.[83] The earliest of these crude devices were notoriously unreliable and many IRA volunteers were killed due to premature explosions. August 1972 was considered the worst month for such casualties.[84] By the following year, more than sixty volunteers had been killed in such a way.[85] This spike in 'own goal' deaths could be due to the involvement of a younger generation of volunteers following internment and Operation Motorman, a particularly bad batch of unstable explosives, British Army tampering or a combination of the three. Former IRA volunteer, Shane Paul O'Doherty, said of the period that those who volunteered to work with explosives 'were regarded either as "nutty professors" or as stark, raving mad'.[86] To minimise such casualties, the IRA centralised manufacture of the chief components. Engineers attached to each unit were required to have the necessary training to be able to complete the devices.[87]

With the crackdown on the availability of commercial explosives in the South, media reports on gelignite raids were largely replaced by reports on the discovery of fertiliser-boiling and related activities. Fertiliser-boiling was a dangerous and painstaking process. It involved the application of constant low heat to fertiliser which was spread out in a trough or similar container. The heat was applied from underneath and the fertiliser was turned regularly. This ensured the clean separation of the various constituent parts of the fertiliser to extract the ammonium nitrate, an essential ingredient in HMEs. When mixed with kerosene and sugar, it formed a substance nicknamed 'anfo', used in the major car bombs employed by the Provisional IRA during the early 1970s.[88] Boiling occurred almost exclusively in the South, particularly Munster.[89] During late summer 1972, the Southern government moved to classify nitro benzene, sodium chlorate and ammonium nitrate under the Explosives Act (1875). This was a result of intelligence received linking these products with the HMEs of the Provisional IRA. As a government report noted, 'the substance [nitro benzene] used in the dyeing industry and according to the Department of Justice is not of great importance to the industry ... Nitro-benzene is understood to have been used recently as an explosive in the Six Counties ... information as to the use of the substance only recently became available'.[90] Such was the extent of fertiliser-boiling by the Provisional IRA in Munster that Gearóid MacCárthaigh used to jokingly refer to the IRA there as *óglaigh na boilglaigh*.[91] Reportedly, IRA volunteers in Belfast began developing a rash from the near constant handling of 'anfo', such were the quantities being produced in the South.[92] Regular contact with reduced fertiliser and gelignite also led to the dreaded 'gelly head'; a pounding migraine accompanied by weeping nose and eyes.[93] This was not a new phenomenon, as one historian noted of the Anglo-Irish War: 'careless handling [of gelignite] with bare hands or letting it touch skin allowed the oily residue to absorb into the skin, causing headaches, vertigo or nausea, symptoms known to the rebels as "gelignite head"'.[94] The output of Southern 'bomb factories' determined activity in the North to a great extent. Evidently, the Northern IRA was using as much of the explosives as they could. *Hibernia* estimated that in the first six months of 1973 alone, 48,000lbs of explosives had been detonated there.[95]

Early Provisional IRA Arms Acquisitions

The bombing campaign was one prong of the IRA's military strategy. British forces were also targeted by IRA volunteers using conventional small arms. The acquisition of these weapons was another task that fell largely on Southern republicans. Seán MacStiofáin wrote in his memoir that, immediately following the split in the republican movement, three substantial arms dumps in the South were turned over to the Provisionals.[96] He noted that the South was 'scoured' thrice by the Provisionals for the campaign in the north; in August 1969, early in 1970 and in the immediate post-internment period. The prior existence of such arms dumps was crucial to the arming of the Provisional IRA. As MacStiofáin noted: 'twice we were certain that the Twenty-six counties had been scoured clean, in August 1969 and again in 1970 ... Two months after internment, the south was still producing ... This material from the south ... formed the basis of the equipment issued to the northern units.'[97] As discussed in the first chapter, scattered across various Southern arms dumps in August 1969 was a substantial quantity of arms, certainly more than is often recognised, albeit often of Second World War vintage or just beyond. A Belfast account of this period complements MacStiofáin's recollection. The official record of the Belfast Brigade's D Company noted the unit's total armament in early 1970 as one .303 rifle, one Martini-Henry rifle, one Thompson submachine gun 'and a few aged short arms'. Just a short time later, their armoury had increased to the extent that regular military operations could take place against British forces. The account continues: 'By May 1971, the "Dogs" had received their first armalites.'[98]

For this last acquisition, the IRA had looked farther afield, to the Irish-American communities in the USA. Contact was first made in the spring of 1970 when Daithi Ó Conaill travelled to New York and met veteran IRA arms smuggler, George Harrison. Through his contacts, Harrison was able to supply the Provisionals with modern rifles, primarily Belgian FNs and American M1 carbines. These weapons began to arrive in Ireland in late summer of that same year. Initially, they came in small quantities, in sea freight, false-bottomed cases or smuggled in through Shannon Airport by sympathetic Irish-American aircrews.[99] Upwards of one-quarter of the population of Shannon town during this period was from Northern Ireland. There existed considerable support for militant republicanism in the area.[100] Cork's harbours were also regularly used as ports of entry for smuggling weapons from the USA. When the QE2 docked at the customs shed in Cobh in October 1971, it was found to contain six unclaimed bags that, when opened, revealed 'rifles, guns and explosives'.[101] Conservative estimates credit George Harrison's sources as providing the Provisional IRA with 2,500 weapons and a million rounds of ammunition.[102] Ó Conaill would later visit continental Europe in an attempt to open alternative channels for arms acquisition.[103]

The South's contribution as regards locally sourced guns was also substantial, even if these weapons were not always of the best quality. From the outset, the IRA's approach in the South appeared to be a pragmatic one of beg, steal or borrow anything to send up to the border so long as it was workable. In a similar vein to gelignite raids, a pattern emerged across the state revealing a concerted effort to acquire arms. In February 1970, a raid on a Forsa Cosanta Aitiuil (FCA) barracks in Midleton, County Cork, netted a Vickers machine gun, two Bren guns and six converted .303 rifles.[104] A similar raid took place on an FCA hall in Dungarvan the previous week.[105] In April, an FCA officer was held up in his Bandon home by an armed man. This followed on from an incident where he was threatened by a car full of men a few days earlier. Gardaí believed the two incidents to be linked to an earlier occurrence when the officer disturbed a night-time 'prowler' while on guard duty at the Inniscara dam.[106] The dam stored commercial explosives. The following year at Roundwood reservoir, County Wicklow, a night-time intruder managed to beat off three FCA sentries with an iron bar before escaping.[107] Small arms were also being reported missing from regular army barracks, with one man receiving a six-month prison sentence for the theft of an FN rifle from Liam Mellows barracks in Galway city. This weapon was recovered in Donegal by Gardaí in a raid on border homes during Christmas 1971.[108]

It is difficult to determine whether any of these thefts were carried out with the connivance of soldiers. Suspicions were raised periodically as to the extent of collusion between recruits and republicans. There are accounts dating back to the 1930s of members of the Irish Defence Forces supplying the IRA with ammunition.[109] When the 1969/70 split came to Cork city, two of the first four IRA volunteers to side with the Provisionals were members of the FCA.[110] Arms dealers and private homes suffered their share of break-ins and thefts during this period. In Dublin alone, homes from Raheny to Foxrock were raided for privately owned arms. That these burglaries were often successful again indicates local knowledge. In the case of the Foxrock burglary, a substantial amount of rifle ammunition (500 rounds) was also taken.[111] Even an arms dealer on Parliament Street, a stone's throw from Dublin castle, was broken into in 1970 in the search for arms.[112] Rather than being solely the work of locals, or even Southerners, there was a degree of Northern involvement in at least some of these arms thefts. One young Derryman received a six-year sentence in December 1971 for his part in an armed raid on a gun shop in Tullamore. In that raid, sixteen firearms including rifles and twelve-bore shotguns were taken, as well as 12,000 rounds of ammunition.[113] During the trial, the approaches to the courthouse in Dublin were picketed by people with placards calling for the release of 'this Derry freedom fighter'.[114] After another raid on a midlands gun shop, this time in Kilkenny city, the Gardaí had no leads and were reduced to 'checking out statements on movement by well-known republicans in the county and the Midlands'.[115]

A highly publicised case around this period involved Captain Joe Keohane, an officer in the FCA (and formerly of the Irish Defence Forces) based at Sarsfield Barracks, Limerick City. Keohane was arrested in September 1971 for suspected misappropriation of rounds while on military manoeuvres.[116] Over the following days, several other officers in barracks across the state were closely questioned by members of G2 (Army Intelligence). Keohane was a GAA legend, a household name for many, having won his first senior all-Ireland football medal for Kerry at just seventeen. In total, the Kerry team with Keohane in the full-back position won five all-Ireland trophies. Keohane had joined the Irish Defence Forces during the Second World War while several of his Kerry teammates were interned due to suspected IRA membership.[117] Although retiring from military service in the mid-1950s and becoming a Munster organiser for Gael Linn, Keohane was called up as a front-line reserve officer when sectarian violence flared in the North during the summer of 1969. He subsequently spent time on border duties with the defence forces before returning to Munster to train FCA recruits.[118] At his court martial, Joe Keohane was charged with over a dozen counts of fraud, misapplication of rounds and acting 'to the prejudice of good order and conduct' between the dates of 1 and 20 of the previous July.[119] By arguing that his client had initially only faced four charges and that this had risen to thirteen just days before the trial, Keohane's solicitor successfully sought an adjournment for several months.[120]

The court martial finally opened on 7 March 1972, with the defendant denying all charges levelled against him.[121] The senior counsel sought by Keohane's solicitor turned out to be none other than veteran legal representative and former IRA Chief-of-Staff, Seán MacBride. Concerning the misapplication of rounds, MacBride argued that this was due to them being considered 'buckshee' ammunition. Questioning other officers and NCOs, he noted that it was common practice for officers to utilise less of the ammunition during target practice than had originally been signed for.

This was done so that extra (or 'buckshee') ammunition could be provided to members of battalion shooting teams to enable them to have additional practice prior to competitions, furthermore, that it was quite common for men who were not officially accounted for on sign-in sheets to take part in shoot-offs for this same purpose. So common was this practice of hoarding ammunition for subsequent, unregistered target practice that some witnesses refused to answer questions on it – on the advice of Commandant Jordan, judge advocate – due to the likelihood of their incriminating themselves.[122] As the *Kerryman* rather dryly noted of this practice of buckshee, 'everyone had heard of it, but it was a different question when it came to anyone who had personal experience of it'.[123]

Despite MacBride's defence, Keohane was found guilty on nine of the thirteen charges levelled against him. He was severely reprimanded, discharged and fined £25.[124] Aontacht Éireann TD Kevin Boland and former IRA Chief-of-Staff Tom Barry had provided character references during the trial.[125] Boland stated that, as a former Minister for Defence, he was well aware of the practice of accumulating surplus ammunition, adding 'it was general knowledge that the most successful shooting teams had as their training officers who were able to arrange for extra practise with live ammunition'.[126] Barry described the verdict as 'saddening'; adding 'Men of my age – I am 75 now – never thought we would see the day when the Irish Army would parade a man like this.'[127] It was Barry's opinion that Keohane had been scapegoated at a time of heightened political tension due to the ongoing and rapidly escalating conflict in the North. In a seeming snub to the Irish Defence Forces and government, several days before the trial's commencement Keohane was unanimously selected as the Kerry senior football trainer and manager.[128]

The Early Politics of the Provisional Republican Movement

While this study is primarily a history of the Provisional IRA, it is pertinent to include a summation of republican political developments in these early years. While not coterminous, the two organisations occasionally overlapped in membership. Policy was also common to both organisations, at least ostensibly. Following the split, political activity took place south of the border in tandem with military preparations. In some areas, the two were inextricably linked. In a 1973 obituary for a north Kerry republican, for example, the deceased was referred to as 'commandant I.R.A. (Provisional) and President Kerry Sinn Féin'.[129] As 1970 progressed, Sinn Féin cumainn were established across the South. While the party had set out its principal pillars in the document *Where Sinn Féin Stands*, it still required official policy. Éire Nua was the major initiative in this respect, arising out of an experimental meeting of 'Dáil Uladh' in Monaghan in the autumn of 1971. The Éire Nua document proposed a federal Ireland divided along traditional provincial lines. The Dáil Uladh conference was attended by several groupings which *Hibernia* described as 'broadly representative' (presumably of the non-unionist spectrum).[130] Similar meetings later organised in the three other provinces were attended by hundreds of delegates respectively, with representation ranging from Aontacht Éireann to the ITGWU and the Cork Communist Organisation.[131] To propagate the new policies effectively, two principal publications were established: *An Phoblacht* in the South and *Republican News* in the North, both making their first appearance in early 1970.

Opinions vary on the worth and stance of these distinct publications. Kevin Kelley wrote that the newspapers represented two broad republican blocs: *Republican News* was generally livelier and more analytical while *An Phoblacht* remained dedicated to the traditionalist outlook of Irish-Irelandism associated with the early leadership of the Provisionals.[132] Kelley's opinion is broadly shared by Ed Moloney.[133] This analysis lacks some depth, however. As early as May 1970, *An Phoblacht* was calling for republicans to become involved in trade unionism.[134] This is not untypical for the newspaper, which often blended militant trade unionism with an Irish republican slant on back-to-the-land thinking. Indeed, one former volunteer in Belfast stated that *An Phoblacht* was the less conservative of the two, stating 'the Dublin paper was always much more radical than its Belfast counterpart *Republican News*. Sean O'Bradaigh would have appreciated the value of non-military political activity but he was trumped by Twomey in 1973'.[135] The simple fact is that neither of the two principal Provisional newspapers can be ideologically, culturally or socially pigeonholed. No more can their readership.[136] Some measure of the interest in the Provisional's political position in the South can be gauged through the rapid expansion of cumainn. This is reflected in delegate attendance at ardfheiseanna: 400 in 1970, 'almost 500' in 1971 and 1,000 in 1972.[137] Linking this and the Provisional IRA, at the 1971 Bodenstown commemoration, an attendance of 10,000 was reported.[138] Ruairí Ó Brádaigh and Daithi Ó Conaill were especially eager to create a progressive socio-political policy. There were legitimate concerns that the organisation would be portrayed as mere mindless militants.[139] According to *Hibernia*, such fears of the Provisionals' total absorption in the 'military programme' existed as far back as the spring of 1970, long before their armed offensive.[140] An early Sinn Féin political campaign in the South was their opposition to the state's bid for membership of the European Economic Community (EEC). The campaign was led by Ó Conaill and, though ultimately unsuccessful, involved the printing of tens of thousands of leaflets and the canvassing of homes across the Twenty-Six Counties. The effort put into the creation and propagation of the Éire Nua policy further indicates the considerable number of serious-minded 'politicals' within the movement.

Ultimately, however, the Provisionals' military campaign during the 1970s meant that political education was never a priority. As noted, the relationship between Sinn Féin and the IRA varied widely across areas. When north Kerry split from the mainstream republican movement in the late 1960s, MacCárthaigh advised them to 'maintain their unit and cumainn', suggesting a close relationship existed between the two.[141] The situation was very different in Belfast, where Gerry Bradley stated that during the early years in particular, there was little to no overlap between Sinn Féin and the Provisional IRA in Belfast.[142] In 1973, *Hibernia* noted that in the North in general, the party was considered 'a pasture for the harmless and elderly'; the notion that involvement in Sinn Féin was considered 'draft-dodging' prevailed in many areas, North and South.[143] The attitude of the commanding officer of the Provisional IRA in Youghal during the early 1970s was probably quite common. He remarked of Sinn Féin that they were 'handy, but they're not needed'.[144] Efforts to redress this elitism took place sporadically. For example, the front page of a 1974 edition of *Republican News* stressed that membership of Sinn Féin did not equate to second-class citizenship within the republican movement.[145] It is debatable whether any such campaigns had any kind of effect, at least before the latter part of the decade.

Toleration and Expressed Sympathy in the Republic of Ireland

Several studies in recent years have considered the level of support and sympathy the Provisional IRA enjoyed during the early 'Troubles'. Some, such as Patrick Mulroe's recent book, maintain that support decreased considerably as the conflict continued.[146] Whether this occurred, or whether previously overt displays of support simply decreased, remains open to debate. Throughout the 'Troubles', opinion polls consistently showed majority support in the South for the IRA's ultimate goal of a British withdrawal and reunification, if not outright support for the organisation. This crossed political boundaries. In 1970 upwards of 70 per cent of Southerners expressed a desire for reunification, while up to one-quarter of Labour Party members were in support of providing weapons to Northern nationalists.[147] The sharp escalation of violence in the following two years seems not to have unduly affected this majority desire. Eighty per cent of people polled during the worst period of the conflict (August 1972–April 1973) still accepted the notion of reunification, 64 per cent specifically desiring it.[148] These figures formed part of a much larger social survey conducted by Fr Míchéal MacGréil, a Jesuit priest and sociologist. In total, over 2,300 Dubliners (not all of whom were born or reared in the city) were surveyed. The results are notable first and foremost for the paucity of outright condemnation of republican groups: only 3.1 and 2.1 per cent of people outright refused to have any social contact with members of the Provisional and Official IRA respectively.[149] Conversely, 41 and 38 per cent of respondents were willing to admit members of Official and Provisional Sinn Féin into their families, while 35 and 37 per cent would do the same for their respective military wings.[150]

There is no reason to assume that such levels of what could at least be classed as tolerance were atypical across the Republic. This likely represents a considerable factor in the longevity of the Provisional IRA's campaign. Who such people were is difficult to classify. J.B. Bell's description of poverty-stricken 'little old men' living in ramshackle cottages scattered across isolated rural areas is often taken to portray the stock IRA supporter.[151] Such a stereotype distorts the true picture of militant republican support. Brigid Makowski wrote in her autobiography that those who provided safe houses for the republican movement in 1969 included Fianna Fáil and Fine Gael members, as well as elected officials.[152] A similar assertion was made by IRA veteran, Gerry Kelly, many years later. He recalled how he and other escapees from the H-Blocks in 1983 stayed in the homes of prominent Fianna Fáil and Fine Gael members.[153] One former IRA volunteer remarked that Fianna Fáil cumann members in County Limerick willingly held guns for the Provisionals during the 1970s.[154] Many years later, a Fianna Fáil member from north-east County Limerick – an area that had been used as an intensive IRA training area – good-naturedly remarked to another interviewee: 'sure, we all knew what ye were at, we all knew'.[155] In later years, even supporters of the Progressive Democrats were reported to have aided the IRA.[156] Despite public disavowals and policy statements, no political party in the South had a membership or support base that rejected militant republicanism in its entirety. One cannot base assertions of IRA support on Sinn Féin's electoral performances.

Indeed, it is likely that IRA support during the 'Troubles' will never be conclusively quantified. It is possible, however, to identify the increasingly harsh measures employed by the state which made overt republican support very unwise. Such measures – to be discussed in later chapters – were markedly absent during the conflict's early years. Two incidents recounted in IRA veteran Joe Cahill's biography illustrate this. In the first instance, in the aftermath of August 1969, two Special Branchmen allegedly approached Cahill and several others collecting arms in the South. According to this account, one of the men handed his own pistol and ammunition to Cahill. In another incident, two Gardaí approached Cahill in a restaurant in Lisdoonvarna, shortly after his 1971 deportation from the USA, and donated five pounds each to the republican movement.[157] Accounts such as this are common in republican memoirs. Kieran Conway wrote that veteran Laois republican, Sean Treacy, was allowed to proceed through a Garda roadblock with an unlicensed submachine gun.[158] In Cork, Gearóid MacCárthaigh spoke of being engaged in an unlicensed collection shortly after internment. Two young Gardaí saluted him as they passed by.[159] It has also been reported that IRA prisoners in Mountjoy had access to alcohol with the knowledge of the warders, while both Martin Ferris in Kerry and Kevin Mallon in Monaghan were allowed to send out for stout, beer and cigarettes when under arrest and supposedly under interrogation.[160] In the case of Mallon, an American photographer accompanying him ('embedded' with a Tyrone active service unit) recounted a more sinister incident which occurred earlier in the day. The unit was pulled over near the border by Gardaí who informed them of an RUC patrol ahead. One Garda reportedly asked: 'Are you going to have a go at them?' to which Mallon replied: 'We might, and where would you be?' The Garda assured him, 'Well if you do, I'll be off having my tea' and waved them on.[161] One possible explanation for the co-operation of some Gardaí is geographical considerations. Based on interviews and other first-hand accounts, members of the force in cities were less likely to show sympathy or support for republicanism. An account from one interviewee is illustrative:

> The sergeant when I came here first he came to me and he said 'Whatever you're doing here, will you keep it out my way. Because if I'm sent to arrest you and I don't, I'll lose my job. And someone else will come out and do it anyway.' I was talking to an ex-detective down in the GAA club [named town] and I was down looking at a match one night, and I was saying I was talking to a few lads in Wexford and I came to the conclusion that the guards, they must have turned a blind eye to a lot of things about republicanism. And he says to me, 'Sure aren't we all republicans?' Now he was the local guard down here. Now I was always on friendly terms with him because being in the GAA. I mean you can't hardly go fight fellows that you know well.[162]

Such qualitative accounts paint a picture of the Southern republican experience which could hardly be put more comprehensively through studies or surveys. The reality was that pressure certainly existed on many Gardaí working in small, tight-knit communities. Where they lived cheek and jowl with republicans, the temptation to adapt to some sort of unofficial live-and-let-live policy, coupled perhaps with personal feelings regarding British activities in Northern Ireland were factors which should not be underestimated.[163] Thus, when the need for Garda coercion of republican suspects did arise, steps were often taken to move Gardaí around outside their usual areas or to bring suspects to remote stations for questioning.[164] A recurring theme of British assessments on cooperation between their forces and the security forces of the Irish Republic was that the Gardaí were far more cooperative than the Irish Defence Forces.[165] At best, successive generations of recruits within this force were capable of displaying a wide variety of opinions towards contemporary militant republicanism.[166] As one IRA veteran recalled of the 1940s, for example: 'the Free State soldiers used to have practise shoots at Renmore [Galway] in trenches, and we used to go out and they would leave the bullets in the trenches in rabbit holes for us. At night some of the soldiers would fling 303.'s over the wall.'[167] As will be noted in later chapters, IRA infiltration or simply republican support within the Irish Defence Forces and FCA (reserves) represented a considerable threat. While public declarations of support for militant republicanism were less common from public figures, they were not unheard of. In the autumn of 1971, the Lord Mayor of Cork sent a representative to the funeral of a Provisional IRA officer in Belfast, remarking of the scattered outrage 'What is wrong with the Provisionals anyway?'[168] Kevin Boland, who was embroiled in the Arms Crisis and later made no secret of his endorsement of the IRA, claimed in one book: 'Throughout the whole of the 1970s, I could scarcely walk a hundred yards in any town in Ireland without people stopping me to tell me they knew what I said was right but thought it better to stay on because, as they put it, "I couldn't let the Blueshirts back."'[169]

Internment in Northern Ireland

By late summer 1971, the Provisional IRA was committed to stage three of its strategy. Sufficient training and arming of volunteers allowed members to go on the offensive in Northern Ireland. Bombings and shootings escalated dramatically. In response, on 9 August, internment was implemented in the North. In the ensuing forty-eight hours, eleven nationalist civilians were shot dead by the British Army in a small area of Belfast. While it does not hold so strong a place in collective memory as Bloody Sunday, the shootings caused immense anger at the time. One Southerner who subsequently joined the IRA remarked: 'In many ways it was much worse than Bloody Sunday because, Bloody Sunday, it all happened in a fairly concentrated period; they just opened fire on a civil rights march. But in the Ballymurphy one … they shot people in ones and twos in different places all over the streets.'[170] As an immediate response to the implementation of internment, all Garda holiday leave was cancelled and all Gardaí then on holiday, whether at home or abroad, were ordered to report back for duty.[171] Internment had a major impact on public and private opinion in the South. Once again, refugees fled across the border. Their accounts, the blatantly partisan nature of the round-up and the signal it gave to loyalist paramilitaries to engage in another major round of pogroms, inflamed public opinion.[172] For republicans, it was a call to action. An Official IRA training camp that was taking place in south Kerry was broken up upon hearing the news: 'When internment came in I was actually on a training camp in mountains in Kerry. That's with the Official IRA. And there was twenty-odd in that camp, and that camp was broke up because there was weapons on it and they thought they were probably needed.'[173] Maria McGuire wrote that crowds of people appeared at the Dublin Sinn Féin offices on Kevin Street seeking to join the Provisional IRA.[174] There were other surprises in store: 'a wizened old man came into Kevin Street and produced various parts of a rusty Thompson gun out of a brown paper parcel. "'Tis a present from the boys in Cork," he announced'; he was one of J.B. Bell's old men 'with a bit of gear in the car and no contact'.[175] A protest rally called by Provisional Sinn Féin outside the General Post Office (GPO) on O'Connell Street several days later was attended by a crowd of at least 2,000.[176]

One former IRA volunteer who was in England on a personal visit when internment was introduced returned to Cork to discover that members of his unit had already been sent up to the border at the request of the Chief-of-Staff.[177] This account tallies with that of Gearóid MacCárthaigh. He recalled that MacStiofáin ordered him to send two of his 'best volunteers', armed, up to the border at this time. The two young men, Dermot Crowley and Donal McCarthy, were provided with revolvers, which was all the unit in the city had at the time.[178] The introduction of internment reportedly led to an 'influx of recruits' into the Provisional IRA (and also the Officials) in Cork city.[179] The situation was similar in Limerick, where one interviewee who joined the Provisionals just prior to internment noted that it had a significant effect on recruitment, adding that upwards of fifty men from the city area were involved in the Provisional IRA during this period.[180] As noted, the influx of displaced persons into the South following internment contributed to the atmosphere of outrage as first-hand accounts from Northerners emerged of brutal interrogation techniques. Such was the level of public anger that one newspaper reported on how, in Cork city 'the

Officials, who have appealed publicly for arms and for new recruits to the I.R.A., are collecting funds outside the Guinness office ... at another table with a placard box beside it saying "People of Ireland join the I.R.A."[181] Earlier that week, senior Official IRA man, Jack Lynch, exhorted a crowd one thousand-strong: 'I ask you anyone that wants to help to give us guns.'[182]

As with August 1969, there were localised outbreaks of both sectarian and anti-British attacks and intimidations following internment. In Gorey, County Wexford, several Protestant-owned shops were singled out for vandalism, with 'I.R.A.' being daubed on doors, walls and windows. Local branches of both Sinn Féin organisations condemned the incident.[183] In April of that year, the British Ambassador to the Republic protested the destruction of a Royal Navy survey party launch and dinghy. Both crafts had been based at Baltimore, County Cork, at the request of the Irish government and were destroyed by explosives.[184] Several months later, a number of British-linked buildings were destroyed or attacked: a bomb was planted at the Department of Health and Social Security Offices in Cork city, and a fire bomb was pushed through the letterbox of the British Legion in Dublin. The former attack was claimed by the Official IRA. That organisation published a statement alleging that the building was targeted due to British Army officers using the office facilities and personnel to contact and entice Irishmen who had deserted from the British Army to re-join. The British Embassy in Dublin dismissed this allegation as 'patently ridiculous', adding 'DHSS, Cork, is essentially a welfare office. It deals mainly with claims of war pensioners and their widows, and to a lesser extent with medical boarding in connection with industrial injury awards.'[185] That same month, the British Legion hall in Charleville, County Cork, was destroyed by a fire believed to have been maliciously started.[186] In October 1971, the Cork-based Saor Éire blew up a British ship docked in the city's port.[187] According to a statement released by the group:

> The reason [for the attack] being to draw to the attention of the people of Cork the scandalous situation as allowed by the Free State authorities to exist in our city. This is to stamp out prostitution and the allowing of young girls on board these foreign ships. This is the start of a campaign against prostitution and drug traffic. Police can raid homes, arrest men, but they cannot go on board ships to rescue 14- or 15-year-old girls.[188]

One interviewee backed up this statement. He claimed that, given the poverty in the locality, young girls were indeed employed as prostitutes along the harbour. Due to their taking such a forthright stance against this activity, Saor Éire subsequently benefited from a level of support in the city which belied the numbers involved in that organisation.[189] In assessing republican attacks on British-linked properties post-internment, the British government concluded that they would not continue with equal vigour. The Provisional IRA, which by this time was clearly emerging as numerically superior, was viewed as 'less theoretical; they prefer the simpler doctrine that shooting enough British soldiers means that all will be vouchsafed unto you, so by definition they are less inclined to action in the South'.[190] No major preventative measures were introduced.

***

With the introduction of internment, the conflict escalated sharply in Northern Ireland. During this time, the Republic continued to play a key role for the IRA. Indeed, recruitment, training, arming and funding in the South fuelled the escalation. If Belfast was the 'cockpit' of the Provisional's campaign during these years, the South was certainly the engine. New recruits from Fermanagh, Tyrone and Dublin were travelling to Louth or Galway or Kerry to receive instructions in arms and explosives from a Tipperary or Derry training officer. This geographical spread, coupled with the endorsement of republicans from previous campaigns, surely influenced recruits. They became imbued with a sense of historical legitimacy and a knowledge that their actions and intent were not simply localised. Knowing that one was part of an effective working structure for an organisation whose base stretched across the entire island, and indeed overseas, must have been heady.[191] As a new year progressed, British Army blunders as in Derry city on 30 January further fuelled nationalist outrage North and South. Perceived victories such as the proroguing of Stormont served as fresh inducement for republican militarism. The Provisional IRA's campaign escalated, fuelled as before by its members' and supporters' activities in the South.

4

Explosion, 1972

The last quarter of 1971 served as the harbinger to the bloodiest year of the conflict. Acts of violence increased exponentially post-internment. In the first eight months of 1971, a total of thirteen soldiers, two policemen and sixteen civilians had been killed, whereas by its end, 174 people were dead and 2,375 injured.[1] As well as attacks in the urban areas of the North, IRA border activity significantly increased post-internment. This was of grave concern to Britain, whose armed forces engaged upon a strategy of cratering 'unapproved roads'. The intention was to shut down the supply routes to the IRA coming from the Republic. The destruction of these roads was felt most by locals, for whom it caused widespread social and economic disruption. This fuelled resentment of the British Army, leading to clashes with nationalist civilians on the border and further support for militant republicanism. Proximity to British Army misdeeds was not a prerequisite for the growth in IRA support. The shooting of more than two dozen civilians at a civil rights march in Derry in January 1972 led to massive protests across the Republic. Many protestors would subsequently join or otherwise assist the IRA, whose campaign peaked in 1972 in terms of activity. It was during this period of intense activity, North and South, that the first discernible geographic tensions emerged within the Provisionals. The Fianna Fáil government, increasingly concerned at the level of tolerance within their own establishment towards militant republicanism, began to introduce legislative measures to combat the IRA and Sinn Féin.

Bloody Sunday

The deliberate British Army targeting of civilians at a civil rights march in Derry city on 30 January 1972 caused public outrage across the Republic of Ireland.[2] As the historian J.B. Bell noted, Bloody Sunday was the most dangerous moment for the Fianna Fáil government. With the 'mob' in the street, the IRA was immune.[3] Within hours of the massacre, a crowd of several dozen protestors were picketing the British Embassy in Merrion Square, Dublin.[4] By the following morning, the numbers had swelled into the thousands, representative of all sections of society.[5] By Monday evening, the first petrol bombs were thrown at the embassy, emerging from the middle of the Union of Students in Ireland contingent.[6] The Gardaí were forced to baton-charge the crowd when they refused to allow fire trucks access to the front of the embassy to extinguish the fires.[7] Across the state there were similar reports of protest and civil disobedience. Ten thousand people marched in Cork city on the Monday, prompted by a mass walkout of hundreds of dockworkers that morning. Union flags were burned on Patrick Street and the Ulster Bank in the city was evacuated as a result of a bomb scare. The following day on Patrick Street, an effigy of Northern Premier Brian Faulkner was burned. More bomb scares were reported at the British Rail office, Woolworths and the Royal Insurance group.[8] In Limerick, protests were held at the city gaol where republicans were being held for non-payment of fines. A Garda Superintendent was hospitalised following an attack on his headquarters at William Street. The British Rail office on O'Connell Street was petrol-bombed that same day.[9] In Waterford, the docks office on the quays was blown up. This was 'greeted with jubilation by the port workers'.[10] The following day, 20,000 people attended a rally in the city.[11]

Disruption was widespread. *The Irish Times* reported disturbances in Ballinasloe, Ballina, Ballyhaunis, Birr, Carrickmacross, Cashel, Ennis, Limerick, Longford, Monaghan, Mullingar, Rosslare, Sligo, Thurles, Tralee, Waterford and the west Donegal area.[12] As protests took place across the state, the hostile vigil outside the British Embassy in Dublin continued. The *Irish Independent* reported on 'a wave of petrol bombings' directed at the embassy as well as British-owned businesses across the city.[13] The embassy was also targeted with a gelignite bomb planted by the Official IRA which destroyed the steel-reinforced front door.[14] The building was finally burned down by the Provisionals on the night of 2 February following four hours of petrol bombing. This was greeted with delight by the crowd of approximately 25,000. When fire trucks arrived to extinguish the flames, protestors charged the Gardaí who were protecting the firemen and managed to cut the water pumps, ensuring the building's destruction.[15]

What made these demonstrations so worrying for the government was the sheer diversity of the crowd. The mob might have been in the street, but what an odd collection it was: students, housewives, factory workers and office girls; schoolboys, socialists, republicans and people of no particular group.[16] Inflammatory rhetoric accompanied the demonstrations. One man with a loudspeaker walked amongst the crowd in Dublin 'urging support for the Provisional IRA'.[17] In Cork city, veteran IRA commander, Tom Barry, exhorted the people not to let the street demonstrations be the end of their activism: 'Parades, protests and passing revolutions were good in their own way, but they were absolutely useless unless the whole nation was united behind a final effort and stood "behind the men who will meet these people with arms".[18] As well as violent demonstrations, a great many people simply wished to express their disgust at the Derry shootings through civil disobedience. On the day of the funerals, all flights were grounded at Irish airports for several hours, ostensibly to allow for airport employees to attend services. In reality, staff at Dublin, Shannon and Cork airports had refused to handle aircraft or luggage from any British airline.[19] Similarly, the RTÉ branch of the Irish Transport and General Workers' Union (ITGWU) advised its 200-odd members to refuse to work on any news bulletin or programme that did not deal with the Northern crisis on the day of the funerals.[20] British-owned businesses in the Republic were not the only targets in the days following the shootings in Derry. British citizens were also at risk from republicans or those using the mantle of the IRA. The distinction is often difficult to discern. One interviewee claimed to have had to conduct investigations into disgruntled former employees of British bosses making threats in the name of the republican movement.[21] Similarly, men traded on family involvement in republicanism to threaten British civilians. Following Bloody Sunday, the Official IRA released a statement which read:

> It has come to the attention of the general headquarters staff of the
> Irish Republican Army that threats have been made in the name of the
> I.R.A. against English workers in the Twenty-six counties. We wish it
> to be made known that these threats do not emanate from the I.R.A.
> ... We ask the news media to give this statement full coverage in the
> interests of public safety.[22]

The statement denied the involvement of republicans in these threats,
blaming agent provocateurs.[23] Irishmen who served in the British armed
forces were at risk. Shortly after Bloody Sunday, a young British soldier
from Dublin was abducted from outside a public house on Lower Stephen
Street in the capital. His body was found the next day near the border in
County Fermanagh. He had been bound, gagged and shot in the head.
British Army and embassy officials were requested to stay away from the
funeral which was attended by a small number of neighbours and friends of
the victim.[24] No organisation claimed responsibility for the killing.

Although anger across the South was genuine and palpable following
Bloody Sunday, republicans were under no illusion as to its long-term
impact. The burning of the embassy was no more than 'the government
allowing people to let off a bit of steam'.[25] To Seán MacStiofáin, it was
merely a ploy on the government's part: 'Lynch let the building burn and
the massive wave of emotion with it. It was better for Fianna Fáil to have
all the anger concentrated on one symbol instead of serious anti-British
rioting all over the place. It was a lot cheaper, too.'[26] Taoiseach Jack Lynch
also struck all the right notes. He briefly recalled the Irish ambassador
from London, announced a day of mourning for the victims and pushed
for the closure of the Irish stock market for a day.[27] The country responded
in kind. Announcements of business closures in the South for the day
of mourning took up three full pages in the *Irish Independent*.[28] For the
most part, the ardour and anger did indeed cool along with the ashes of
the British embassy in Dublin. Martin Ferris was aware of this fleeting
sentiment:

> I knew at that point in time that t'was only going to last for a short
> period, the emotions of the last atrocity ... But when all that died
> down and so forth, tis then only you'd really see the substance of

what I would consider people prepared to do something about it. That's republican, real republican unemotional politics of struggle, that sort of thing. And there was a few of us, like there was at that time, if you were recruiting for the IRA on the days following Bloody Sunday you would have every single young person, man or woman, queuing up to try and join the IRA at that point in time. But five or six weeks later that number would be very small, you know what I mean, the people wouldn't have the courage or the conviction to see it through.[29]

As noted previously, Kieran Conway was aware of scores of applicants to the Dublin Brigade of the Provisional IRA in the aftermath of Bloody Sunday.[30] The importance of an unemotional factor is echoed in the testimony of a former IRA volunteer interviewed by Robert White, who stated: 'Bloody Sunday, then, didn't change my attitude, and, in particular, it wasn't an emotional response that "I hate the Brits and it's about time I did something ..." I'd always been concerned, I'd always been motivated.'[31] There is a converse to this, however. It is true that most Southerners caught up in the emotional flux of outrages such as Bloody Sunday did not become fully active in the republican movement ('after that then it probably weaned away to the people that were republicans prior to it, and people that stayed on').[32] However, the memories of the Derry killings, coupled with a general sense of incomplete national aspirations, ensured a measure of tolerance across the state for the IRA's campaign in subsequent years.

Financing and Arming the Provisional IRA, 1972

As well as a recruitment boon, both IRAs benefited from increasing financial support following Bloody Sunday. Although the USA was undoubtedly a source of considerable finance for the Provisionals, some maintain that finance from overseas was exaggerated. J.B. Bell wrote of the constant overestimation from Washington, London and Dublin about the impact of the Irish diaspora on IRA coffers, referring to it as 'bits and drabs, a matter of cake-bake sales and dances in suburban halls, crumpled bills in bars, and almost never great cheques signed with a flourish. The Zionists could raise more in New York over a weekend than Noraid [the US-based Irish

Northern Aid Committee] managed in a generation.'[33] Legislation in the United States – particularly following the 1973 Foreign Agents Registration Act (FARA) investigations – severely curtailed opportunities for republican fundraising.[34] One estimate is that over a sixteen-year period (1970–86), NORAID provided the Provisionals with $3m, an average of $187,500 annually which was said to have constituted a major source of Provisional IRA revenue.[35] Ed Moloney similarly believes that money raised in 'Irish-America' accounted for 'a significant amount of the IRA's income'.[36] Republicans demur. As one interviewee stated: 'they make out there was finance coming from America. They shut… that stopped in the seventies, in the early seventies. The amount of money you'd be getting from there would be very minute, well; I wouldn't say it was minute, but it was small, like.'[37]

> Belfast ran itself for years on its [social] clubs. You know the clubs? They formed the clubs, earlier on they formed it and … the car parks, you know, not building them but taking over areas and running them as car parks. There was no one to say how much you took in and how much you took out and so, you know, if there was twenty-thousand coming in every week you could say there's twelve-thousand coming in and then there's eight-thousand going one way, and you paid your people and say there's so much going every week. And that financed the movement.[38]

According to several interviewees, the bulk of the money needed for the IRA's campaign was obtained from within Ireland, on the initiative of each individual area or unit: 'Basically, we funded ourselves from within', while Belfast was largely responsible for funding the lion's share of what became Northern Command.[39]

Both the Official and Provisional IRA needed significant sums to fund their campaigns during the early 1970s. It is therefore no surprise that the number of bank robberies in the South rose by more than 200 per cent between 1971 and 1972.[40] It was reported that £188,000 had been taken in armed robberies during 1971. As substantial as this figure was, it was but £1,000 more than the sum taken during the same period in the lawless North.[41] A memo from the British Embassy noted:

I have given up trying to keep a record of such events [bank raids and crimes against property] for the simple reason that I know in advance what the outcome will be: - no arrests. The reason why there are no arrests is simply the unwillingness of ordinary members of the public to come forward and give evidence in public against the perpetrators.[42]

Much of the money raised by the Provisionals during this period was directed to the usual republican outlets: prisoner welfare, propaganda campaigns and conventional arms purchases. However, the IRA also sought effective modern armaments for which considerable capital was required. In 1972, inclement weather forced a light aeroplane to reroute to Shannon Airport from Farranfore in County Kerry, where IRA volunteers had been awaiting its arrival. The plane, piloted by a Canadian, had flown from Libya with at least one cargo of arms that included RPG-7 rocket launchers. Its unexpected arrival at Shannon and the subsequent panicked smuggling of the arms into waiting safe houses was facilitated by sympathetic airport workers.[43] The British government had earlier noted that airport's role in arms imports from the USA:

[Arms] are flown in into Ireland in small quantities, frequently on Aer Lingus direct from Chicago and New York to Shannon. Irish businessmen and others flying back to Ireland are often prevailed upon to conceal a gun or two in their personal luggage. The IRA have sympathetic contacts in the Irish customs service at Shannon where such people are often 'seen through customs' without examination.[44]

The Provisional IRA sought to expand their North American sources beyond the United States. In February 1972, the British Foreign Office reported:

A friendly and generally reliable contact has reported overhearing a conversation in a Hull (Québec) bar last night in French which was apparently concerned with an arms delivery to Northern Ireland. Two of the three participants were somewhat loosened up by drink to the evident concern of the third who tried to get them to moderate their voices. Contact, whose French is excellent, heard distinct references to arms including bazookas and the following place names: Bundoran, Rathlin Island and Garron Point. There was also mention of quote Wednesday unquote, but contact is not certain which date.[45]

Some months later, an Israeli journalist reported to British authorities that the IRA was importing machine guns in large quantities, and even claimed to have witnessed one such landing. The landing area was purportedly in Northern Ireland although both the journalist and authorities suspected this was a ruse and the real location was 'at a point some 20 minutes' journey south of Bray, Co. Wicklow, close to a headland which "juts out like a beak". This could be Bray Head.' The journalist also reported that the landing place had been used a number of times already and was likely to be used again. During these importations, 'a substantial number of crates are put ashore at the landing, each holding six or eight machine guns. Crates seem to come from Germany...'[46] As for the successful importation of Libyan RPG-7s, a special training camp was subsequently established in the rural South, overseen by an ex-British soldier from Belfast. The training officer expressed concern that insufficient time had been allocated for training in the use of these weapons. His objections were overruled by a senior Belfast IRA officer who wanted the rockets utilised as early as possible.[47] The discovery of one of these weapons in Derry city days prior to their scheduled use across Northern Ireland, coupled with insufficient training, stripped the weapon of its tactical effectiveness.[48] The RUC and British Army rapidly upgraded their armoured vehicles to cope with rocket attacks.[49] The limitations of volunteers in the use of this weapon were not missed by the British Army either; a later internal report stating that 'inadequate training had resulted in the mishandling of the RPG-7'.[50] Although it was widely accepted that the rocket-launchers had come to Northern Ireland via the South, Fianna Fáil minister Brian Lenihan emphatically denied such claims, insisting rather implausibly that the weapons could only have come through the North.[51]

North–South Divisions

Tensions within the Provisional republican movement were evident along a broadly North–South divide from an early stage.[52] Although Southern volunteers played a frontline role in the conflict from the outset, as time passed this became less and less the case. A greater focus on subsidiary roles came to define their involvement.[53] This fed into notions of Northern superiority, particularly directed at the leadership. Martin Meehan and others in Belfast contemptuously referred to the Dublin-based leadership as the 'long rifles', while MacStiofáin's allegedly self-important demeanour when visiting beleaguered north Belfast was very badly received.[54] The promotion of Southerners to local positions of command, as happened in Tyrone, led to considerable resentment. In some cases, the result was localised unsanctioned replacements.[55] The disconnect continued, with large operations often undertaken with no input or prior knowledge from GHQ. In such cases, the leadership had little choice but to retroactively sanction them. The Provisional IRA's London bombings in 1973 – the first such of their kind for over thirty years – are an example.[56] Maria McGuire, a Sinn Féin activist during the early 1970s, noted Ó Brádaigh's demoralised realisation at being so removed from the on-the-ground knowledge and planning of the campaign.[57] By late 1972, Daithí Ó Conaill was reported by one informer as being 'pissed off … He thinks the IRA are a northern organisation now. He feels like surplus baggage, very disillusioned.'[58]

As previously noted, the logic in situating GHQ in the South was sound for practical purposes. However, as time passed, more and more Northerners felt that the movement in the South, with some exceptions, simply did not understand the nature of the conflict. Belfast volunteer Brendan Hughes said of it:

We believed, and this might have been an elitist thing, that we knew how to run the war, not those people sitting in Dublin in their safe houses; people like Daithi Ó Conaill, Ruairi O Bradaigh, who were never in any danger. Daithi O Conaill had not visited Belfast except during the [1972] ceasefire. I remember having arguments with him, that we knew how to run the war, and they didn't … there was always that conflict between Belfast and the Dublin leadership especially with Daithi. He was a tall, good-looking, dashing figure who saw himself as – and he was – very articulate. *But he was not involved in the war*, not involved in places like Derry or Belfast or Armagh. He was sitting in Dublin directing. And there was a fair deal of resentment …[59]

Conversely, Hughes spoke of the hostility among Cork and Kerry republicans (possibly meaning Munster as a whole) at what they felt to be the intrusion of Northerner, Pat Doherty, in his alleged capacity as Director of Intelligence whenever he travelled south.[60] Frustration and friction clearly rubbed both ways. On geographic cliques in the prison system, one Southern interviewee stated:

> You always had your cliques like, I mean, I got caught in Derry, so I would always stay with the Derry lads. And, you know, it's kind of like a Dublin–Limerick thing; the Belfast people thought everyone else were 'culchies', and they thought everything was happening in Belfast, and the Tyrone lads, everyone would kind of stay with themselves like.[61]

Divisions were evidently not so simple, or perhaps imprisonment introduced new dynamics. Southerners imprisoned in Long Kesh were well received by other prisoners and were instrumental in establishing Irish language classes there.[62] Similarly, a Northern interviewee imprisoned in Portlaoise stated:

> [T]here wasn't a north–south split. And what's probably more likely to happen in a place like that, there wasn't even an urban–rural split. You'd certainly, what you would get is maybe in some cells you'd get two or three Tyrone people sitting and talking. Maybe some of the Dubs would have broken down into the areas they'd come from or who'd they known outside. But there was no noticeable divisions into parochial or geographical areas … I mightn't have seen that as often or I mightn't have seen it where others did, but I certainly never noticed it to any great extent.[63]

Hostility on the outside possibly stemmed from grassroots mistrust of GHQ, another contributing factor being rural contrariness towards an urban-based leadership. As one interviewee said, 'Overall these things were happening, and it was no different from the way people in Cork would look at things, to people in Clare and Limerick, you know. See we're very tribal, but in all that, in the whole country, there was really good people rose above all that.'[64]

Clashes with the Southern State

Linked to North–South divisions was the belligerent attitude some Northerners felt towards the Southern state, particularly as represented by its security forces. It was often difficult to convince such volunteers that the Twenty-Six Counties was a useful base and that antagonising the Gardaí was unwise.[65] Border IRA volunteers were particularly nonplussed at being forced to tolerate arrests and ill-treatment in the South while being directed to attack the RUC in the North.[66] Such frustration could manifest itself in various ways. On one occasion, two Derry volunteers stole a Garda car, tied its owners up and stripped them of their uniforms after a heavy-drinking session.[67] In more serious incidents, IRA volunteers occasionally engaged in military action against the Irish Defence Forces. One such clash occurred as an IRA unit withdrew over the border following an attack on British soldiers near Forkhill, County Armagh.[68] There were no casualties. As the conflict in Northern Ireland intensified during the latter part of 1971, and the likelihood of such incidents increased, the Dublin government introduced measures to curb the influence of paramilitary groupings. Section 31 of the Broadcasting Authority Act (1960) – popularly known as 'Section 31' – was a measure of media censorship introduced by Fianna Fáil in 1971.[69] This act prohibited the national broadcaster RTÉ from broadcasting anything that could be interpreted as supporting the aims or activities of organisations that 'engage in, promote, encourage or advocate the attaining of any political objective by violent means'.[70] Such interpretation was loosely defined and increasingly arbitrary as the conflict wore on. From its implementation, the government expressed commitment to the ban. In 1972, the entire RTÉ authority was summarily dismissed by the government for breaching Section 31 by allowing the broadcast of an interview with a member of the Provisional IRA.[71] The journalist who conducted the interview was imprisoned for contempt of court when he refused to disclose the identity of the interviewee.[72]

The republican movement's inability to address the public via broadcast media was a significant frustration during periods of heightened tension, as with prison crises. On 19 May 1972, for example, a major riot broke out in Mountjoy Prison involving approximately 100 republican prisoners. The riot was supported by approximately 1,000 republican supporters outside the prison. The latter riot was put down only after the involvement of 200 soldiers and several hundred Gardaí.[73] Interestingly, both Official and Provisional prisoners were involved. As well as indicating amicable relations between the two groups, it also reveals that segregation was not enforced along factional lines in Mountjoy.[74] The source of the riot was allegedly the sacking of a sympathetic warder who had allowed Provisional prisoners to visit a public house en route to court; it was an escalation on both sides then leading to a more acute expression of various other grievances.[75] At the time, there was a de facto 'political' status for republican prisoners in the Republic as a result of a hunger strike by several prisoners earlier in the year. This was, however, denied by the Irish Government at the time.[76] When a similar hunger strike took place in Crumlin Road Gaol in June 1972, led by Billy McKee, the British Government sought the advice of their Irish counterparts. They too were awarded a de facto 'political' status, subsequently, the later infamous Special Category Status. During the Belfast hunger strike, the heads of the three largest unions in Ireland wrote to the British Prime Minister in support of political status. Brendan Corish, then leader of the Labour Party of Ireland, did the same.[77]

A number of republican prisoners were transferred to the Curragh Camp during the summer of 1972, where the government had recently spent £200,000 on security and infrastructure upgrades.[78] The Curragh had been used in previous decades as an internment camp for IRA volunteers due to its remote location. A likely expectation was that this remoteness would preclude riots such as that outside Mountjoy. However, a major clash took place there on 9 July 1972. As with previous disturbances, prisoner treatment was at the core of the grievances. The spark in this instance was the denial of parole to a Belfast prisoner who was due to be married. It began as a peaceful demonstration, organised by Provisional Sinn Féin and attended by approximately 2,000 people. Cabhair Uladh and People's Democracy were also officially represented. A large group of mostly young people broke away from the main parade to confront soldiers kitted out in riot gear (the first time such troops were deployed in the Republic of Ireland). Equipped with Perspex shields and batons, as well as guns to fire CS gas canister and rubber-bullet guns, these men stood behind wire entanglements at key points leading to the prison. A section of demonstrators managed to cut through the barbed wire and were attacked by Gardaí and riot troops. The crowd responded with petrol bombs and thunderflashes and set fire to a building at the complex. At approximately 6pm, the last of the demonstrators – some 200 people – were dispersed by a large baton-charge. Despite the ferocity of the riot, casualties were low; six soldiers, two Gardaí and several rioters were injured.[79] Two months later, another hunger strike in the Curragh led to serious rioting in Dundalk, the home town of one of the prisoners. Two Garda stations were attacked with stones and petrol bombs. One was destroyed by fire. Several businesses were also seriously damaged and private cars burned out. Riot troops eventually dispersed the crowds with baton-charges but the total costs of damage for the riot were estimated at £25,000.[80] The Provisional IRA denied responsibility for orchestrating the violence.[81]

Clashes with IRA prisoners and supporters on this scale represented an alarming development for the Southern state. Scenes captured on newsreel and press photographs were uncomfortably reminiscent of riots in Belfast and Derry. British blunders such as internment and Bloody Sunday fuelled Southern outrage and undoubtedly fed into support for the IRA. While many establishment figures may also have been so inclined, threats to the state would need to be met head-on, particularly as appendages of the state were often all too ready to demonstrate tolerance for the IRA campaign. A newspaper report from 1971 noted a recent court case in Dundalk where jurors shook hands with IRA defendants following their acquittal.[82] Several months earlier, a County Mayo farmer was acquitted of unlawful possession of arms and ammunition. The man had been found in possession of a Thompson submachine gun, five rifles, two automatic pistols and 2,295 rounds. Having deliberated for thirty-five minutes, the jury returned a verdict of not guilty, to which the judge added: 'whether he is a member of an illegal organisation or not is a matter for himself and does not concern the jury or myself in this case'.[83] The verdict was greeted with cheers by members of Provisional Sinn Féin who had picketed the courthouse throughout the trial. The British Embassy, which avidly followed republican trials, referred to the verdict as 'unsatisfactory'.[84] Another judge in County Mayo dismissed a charge of IRA membership against two young men from Belfast. Although the IRA was a proscribed organisation in both states, Justice Hugh McGahon threw out the charges on the basis that they specifically referred to the Belfast Brigade of the IRA, an area over which neither he nor his court had any jurisdiction.[85] Of a similar acquittal in Donegal, a British Embassy memo noted: 'This is clearly another case in which a black mark goes to an Irish jury.'[86] Many members of the security forces in the Republic of Ireland were equally frustrated. During the winter of 1971, Gardaí in Munster had held an unofficial congress in Mitchelstown, County Cork. Among the principal grievances aired was that, during the previous twelve months, perhaps twenty people facing serious charges of arms possession received suspended sentences.[87] For their part, and in order to present a formal expression of concern to the Irish Government, the British had been compiling a 'scorecard' of acquittals and lenient sentencing issued by judges in the Republic.[88] Excerpts from the 1970–1 period include:

- 17 November 1970: eight County Antrim men told a Dublin Judge that they refused to recognise the Court, and one, Kevin Murphy, accepted full responsibility for the arms found in their possession near Dublin. The arms found were two rifles, a pistol and 337 rounds of ammunition. Each man fined £20.
- 25 November 1970: fourteen men were charged at Dundalk Court with having in their possession three sub-machine guns, one revolver, two pistols, one .303 rifle and a quantity of assorted ammunition without a firearms certificate. Justice Dunleary dismissed the charges.
- 8 January 1971: the Chairman of Newry Civil Rights Association was charged with the men at 'B' [the case immediately above this] and, in addition, having in his possession a bomb, 3½lbs of gelignite. Jury returned a verdict of not guilty. Applause in Court.
- 12 January 1971: Cathal Goulding and Michael O'Driscoll [Official IRA Chief-of-Staff and Quartermaster General, respectively] were charged at Dublin Court with stealing a lorry valued £400. Owner of lorry said he would not have informed Gardaí had he known Goulding was using the lorry to take 'stuff' to the border. Judge Conroy directed the jury to find the two men not guilty.
- 17 March 1971: a man who admitted being a member of the Provisional IRA and firing a shot into a Dundalk bar was charged with having no firearms certificate. Fined in Dundalk Court £5.

- 22 April 1971: Peter Donnelly charged at Clones Court with having a Thompson sub-machine gun with intent to endanger life and without a firearms certificate. District Justice Shaw dismissed the three charges on the grounds that the search warrant used was invalid. Loud cheering by demonstrators.
- 13 May 1971: an ex-Provisional IRA member was charged at Dundalk Court with being in possession of a pistol and two rounds of ammunition on November 1, in possession of 152 rounds of ammunition at his house on November 2 and being in possession of 15 detonators and 38 feet of safety fuse. Pleaded guilty and Probation Act applied.
- 15 July 1971: [The acquittal of the Mayo farmer, cited above]
- 26 July 1971: a Londonderry man accepted full responsibility for two hand grenades found in his possession when charged at Donegal Court. Cleared by jury. Applause in Court. Judge Ryan commented, 'I'm glad, gentlemen, that that's your verdict, not mine.'
- 29 September 1971: applications for extradition orders against three young Dungannon men for failing to answer bail granted them in Northern Ireland on charges in connection with the possession of explosives were heard by District Justice Shaw at Monaghan Court. The applications were dismissed. District Justice Shaw, when asked, said he was not obliged to give any reason.
- 11 October 1971: four men were charged with possessing firearms and ammunition without certificates on the Louth/Armagh border at Dundalk Court. The men had fired shots across the border at the British Army. They were sentenced to 14 days from date of arrest and were released immediately.

Such judicial leniency alarmed the British and Irish governments, as well as sections of the Gardaí and legal establishment. Already by this period the Special Branch of an Garda Síochána had been expanded to perhaps 600 members in response to the escalating violence.[89] In a summary internal memo of the first five months of 1972, the British reported: 'Acquittals have resulted mainly from willingness on the part of juries to give the accused too much benefit of the doubt', adding that 'District Justices Dunleavy, in Louth, and Shaw, in Monaghan, have both discharged defendants in inexcusable circumstances before trial.'[90] The Irish government was just as concerned at the actions of their judges in Dundalk, in particular. From January 1972, a number of outstanding court cases against suspected IRA members were transferred from there to the Central Criminal Court in Dublin. The British noted that it 'may be a sign of Government efforts to bring IRA defendants to justice, for [IRA suspects] are likely to encounter in Dublin a court less sympathetic to their plights'.[91] Indeed, during a conversation with the British Ambassador to Ireland during this period, Taoiseach Jack Lynch named several judges who he agreed were overly sympathetic to the IRA; referring to them as 'bad' or 'weak'.[92] Aside from the extraordinary and unprecedented nature of the Taoiseach's comments to the representative of a foreign state, this account is revealing of another concern. Both parties to the discussion acknowledged support for or tolerance of the IRA being a major challenge in court cases. In particular, regional courts and juries hindered the successful prosecution of republicans. In May 1972, in response to repeated British requests and the very significant escalation of violence in the North, the Irish government re-introduced the juryless Special Criminal Court. This had previously been used during the Second World War.[93] The most vocal supporters of this measure, such as Conor Cruise O'Brien, stressed the ever-present threat of jury intimidation as being the primary driver of juryless courts. Such declarations blithely ignored the reality of the numerous acquittals which preceded its re-introduction.[94] It is worth noting that, during parliamentary debates preceding its re-introduction, the Irish government refused to demonstrate to deputies Michael O'Leary and Noel Browne how the current system had been shown to be inadequate. Such a demonstration was in fact a constitutional requirement.[95]

Of itself, the re-introduction of the Special Criminal Court had no immediately discernible impact on republican activities in the South or subsequent capabilities in the North. Between 26 May and 1 October 1972, it dealt with sixty-five republicans, of whom sixteen were acquitted. Individuals brought before the court were members of Saor Éire, the Official and Provisional republican movements, and were referred to by the British as 'relatively small fry'.[96] Given the breadth of tolerance and support militant republicanism continued to benefit from, the Dublin government felt compelled to assert further control. Towards the end of

1972, they announced that amendments to the existing Offences against the State Act were to be introduced. Among these was the allowance that any Garda from the rank of Chief Superintendent upwards could present as evidence for an individual's IRA membership merely their own assertion.[97] This legislation met with fierce opposition in the Dáil, including from many TDs of the ruling party, Fianna Fáil. It seemed likely that the bill would fail when presented to the Dáil for a vote on 1 December 1972. As parliamentary debate took place, two car bombs exploded in Dublin city centre, on Eden Quay and Sackville Place. In the latter explosion, two Córas Iompair Éireann (CIÉ) workers were killed. The bombs could be heard in the Dáil chambers. Voting on the legislation took place as reports of the casualties from the attacks were filtering in. Many previous opponents of the bill voted in its favour and it was approved. There are reasonable suspicions that elements of British intelligence played a key role in these bombings, as noted by the Barron Report.[98] In the final three months of 1972, there had in fact been numerous bombs planted by British loyalists in the Republic. In October, four hotels in Dublin were damaged by incendiary bombs while a 12lb bomb was discovered in Connolly Station and dismantled by an army explosives expert. That same month, another unexploded bomb was discovered in Letterkenny Court House while a car bomb seriously injured a man in Clones, County Monaghan, and a fertiliser store was damaged by a bomb in Carrigans, County Donegal. In the following month, bombs were planted or detonated in counties Mayo, Donegal and Dublin.[99] What marked out the 1 December bombs in Dublin was their relative professionalism.

**

By the close of 1972, nearly 700 people had lost their lives in the 'Troubles'. The majority of deaths occurred that very year. The Provisional IRA had proven themselves capable of launching a multi-pronged military offensive in Northern Ireland. Civilian casualties were an inevitable result of the crudity of some IRA tactics, particularly those employed in urban areas. The British had equally demonstrated their willingness to use brute force in striking at republicans and the broader nationalist community through their armed forces and loyalist proxies. By the year's end, the broader population in the Republic of Ireland was also reeling. There was residual public anger due to atrocities such as Bloody Sunday. However, IRA bombings – Official and Provisional – which killed numerous civilians in Northern Ireland and Britain equally revulsed. Despite this, widespread support for militant republicanism still existed across the state. Indeed, major community organisations such as the GAA continued to be vocally supportive of militant republicanism for many years to come. With changes in legislation and the judiciary, prosecution – as well as ill-treatment – of republicans increased year on year throughout the decade from this time. While deaths from IRA activity in the North peaked in 1972, activity in the South arguably increased in subsequent years. If anything could measurably be said of republican support and sympathy, it was that overt displays become less commonplace and this nebulous community went underground to a large extent. As will be discussed in later chapters, however, the potential for this community to become a mass movement remained.

Stalemate and Peace Overtures, 1973–4

On 21 July 1972, the Provisional IRA detonated over two dozen bombs across Belfast city centre with wholly inadequate warnings. Nine people were killed and scores more injured. Ten days later, the British Army launched Operation Motorman, their largest military operation since the Suez invasion of 1956. Troops, tanks and armoured cars moved into the barricaded 'no go' areas that had been established in nationalist areas of Derry, Belfast and other large towns. As a consequence of the dismantling of these barricades, and subsequent heavy army presence, IRA operations became more focused on rural areas in 1973. The lack of 'no go' areas in the North also led to a reduction of regular, large-scale bombings. It was no longer logistically possible to prepare such operations due to regular security force patrols in nationalist areas. The year 1973 saw the first IRA bombs in England for over a generation. While IRA operations – and British Army casualties – declined that year relative to 1972, there was a noticeable increase in the IRA's efficiency in other areas. In the South, for example, this could be seen in the regularity and sophistication of training camps. There were also increased efforts to acquire more weapons, explosives and finance. Support and sympathy for militant republicanism remained a constant in the South during this period. The beginnings of a broader negative reaction among the public to IRA activity could also be discerned. Whether this was caused by general war weariness or reactions to specific IRA atrocities is open to debate. A general election in the Republic of Ireland in 1973 saw Fianna Fáil replaced by a coalition of Fine Gael and Labour. There was a significant change in rhetoric and action from this government as regards the Northern conflict. Relations with the British government improved, and Irish republicans became the subject of increasing pressure and repression. Indeed, the seeds of those dark days for civil liberties in the Irish Republic – namely, the mid-1970s – were laid in the early years of this government's tenure. By the close of 1974, a military stalemate existed between the British and Provisional IRA. Peace attempts which deliberately excluded the Provisionals earlier that year were a signal failure. However, the coalition government in the South was determined to wreck any bilateral peace attempts between those two parties. This chapter discusses all these issues, concluding with the IRA ceasefire of 1975.

Arms Importation and Acquisition Attempts

In summarising IRA arms capabilities for the preceding years, a 1976 British government report stated: 'Evidence suggests that for the period 1972–1974 some 85 per cent of modern weapons used by the IRA were of American origin. This figure has been quoted publicly but it is now out of date; the current figure may be less than 50 per cent.'[1] The IRA continued to receive a small but steady stream of arms from the USA throughout the decade. However, by 1973, they were making serious – and often successful – attempts to open alternative channels. Of these, the two best known were the unsuccessful *Claudia* shipment in 1973 and the acquisition of RPG-7 rocket launchers discussed in the previous chapter.[2] In both cases, the Republic of Ireland served as the delivery point. The *Claudia* was a Cypriot-registered boat used to transport Libyan arms to Ireland: a 'gift' from Colonel Gaddafi of Libya.[3] The *Claudia* was intercepted off the Waterford coast in March 1973 by the Irish Navy and found to contain five tons of weaponry.[4] This included general-purpose machine guns, modern assault rifles and grenades. Of the six IRA volunteers onboard, all but one was from Munster. They included the then-Chief-of-Staff, Joe Cahill, from Belfast and QMG, Denis McInerney, from County Clare. Rumours circulated that another man, a vocational teacher from Monaghan, was also on board but managed to escape in the ship's launch. Patrick Donegal, Minister for Defence, reported that this man subsequently went to Boston to raise funds for the IRA. This account is unlikely.[5] Before the ship was boarded by the Irish Navy, McInerney managed to cast a suitcase containing a substantial amount of money as well as the names and addresses of IRA contacts into the sea. Naval attempts to retrieve the case were unsuccessful. However, enterprising locals marked the spot where the suitcase entered the water with a buoy and studied tidal patterns. Later, a trawler manned by local fishermen located the case and pulled it up with the aid of a grappling hook. The money and contact lists were allegedly returned to the IRA in a field outside Dungarvan sometime later.[6] Although this *Claudia* attempt represented an operational failure for the IRA, it is worth noting the underlying logistics which indicate the resources available to them on such occasions. According to a later account of the events:

> The boat reached the Waterford coast but the republicans were frustrated when they were forced to stay at sea for another 24 hours due to adverse weather conditions. Equally frustrated were the awaiting groups at Helvick Head, watching out for The Claudia (…) The land operation had its headquarters in a house overlooking Helvick Harbour. An Abbeyside man was Officer in Command and there was also an active service unit to escort the arms to dumps. In all, there was a 50-person plus team involved in the onshore operation.[7]

Aside from Cahill and McInerney, those arrested were Gerard Walsh (Dungarvan, County Waterford), Donal Whelan (Kilmacthomas, County Kilkenny) and Seán Garvey (Cahirciveen, County Kerry). All faced trial, with charges ranging from IRA membership to conspiracy to import arms and ammunition. As with previous high-profile IRA trials, the public support for the defendants was alarming. The national GAA congress, for example, voted unanimously to 'strive by every means at its disposal for the reinstatement of Donal Whelan'.[8] Whelan had been dismissed from his position as headmaster of a Waterford vocational school. One former president of the GAA was quoted as saying of him: 'this man is of greater value to this nation than many of the people now strutting the country whom I can only describe as being disciples of apostasy'.[9] The GAA was not the only organisation active in Whelan's reinstatement campaign. Among the representations made to the Taoiseach were those from the Transport Union of Ireland, Irish National Teachers' Organisation, the County Waterford Vocational Education Committee, Dungarvan Urban

District Council, Kilmacthomas Parents' Committee and Past Pupils' Union, the Irish Countrywoman's Association as well as the East and West Waterford GAA boards.[10] Such was the level of vocal support in the courtroom that, by the second day of the trial, the presiding judge was reduced to threatening to clear the public galleries in the event of further interruptions.[11] Cahill attempted to take full responsibility for the shipment, stating that the crew and accused had no knowledge of the operation or cargo. When asked if he had a license for importing the arms, Cahill replied that he had not. After a short trial, all but Gerard Walsh – who was acquitted – were found guilty of conspiracy to import arms and ammunition, with attempting to import arms and ammunition, and with having control over ammunition and explosive substances to enable other persons to endanger life.

Cahill received three years' penal servitude for the importation conviction and an additional twelve months for IRA membership. Whelan and Murphy received suspended sentences while McInerney and Garvey were both sentenced to two years for the importation conviction and twelve months for IRA membership. Cahill used the opportunity of the considerable media coverage to make a speech from the dock: 'If I am guilty of any crime, it is that I did not succeed in getting the contents of the Claudia into the hands of the freedom-fighters in this country. And I believe that national treachery was committed off Helvic when the Free State forces conspired with our British enemies to deprive our freedom-fighters of the weapons of war.' Garvey brought a local dimension to his statement, saying that he would not deny that it was love of his country that brought him to Helvic Head, as it was love of freedom that brought Roger Casement to Banna Strand. He added: 'Do your damndest.' Of the defendants, McInerney was the most laconic, if impactful. He merely stated 'Joe Cahill has spoken for me. Now go earn your 30 pieces of silver.' He followed this up by throwing a handful of smuggled shillings at the judge.[12] Later that year, Dáil Éireann was the scene of ignominy when, during a spat regarding the Claudia arms importation, a north Cork Fianna Fáil TD shouted across the chamber 'More guns we want. Bags of guns.'[13] Several months prior, a former Fianna Fáil TD for Mayo spoke to a reporter of his certainty that the Claudia shipment was a decoy. He added:

I am delighted that the IRA got away with it. I have always been in favour of the IRA. It is about time that our people got in some guns to defend our people. If the British can take in arms to this country, why can't our people do it ... We would not hand over any information to the Gardaí. If they come to me, the answer they will get is no.[14]

Indeed, government elation from the seizure of the *Claudia* soon gave way to nervous expectancy that other shipments could be en route at any time. This anxiety peaked the following year when an unidentified ship of 2,000 tons dropped anchor between Hook lighthouse and Dunmore East in the south-east, leading to a full-scale security alert. A contemporary news report described the ship's unusual actions: 'After about two hours in Waterford harbour the ship hauled up anchor and headed for Tramore bay where she again anchored. Early yesterday she set course for Ballycotton when she again dropped anchor.'[15] Ultimately, the fears were unfounded. A similar issue was raised in the Dáil the following April with reports of a submarine off the coast of Clonakilty. A fruitless search of 100 acres of marram grass on the Saltee Islands, County Wexford, by the Gardaí and Irish Defence Forces kept tensions simmering.[16] Anxiety occasionally spilled over into full-scale paranoia; two newspapers ran stories during this period headlined 'IRA buying Nigerian arms' and 'Biafran arms for the IRA?'[17] Overall, government fears following the capture of the *Claudia* were understandable. It was widely believed that several IRA arms shipments were successfully landed in the Republic of Ireland the previous year.[18] This includes the rocket-launchers brought in through Shannon Airport. Two months after the *Claudia* arms trial, a Monaghan man was arrested upon arrival at Dublin Airport from Montreal. This was in connection with the seizure of seventeen rifles, 29,000 rounds of ammunition and sixty pounds of explosives from a ship docking at Dublin. The ship's papers had the arms listed as 'cases of machinery' and they were being forwarded care of Toronto to a fictitious Dublin company, 'Leinster Manufacturing Co'.[19] The security forces of the Republic scored a number of new victories the following year. Seizures included the following:

- January 1974: 1,200 rounds of assorted ammunition, including 340 armour-piercing bullets on the Monaghan border.

- January 1974: Bombs, gelignite, detonators, two revolvers, 3,000 rounds of assorted ammunition, radio equipment and combat jackets near Castleblayney, Monaghan.
- February 1974: Home-made mortars, 110lbs of sodium chlorate, 50lbs of chloride nitro-benzine mixture, fourteen 3lb bags of another mixture and thirty feet of Cordtex in vacant houses north of Dundalk.
- February 1974: Home-made mortar bombs, 4,000 rounds of ammunition, remote-control explosive devices, and a quantity of detonators near the shoreline at Moville, Donegal
- February 1974: Five rifles, an obsolete anti-aircraft machine gun, one rocket-launcher, rifle ammunition, dozens of parachute flares, 200 empty small arms cases, two tons of nitrate and soda, a half-ton of NET nitrate, eight hundredweight of nitric acid, five-gallon drum of acid, 'a large number of containers containing assorted chemicals – not yet fully analysed', batteries, boxes of paraffin wax, electric drill, plastic dustbins, 'a quantity of other bomb-making material', an assorted number of maps of the Republic and Northern Ireland, and numerous other paraphernalia near Slane, Meath.
- April 1974: Bomb-making material, 40–50,000 rounds of assorted ammunition divided and ready for distribution, four revolvers, army training manuals, electric detonators 'in the unoccupied former home of the late Jack McCabe', the first Quartermaster General of the Provisional IRA.[20]

Gardaí also made significant arrests for fertiliser-boiling and explosives-manufacture. In October 1974, four men were discovered with explosive material at a derelict farmhouse outside Ennis, County Clare. Gardaí reported many bags of fertilisers in front of and behind the house with 'two steel troughs more than half full with a white crystalline substance' at the rear of the house.[21] The following month, a 'bomb factory' was discovered in the hilly border region of Clare and Galway. The find contained 33,600lbs of fertiliser, 6lbs of gelignite, two Webley pistols, rockets, rocket launchers, grenades, an assortment of ammunition and combat jackets hidden among bushes. Gardaí and detectives also discovered an old-fashioned iron bath and gas cylinders used to 'boil' the fertiliser to extract crystals for use in bomb-making. The fertiliser had already been boiled and was ready for use as explosives.[22] As noted, boiled fertiliser was often the main component of IRA bombs, with conventional explosives like gelignite serving primarily as a booster.[23]

Following the ousting of Fianna Fáil from power, security cooperation between the Irish and British governments became much more common. In part, this was due to the latter government furnishing their Irish counterparts with an embarrassing catalogue of instances where explosives of Twenty-Six County origin were seized in Northern Ireland.[24] The principal means of identifying the source of commercial explosives was stamping or scratch-marking. The British were eager for the Irish to adopt this measure but were aware that 'the Irish react badly to anything that they regard as pressure from us'.[25] Commandant Boyle of the Irish Defence Forces did in fact appear to show extreme reluctance to introducing a systematic stamping system. Having travelled to Belfast in April 1975 to witness a demonstration of the machine, Boyle had apparently been satisfied of its capability and safety measures. However, in a later call to a British official, he had much changed opinions. A British report on this discussion expressed confusion and frustration at the sudden change of mind, pointing out that each objection Commandant Boyle raised was met with a logical rebuttal.[26] The coalition government was eager to cooperate in this respect, however. The following years saw a far greater number of restrictions imposed on manufacturers and users of commercial explosives. This is discussed in the next chapter.

Southern Provisional IRA volunteers continued to take part in military operations in the North during this period. Several interviewees noted concentrations of Southerners in border IRA units. Kieran Conway spoke of how scores of such men operated over the border from bases in the Republic; his area stretching from mid-Cavan to Donegal.[27] One of the young men sent to the border in 1971 by Gearóid MacCárthaigh (noted in Chapter 3) was killed in the early summer of 1973. His friend and comrade was killed the following month. These were the first two Southern Provisional IRA members to be killed on active service during the 'Troubles'. Dermot Crowley and Anthony Ahern, childhood friends from Cork, had graduated to the IRA from Na Fianna and were based primarily in Leitrim during their time on active service.[28] MacCárthaigh referred to them as 'two of the best recruits I ever met in the army'.[29] Although they did not remain on active service permanently after being sent to the border by MacCárthaigh, both were eager to do so after returning to Cork. Crowley joined the East Tyrone Brigade of the IRA in 1972, at a time when MacCárthaigh had taken over as O/C there. Ahern went to the border early in 1973, although he was still officially considered part of the First Cork Brigade. He was involved in transporting a landmine over the border near Roslea, County Fermanagh, on the night of 10 May when it detonated prematurely, killing him. He was the youngest of several sons, whose father had served in the Irish Defence Forces. According to a Provisional spokesman, 'Aherne [sic] was the first volunteer from the 26 Counties to die on active service in the North since the present troubles began.'[30] His family requested that the funeral be non-political. The esteem in which the young man was held by the republican movement was evident in the wreaths on display, however; some forty-five wreaths – including from IRA units around the country – were sent. More than 2,000 people attended Anthony Ahern's funeral, with hundreds of Gardaí overseeing events. Dermot Crowley was also in attendance.[31] Shortly after the funeral, Crowley returned to Tyrone on active service.

Just a few weeks later, on 25 June, he and two other IRA volunteers – Patrick Carty and Seán Loughran – were transporting a bomb intended for the British Army barracks near Omagh when it exploded prematurely, killing all three. As with Ahern, Dermot Crowley's funeral witnessed a heavy Garda presence, with reinforcements brought in from Limerick, Waterford and Kilkenny. Unlike his friend, Crowley had a republican funeral, with an IRA honour guard led by a pipe band. Members of Cumann na mBan and Na Fianna were also in attendance. Among the approximately 1,300 mourners were a sizable contingent of men and women from Monaghan and Tyrone who knew Crowley from his time on active service. Senior IRA member, J.B. O'Hagan was present and was in fact arrested. Among the fifty-odd wreaths at the funeral were those from IRA units in West Tyrone, Dungannon and North Armagh, the West Cork Brigade and wreaths from prisoners in Crumlin Road, Long Kesh, Mountjoy, Armagh and the Curragh.[32] Other Southerners were captured in Northern Ireland and spent time in Long Kesh and other prisons during this period. Kieran Conway was arrested in Derry in 1971 and imprisoned in Long Kesh until 1974.

Hugh Hehir, a Clareman who was shot dead by Gardaí in 1988, was charged with possession of explosives in 1974 and imprisoned in Long Kesh.[33]

The Southern authorities and Provisionals engaged in a constant struggle of control and improvisation during this period. The latter group sought to manufacture firearms and other offensive weapons. In the early years of the conflict, this included ship's signal rockets with gelignite attached to the top as primitive warheads.[34] IRA engineers also modified .303 rifles to allow them to fire .22 calibre ammunition, as this was more common and easily obtainable.[35] In 1973, a man secretly representing IRA GHQ leased a factory in an industrial estate near the Stannaway Road, County Dublin, under the name Light Machine Services. Ostensibly, the business repaired broken machinery parts for other factories in the vicinity. It was in fact a secret IRA arms-manufacturing factory, all employees being full-time active service volunteers. Standing instructions were that, if ever there was an unexpected knock at the door, all employees were to bury whatever they were working on in a scrap box and put ordinary bits of machinery on their worktops or in the machines. Six crude firearms a day was not an untypical output. The quality of the weapons was never very high, however, being of limited range and prone to jamming or breaking down. Light Machine Services operated until the end of October 1973 when the lease on the premises ran out. Coincidentally, this was the same day as the Mountjoy prison helicopter escape.[36] In 1975, another actual arms factory was discovered by Gardaí while still in use. This one operated in the north Dublin village of Donabate. A British report from their embassy noted: 'it appears to have been a centre for the manufacture of grenades, rockets and mortars. The Provisionals were careful to work "nine to five" hours in order not to attract suspicion'.[37] A follow-up report expressed widely held fears that the factory was not a standalone operation, stating, 'it must be presumed that other factories exist or are planned for this purpose'. Prime Minister Wilson sought to have the Irish government run an automated check on 'every recent factory which has either been let or sold', adding 'Please telegraph your estimate of the chances of getting the Irish authorities to carry out such a check. You should not consult them at this stage'.[38] The proposal was not followed through on.

During the period that Light Machine Services was operating, the IRA also began experimenting with mortars. This weapon was first used against British military targets in County Tyrone in 1973.[39] Their effect was considered unsatisfactory. When discussing the poor results from the use of RPG-7s in August 1973, Daithí Ó Conaill also remarked that 'skilful use of the mortars has yet to be secured' thus leading to the establishment of manufacturing and training camps later that year.[40] Gearóid MacCárthaigh proceeded from supervision of Light Machine Services to leading one of these camps in the south-west of the country. The camps were hosted by a retired bachelor farmer who allowed the IRA to use his land and farmhouse for billets. Most of the farmer's land was rented to neighbours for grazing. Despite the camps likely being public knowledge locally, there was never any disturbance from the Gardaí. From 31 October to March of the following year ('One of the wettest winters in my lifetime,' according to MacCárthaigh), these mortar training camps were held every four days. The other three days of the week were used by MacCárthaigh to manufacture mortar rounds in the milking parlour and prepare for the next group of recruits. Each day, IRA volunteers left before dawn for the training site and remained there until after dark. Each evening, the farmer had a large pot of stew ready – 'They were very welcome meals,' remarked MacCárthaigh. Blank mortar shells weighted down with sand were used on the camps. Only one live round was fired on the last day of each camp to give IRA volunteers a sense of their impact. This round was usually fired out to sea to kill the sound. By the end of 1973, one newspaper report noted: 'nowadays, the Provos have home-produced mortars which are near professional'; they would soon earn the grudging respect of the British Army.[41] Among the IRA operations where mortars were subsequently used was the May 1974 attack on an Ulster Defence Regiment (UDR) barracks in County Tyrone in which Private Eva Martin (UDR) was killed. This attack is recounted in Seán O'Callaghan's memoir.

Changing Tactics in Financing the Provisional IRA

On 3 August 1973, as IRA volunteers were manufacturing firearms at Light Machine Services, they received an unexpected visit. The callers were two Gardaí canvassing businesses and homes in the area following a recent shooting. Unbeknownst to the men in the factory, only a short distance away a Provisional IRA unit had recently attempted the armed robbery of a vehicle delivering wage packets to the British Leyland factory in the same industrial estate. During the robbery, the unarmed delivery man, James Farrell, was shot dead. Three men subsequently received sentences of penal servitude for life.[42] Upon receiving the Gardaí, Gearóid MacCárthaigh invited them into the factory. That day, six weapons had been completed and were locked in the office. When the Gardaí enquired about access, MacCárthaigh claimed that the boss had the key and was away. Luckily for the Gardaí, they did not insist on getting access. As MacCárthaigh recounted, 'Had they done so, they would never have lived to see any award for what they discovered that day.' He subsequently referred to it as 'one of the narrowest shaves I ever had in my life in the army'.[43]

On IRA financing, a 1976 report by the Northern Ireland Office noted that NORAID had provided an estimated $1,200,000 since 1971. A spike in the wake of Bloody Sunday distorted the average annual amount which was then at about $100,000. The report continued: 'We believe that money from the U.S. represent under 20 per cent of the PIRA total income; by far the greatest amount comes from criminal activities in Ireland, particularly from bank robberies in the Republic. The PIRA campaign is aided by but does not depend on U.S. financial help.'[44] When exactly the IRA began using this tactic remains unclear. By the summer of 1972 armed robberies were certainly being carried out in the North, but the South was slower to adopt this tactic.[45] J.B. Bell, who maintained a number of sources within Irish republicanism from his time researching the IRA in the late 1960s, stated emphatically: 'the Provos undertook their first twenty-six county armed robbery in August 1973'.[46] Bell's assertion does tie in with Seán O'Callaghan's account of the local leadership in Munster being removed in 1973, which facilitated the subsequent planning of armed robberies in the region.[47] In an interview in late 1971, Ruairí Ó Brádaigh claimed that bank robberies were 'completely contrary to the national interest' and that 'this is not the time and the 26 counties is not the place'.[48] Prior to the split, the IRA had carried out an armed robbery near Ballymun in May 1969. This yielded the greatest sum taken from such an operation in the history of the state to that time.[49] As well as this, the small republican group, Saor Éire, had been engaged in armed robberies in the South for several years prior to Ó Brádaigh's statement. Their successes had shown how beneficial it was in terms of a risk-benefit calculation.[50]

It is generally accepted that the Official IRA was responsible for most bank robberies during the first years of the 1970s.[51] According to the Garda Commissioner at the time, almost £2m was stolen in 619 bank robberies in 1973 throughout the whole of Ireland. Although this figure was divided between two states, it represents close to one bank robbery every second day, per state.[52] This drastic spike puts events into perspective should one choose to accept Bell's assertion that 1973 was the year when the Provisionals began to conduct armed robberies. As with arms acquisition and training, the IRA in Munster played a key role in funding, along with the two battalions of the Dublin Brigade, based on either side of the Liffey.[53] In December 1974, a Provisional IRA unit carried out what was then the biggest bank robbery in the history of the state at Shannon, County Clare. The operation netted £140,000.[54] Already in May of that year the *Irish Independent* was referring to a 'wave of robberies' in the South.[55] Indeed the frequency of these crimes led to a claim by the Republic's Minister for Justice Patrick Cooney that lawlessness had reached its peak in the three months ending in June 1974, when £114,000 was stolen in twenty-one armed robberies.[56] Across the state, such incidents became almost commonplace. They served as a huge source of finance for the Provisionals and a principal activity for Southern IRA units. Such was the proliferation of these raids that one study of the period noted how 'armed robberies of post offices, banks and company pay rolls every Friday became something of a national joke' – on one particular Friday, there were four armed robberies in Dublin alone.[57]

Given the unifying motivations for which most Southern volunteers joined the Provisional IRA, the need for armed robberies and people to carry them out was perhaps disheartening for those who sought real 'action'. As J.B. Bell incisively notes, it was far more difficult to persuade idealistic young men to steal than to kill – a soldier's lot – but that necessity made volunteers into armed raiders.[58] Despite substantial involvement in such activities, Southern IRA volunteers refused to equate their actions with criminality. Bell noted that all such robberies were treated as though they were military operations.[59] There is no consensus on the centralisation of funds within the Provisional republican movement. Some analysts claim that all monies had to be processed through central command, while the existence of distinctive finance officers for separate commands indicates a degree of independence.[60] It has been asserted that Provisional IRA units, with rare exceptions, were almost entirely self-financed; particularly in the South, but in several parts of the North also.[61] Surplus money raised by individual units or areas would then serve to feed into the organisation as a whole and contribute to the acquisition of arms and supplies from abroad. The spike in armed robberies in County Kerry for three years preceding the 1984 *Marita Ann* arms importation attempt could be taken as evidence that periodic increases in such activity were driven by intent rather than opportunism.[62] As *The Irish Times* noted for a later arms importation attempt: '"fundraising" activities tend to come in cycles. Where a large sum of money is required, perhaps for an incoming shipment of arms, the raids will be frequent and sustained until the required sum of cash is at hand.'[63]

Continued Support and Toleration in the South

By 1973, public displays of support for militant republicanism were becoming less commonplace. However, a steady but undetermined proportion of the population still refused to equate the IRA with bogeyman status. Indeed, so long as certain transgressions were avoided, attitudes to IRA actions often bordered on the flippant. Following the theft of the entire takings from the Munster senior hurling final in Thurles in 1977, one Clare spectator remarked, 'I'm delighted about it. We [the Clare team] were robbed today, and now the GAA is robbed. If they hadn't charged us as much as they did to go in, all that money would not have been stolen.'[64] *The Irish Times* reported on how spectators received news of the armed robbery, a reception that could be classed as ambivalent at best: 'The news did not stun the crowds when it was broken to them in the packed public houses in the Tipperary town. The raid had simply added drama to a highly emotional occasion.'[65] As for committed republicans, attendance at commemorations remained, as ever, an overt and defiant way to declare their support for the IRA. None more so than the annual commemoration at Bodenstown, County Kildare, on the birthday of Theobald Wolfe Tone, the 'father' of Irish republicanism. While the veracity of the figures can be disputed, *An Phoblacht* reported attendances of 20,000 and 15,000 at the 1973 and 1974 events respectively,[66] the Easter commemorations for that latter year were reportedly 2,000 attendees in Monaghan town, 1,000 in Nenagh, 700 in Limerick city and 'hundreds' in Tralee and Drogheda.[67]

As discussed, particularly egregious incidents such as Bloody Sunday could bring far greater numbers of Southerners out in gestures of support, solidarity or sympathy. One such example was the funeral of IRA prisoner, Michael Gaughan, in June 1974. Gaughan died in Parkhurst Prison on the Isle of Wight from complications arising out of a hunger strike he was engaged upon. He had been serving a prison sentence for his part in an armed robbery in London. Although the robbery was conducted to raise funds for the Official IRA, Gaughan transferred his loyalties to the Provisional IRA while he was imprisoned. His hunger strike was part of a broader campaign among several IRA prisoners in the UK for recognition of their political status and for repatriation to serve their sentences in Ireland. Gaughan's hunger strike had already stirred up significant tensions. His death came just days after the collapse of the exclusionary Sunningdale Agreement, two weeks after the Dublin–Monaghan bombings. As per his wishes, Gaughan was due to be buried in his native County Mayo. Following a funeral in London, attended by 5,000 mourners, his body was flown to Dublin airport; the cortège thus traversed the breadth of the country to reach Mayo. At towns and villages along the route of the procession, people came out in great numbers to pay their respects. This, despite – or perhaps because – Gaughan's coffin was accompanied by a full military guard of honour provided by the IRA. When it reached Mullingar, the procession stretched back more than two miles. By the time Gaughan's body reached its final resting place in the town of Ballina, untold thousands had paid their respects. The coffin was draped in the same tricolour which adorned the coffin of Terence MacSwiney, the IRA volunteer and Sinn Féin Lord Mayor of Cork who died on hunger strike in 1920. What happened on Gaughan's final journey was quite remarkable and a source of great alarm and discomfort to the coalition government. The burial ceremony itself was attended by approximately 10,000 people.[68] Cinemas, public houses and most of the shops in Ballina were closed for the day. Several months later, a tribute song was recorded by Belfast band, The Wolfhounds. Despite being banned from airplay by RTÉ, it sold over 10,000 copies in the South.[69] The previous year, and despite a similar radio ban, a satirical song recounting the Mountjoy helicopter escape spent four weeks at number one in the Republic's music charts.[70]

The refusal of many Southerners to outright reject the IRA, even if they did not actively support them, was a key contributor to their survival.

MacGréil's study of toleration and sympathy for militant republicanism, noted in a previous chapter, was just one of the more quantitative demonstrations of this reality.[71] As one commentator observed of attitudes in the South, toleration 'is easy, comfortable, cost free, traditional and widespread'.[72] Active support was far more worrying for the successive Dublin governments. Particularly, as it occasionally extended to their own political and parliamentary parties, as noted earlier in this chapter. The publisher of a 1973 illegal Provisional IRA booklet, *Freedom Struggle*, was 'a prominent member of the Fianna Fáil party in Drogheda'.[73] Following the government's refusal to reinstate two civil servants arrested onboard the *Claudia*, two Fianna Fáil councillors in Waterford openly declared 'that can't and won't be the end of it' and 'well wait and see'.[74] Of course, Fianna Fáil had long professed to be the most republican of the constitutional parties in the Dáil – notwithstanding the breakaway Aontacht Éireann. Many grassroots members simply saw themselves as carrying on a justifiable tradition of supporting the 'struggle'. Conor Cruise O'Brien sardonically wrote of this phenomenon: '[they have] a sneaking respect for the IRA, the only category of the population not deemed to be less truly Irish than Fianna Fáil. "The boys" might have to be disciplined from time to time, but your heart went out to them all the same. Especially when Fianna Fáil was out of office'.[75] Fianna Fáil members and supporters were often likely to tolerate militant republicanism locally.[76] Other parties were not immune, however. A third interviewee put it thus:

I knew people over the years who were involved in the IRA, people who were involved who were either Fianna Fáil or Fine Gael and so on, you know … a lot of people who were Treaty people in Clare were Treaty because they were against De Valera. And a lot of people who would be now classed as Fine Gael back in the forties and fifties were helping the IRA. Because they were, do you know what I mean, they were Collins people … They were Fine Gael because they had some sort of family connection, but an awful lot of them, and I know an awful lot of them down in, and in no way were they Fianna Fáil… I know places where Fine Gael people brought present-day lads around and put them up and all that, you know.[77]

During one of the IRA hunger strikes of the 1970s, a 67-year-old man wrote to Taoiseach Liam Cosgrave professing to be a lifelong Fine Gael supporter. He added that seeing Cosgrave accept the seal of office in 1973 was one of the proudest moments in his life. The author of the letter went on to say that the marriage of his UCC-graduate daughter to a Northern Catholic businessman in 1963 opened his eyes to the plight of the Northern minority. The letter states: 'I always supported the Treaty ... I still support it of course and will to my last breath ... Let me tell you right now, Mr Cosgrave, that if I was a young man brought up in N.I. I too would be in the IRA.'[78] In his part-sociological account of rural Ireland during the 1970s, John Waters mentioned a similar attitude on the part of his father, a Fine Gael man bitterly hostile to De Valera but supportive of attempts to arm the nationalists in the North following the August 1969 burnings.[79] There is indeed some veracity to these claims in that the 1973 general election highlighted the paradoxical relationship many Southerners held with militant republicanism; an echo of Coogan's droll statement about Fianna Fáil: 'Indeed the late-night Fianna Fáil drinker is quite likely to mutter approvingly about the "boys" – and then go off without a qualm the next day to vote for some Fianna Fáil measure to curb the IRA.'[80] That so many people could mentally divorce two broad issues – the domestic-economic and the age-old struggle with Britain – must be acknowledged if one is to begin to understand the true nature of the Provisional IRA in the South.[81] As one interviewee remarked:

> There's a lot of people ... they'd do anything for you but vote for you. They'd give you their bed. And people around here now, have offered their place to me for use, for arms dumps and things like that. And, you know, I wouldn't go near them in a million years, but they'd offer it ... They'd do anything for you that way, you could hide your guns or you could go hide yourself. But they wouldn't vote for you.[82]

Similar examples exist upcountry, in County Leitrim. Fine Gael families would allegedly purchase fertiliser for the local IRA unit – young men they would have seen grow up – and allow their land and outhouses to be used for making homemade explosives.[83] One of the organisations which endured the most division and bitterness due to its ambiguous relationship with militant republicanism was the GAA. The organisation had been established during the Gaelic revival of the late 1800s and was proud of its historical associations with republicanism. Many of its local branches were named after local or nationally prominent republicans. As a grassroots organisation, it often reflected the attitudes and beliefs of the local population, as discussed above in relation to one of the *Claudia* accused.

Toleration and support for militant republicanism existed among all layers of Irish society, and all professions. The Irish Defence Forces were no more immune to sympathisers and supporters within their ranks than any other workforce. It has been noted that large-scale explosives' raids in the first four years of the conflict led to a serious clampdown on the availability and storage of gelignite. As storage procedures demanded armed guards, revelations soon emerged of soldiers aiding the IRA. In 1974, a significant amount of gelignite was reported missing from the Irish Industrial Explosives factory at Enfield on the Meath–Kildare border. As this factory had been under Garda and military guard for some time, the authorities initially sought a discreet inquiry. The story was leaked, however.[84] The subsequent investigation revealed 'considerable wastage or loss of materials at the factory, which did not have to be accounted for'.[85] Six soldiers appeared in the Special Criminal Court over the theft, four of whom were acquitted. Two others received two and three years' penal servitude respectively.[86] The previous year, a Garda and a staff officer for Cork County Council were sentenced to six months' imprisonment for the theft, possession and suspected transmission of Garda intelligence documents to the IRA.[87] Similarly, a Kerry employee of the Department of Agriculture was sentenced to two years in jail in 1974 for IRA membership.[88] In his history of republicanism in County Leitrim, Cormac Ó Suilleabháin noted a number of similar cases. These include the widow of a Garda offering her home as a safehouse and a retired Irish soldier hosting camps of up to forty IRA volunteers on his land.[89]

State Reaction: Repressive Tactics

By the time they were voted out of office in February 1973, the Fianna Fáil government had begun to take measures clamping down on militant republicanism. The ascension to power of the coalition government marked an escalation in this strategy. One early indicator of a harsher approach was in prison sentencing. In 1974, a man was sentenced to one year's imprisonment for possession of IRA posters.[90] Another received three years' penal servitude for possession of a pistol and ammunition.[91] The contrast with the acquittal of the Mayo farmer noted in the previous chapter is stark. In 1973, the editor of *An Phoblacht*, Éamonn MacTomáis, received a fifteen-month prison sentence for IRA membership. No evidence other than the testimony of a Garda superintendent was proffered as supporting evidence. The trial took place in the Special Criminal Court and was therefore juryless. Eight weeks after his release, the hapless MacTomáis was arrested again and received another fifteen-month sentence for membership and possession of incriminating documents.[92] A previous editor, Colman Ó Muimhneacháin, had also been arrested on such grounds.[93] A contemporary report of the kind of routine raid taking place at the Dublin offices of *An Phoblacht* indicates the principal goal: '[Gardaí] removed documents included a list of subscribers to *An Phoblacht*, a countrywide list of agents who sold the newspaper and documents relating to the prisoners' dependents fund.'[94] Garda brutality and a more wholesale harassment of republicans and their families became commonplace from 1973. It would reach peak levels by 1976. During the autumn of 1973, republican and some mainstream media began reporting of assaults on prisoners in custody. In Mayo, a number of men were reportedly badly beaten by members of the Special Branch; a teenager was beaten, slapped, choked and deprived of sleep.[95] Following the Chase-Manhattan bank robbery in 1974, a Limerick man was arrested and brought to Scariff Garda station in rural County Clare where he was beaten and hung from the banisters.[96] Families experienced harassment also. In the words of one contemporary commentator:

> It is, indeed, a policy of the state, quite unstated, to make life miserable everywhere for republicans. Parents and employers are warned of the dangers of Sinn Féin membership, suspects are questioned where and when the major amount of embarrassment will occur, cars are stopped, tickets given, homes searched, members followed for little other purpose than to cause trouble. When arrests and imprisonments are the policy, often the most vulnerable, men with a new job or a sick wife or a heavy mortgage, are lifted first.[97]

One of the few mainstream publications that sought to highlight these abuses was *Hibernia*. In 1974, they reported on the case of an elderly widow in County Galway who had received a number of hostile visits from the Special Branch. They were seeking the whereabouts of her son regarding the selling of a local republican newspaper. The son, a married man, had been living in a home of his own for a considerable time. This fact was known to the police officers.[98]

That same year, a journalist working for *Hibernia* claimed to have come into possession of an internal government blacklist. The list was fifteen pages long and comprised 250 named Irish people who 'shall be disqualified from holding within seven years of the date of such conviction, any office or employment remunerated out of the central fund or moneys provided by the Oireachtas or by local taxation'.[99] This terminology was employed in legislation barring from state employment – usually for a given number of years – such people as had been convicted under the Offences against the State legislation. However, the list in question contained the names of people acquitted of such crimes as well as those who had never been charged with anything at all. The allegations made by the *Hibernia* journalist have since been vindicated by further testimony. Speaking of his time as Chairman of RTÉ during the 1970s, Todd Andrews recalled being presented by the Special Branch with a list of the names of 'suspect people' working within the organisation.[100] Oliver Maloney, who was the station's General Secretary from 1975 to 1978, similarly stated, 'I got such a [black] list. It was delivered to me by a military officer, and it was marked "top secret". And it contained a list of two and a half pages of individuals who were not considered suitable for appearing on air.'[101] What first struck Maloney as disconcerting was the appearance on the list of several prominent trade unionists who had no criminal convictions.

If the government of the Republic of Ireland were keen to identify and close down IRA support networks, so too were the British. On one occasion, their embassy in Dublin provided the contents of a letter to the Irish authorities written by an English woman resident in Belgium. The woman, who was married to a Belgian man, wrote of how they had sent their son to Ireland since the late 1960s for summer English-language immersion classes. The letter continued: 'It is possible that the addresses at which he stayed were those of IRA sympathisers, if not actually of the IRA. I believed the addresses were obtained through an agency operating from Ostend (for London too ...) "They said they will stop at nothing," said the boy.[102] Undoubtedly, violent incidents committed by the IRA during the tenure of the coalition government fed into the desire to quash militant republicanism and its support base. Whether IRA violence or otherwise, there was always a fear that the conflict proper would spill over into the Republic. Indeed, the greatest single loss of life in one day during the 'Troubles' occurred in the South. In May 1974, bombs exploded in Dublin and Monaghan killing thirty-four people. These were no-warning attacks that, in the case of the Dublin bombs, went off with precise synchronisation. The level of technical skill this entailed likely belies loyalist claims of responsibility, as they signally failed to demonstrate such skill prior or subsequent to these attacks. As with the December 1972 bombings, there is a suggestion that British military intelligence played a part in the making and planting of the bombs. In 2006, an all-party Oireachtas committee concluded that there was no doubt but that collusion between British security forces and loyalist groups was behind many if not all the atrocities considered in their investigations, of which these bombings were included.[103] In the aftermath of the attacks, a candid *Hibernia* editorial stated:

> It is a sad but true fact that not until last Friday's bomb outrage killed thirty-four men, women and children in Dublin and Monaghan did the people of the South come near to appreciating the full extent of suffering, terror and bloodshed, which has been an integral part of everyday life ... in Northern Ireland for the past four years.[104]

Another pivotal event during this period was the killing of Fine Gael Senator, Billy Fox. The popular politician was shot by members of the Provisional IRA in what has been described as a 'confused incident' at the rural Monaghan home of his girlfriend.[105] Although the IRA was undoubtedly responsible for the shooting, the motivation remains unclear to the present day. Fox's religion – he was an Anglican – has led some media commentators to label this as a crude sectarian killing.[106] However, Fox was well-known for being on the liberal side of the Fine Gael party and was widely respected in his border community for opposing the British Army policy of closing border roads, as well as their use of rubber bullets and CS gas during these closures. It has also been claimed that Fox received part of the 'Sinn Féin vote' in two elections.[107] Whatever the truth behind the killing, Senator Fox was the only member of the Oireachtas to be killed during the 'Troubles' and the first serving Irish politician to be killed since the assassination of Kevin O'Higgins in 1927. Understandably, this attack led many TDs and citizens to view the IRA as a legitimate existential threat to the state. The Provisional IRA was also on the back foot in terms of allegations that they were targeting the South's security forces. In May 1974, *An Phoblacht* made official denials regarding attacks on a Garda station and bridge in Swalinbar, County Cavan, as well as the home of a Garda sergeant in County Leitrim.[108]

Republican Prisoner Experiences in the South

In 1973 the Irish government decided to transfer the bulk of republican prisoners to Portlaoise prison. This decision came in the wake of two significant events. The first was the aforementioned riot in May of the previous year at the Curragh. The second major incident was the helicopter escape of three leading Provisionals, J.B. O'Hagan, Kevin Mallon and Seamus Twomey, in October 1973 from Mountjoy prison.[109] The success of this escape was a combination of careful planning and the immediate threat of violence. In the first stage, an IRA volunteer impersonating an American film director phoned an aircraft rental company. This person requested the use of a helicopter and pilot to fly over parts of Leinster for landscape shots. At one point during the flight, the impersonator requested that the pilot land the aircraft in a field in County Laois to collect photographic equipment. Upon landing, two armed and masked men approached the helicopter while the impersonator held the pilot at gunpoint. The impersonator then left with one of the men while the second climbed aboard the helicopter and ordered the pilot to fly to Dublin, landing in the yard of Mountjoy prison while the prisoners were out on exercises. Knowing of the plot in advance, several IRA prisoners worked to restrain nearby warders while others hustled O'Hagan, Twomey and Mallon onboard.[110] Stories such as that of a warder shouting to close the gates of the prison as the helicopter flew away are likely apocryphal. The helicopter was supposed to land at a pitch-and-putt course owned by a republican sympathiser in south Dublin. However, the owner was sick, and the course manager ordered the helicopter off the private property. It subsequently landed at Baldoyle, County Dublin, where the escapees were spirited away by members of the IRA's Dublin Brigade.[111] In Twomey's case, it would be years before he was apprehended. This was not the only example of the IRA using airpower. The following year, Rose Dugdale and several others used a hijacked helicopter to drop two milk churns filled with explosives onto Strabane RUC barracks. Neither bomb hit their target, nor exploded.

The need for a more remote incarceration as much as the need to accommodate rising prisoner numbers thus lay behind the decision to transfer many of the 'politicals' to Portlaoise in 1974. Minister for Justice Paddy Cooney had previously insisted that there was no internment-by-remand system in place in the South. Therefore, the historical implications of using the Curragh for anything more than the detention of a handful of prisoners was too much to contemplate.[112] For a time, however, the number incarcerated in the Curragh did extend into the dozens. In March 1973, the prisoners made a public statement condemning the prison facilities there. Dan Hoban and Martin McGuinness co-signed the statement as prison O/C and Adjutant, respectively.[113] Two months later, a demonstration at the camp by relatives and supporters of the prisoners was attended by up to 1,000 people.[114] According to Tim Pat Coogan's first-hand account, the prison at Portlaoise during the 1970s was 'still the vile place in which Seán McCaughey died' in May 1946, conditions which Seán MacBride had forced the prison coroner at the time to admit he would 'not even keep a dog in'.[115] Martin Ferris, who spent many years incarcerated there, stated that conditions were worse than Long Kesh or the Maidstone prison ship.[116] This same assertion was made by delegates to the 1976 Sinn Féin ardfheis.[117]

As the imprisoned IRA volunteers viewed themselves as members of a legitimate army, escape was a considered priority. During the summer of 1974, Gardaí discovered an elaborate tunnel being dug from outside Portlaoise Prison, beginning at a house 100 foot or so from the perimeter wall, and leading towards the prison. Inside the tunnel were found hacksaws, axes, crowbars, lemmy spades, buckets, ropes and trolleys.[118] Any relief this discovery might have brought was rudely dispelled the following month when nineteen IRA prisoners succeeded in a mass breakout in broad daylight using smuggled explosives. According to contemporary reports, a door and part of the outer wall of the prison were blown up around noon on 18 August with five cars being hijacked locally to facilitate the escapees.[119] Among those who successfully escaped were J.B. O'Hagan and Kevin Mallon, both of whom had been recaptured following the Mountjoy helicopter incident the previous year. Mallon passed the first few days post-escape in a wood near the town of Emo, with seven other escapees and two female volunteers. Local republicans aided their journey to Gorey, via Wicklow.[120] Former IRA prisoner, Christy Burke, has remarked on the likelihood that Mallon allowed himself to be recaptured following the helicopter escape in order to help lead this mass breakout from within.[121] When one considers that Mallon had been captured following an ostentatious appearance at a packed public event in the midlands at a time when he was perhaps the most wanted man in the state, Burke's suspicion seems justified. In seeking information on the escapees, the authorities allegedly used considerable brutality. *An Phoblacht* reported on a young Tipperary man who was savagely beaten by two members of the Special Branch during questioning. Throughout these sessions, the Branchmen refused to allow presence of the Garda desk sergeant, nor to allow the man's family information on where he was being held.[122] Despite extensive follow-up searches, by the end of 1974 sixteen of the escapees were still at large.[123]

Following these incidents, the authorities introduced a much tighter security regime at Portlaoise. Parcels were routinely confiscated and random cell searches took place; additionally, strip searches, became the norm. There was also a big focus at this time on remarks made by Minister for Justice Cooney regarding prisoners and their rights. To quote directly, Cooney stated that 'to talk about prisoners' rights is a misnomer'. This statement was generally taken to mean that Cooney believed prisoners had no rights.[124] According to Gearóid MacCárthaigh, by December 1974 conditions within the prison had deteriorated to the point that the republican leadership within felt compelled to riot to draw attention to their grievances. As well as food parcels not getting through, the prison food within was considered inedible. Tommy McKearney, a prisoner at the time and formerly a butcher, said that the meat they were served was what was used in the manufacture of dogfood; many times the prisoners refused to eat dinner. The planned riot was to take place on the Saturday after Christmas following the rejection of prison O/C Leo Martin's overtures to the authorities on improving conditions. Much preparation went into the riot, with prisoners even producing tallow candles out of kitchen grease in anticipation of the authorities cutting power to the prison. MacCárthaigh stated that, during the riot, Martin and the prison Governor were in the midst of negotiating a resolution when Minister Cooney rang and ordered that the prison be retaken immediately. Aside from the inevitable prisoner–warder violence which arose from this, every piece of private property was confiscated from the inmates; clothes, razors, musical instruments, handkerchiefs. The clothes were eventually returned, though only after being thrown out into the yard during a rainstorm and left there for several days. Conditions within the prison remained as before.[125] It was an inauspicious beginning to the new year and marked a period until 1977 considered the worst for the prison situation in the South.[126]

Peace Attempts

By common consensus, the IRA's 1975 truce was a disaster, bringing the republican movement as close to destruction as it ever came.[127] What has largely escaped serious scrutiny until recent times was why the IRA had ever agreed to the ceasefire. In a 2010 article, Robert White detailed the extent to which the organisation was at an operational and material low point by the end of 1974 when talks began.[128] Successful attacks on British soldiers in the North were decreasing. There was also widespread revulsion of the Birmingham pub bombings in November, which killed twenty-one people, and of the attacks in Guildford, south of London. In the Republic, there was considerable local outrage in Meath following an attempt on the life of a British Army officer. The man was married to a local woman and they were holidaying with their young daughter near Athboy. One night, three rifle shots were fired through the window of their isolated bungalow home. Although the padding of the officer's jacket was hit, he himself suffered no injury. The family left that same night on a ferry back to Britain.[129] As the year drew to a close, Belfast IRA leader Billy McKee insisted that the IRA needed some kind of cessation if it was to have any hope of continuing as a viable force. By this period, with the exception of Armagh, there were allegedly more Northern IRA volunteers imprisoned than active.[130] The state of the Belfast Brigade is a salutary example of republican doldrums. Due to constant arrests, it had had no O/C for the six weeks prior to the ceasefire.[131] On the evening of 9 December 1974, the Provisional leadership met with several Protestant clergymen from Northern Ireland for exploratory peace talks, the implicit understanding being that the clergymen could subsequently act as intermediaries with the British government.

The meeting took place at Smyth's hotel in the remote village of Feakle, County Clare. The Provisional delegation at the meeting comprised Ruairí Ó Brádaigh, Daithi Ó Conaill, Máire Drumm, Seamus Loughran, Billy McKee, Seamus Twomey, Kevin Mallon and J.B. O'Hagan.[132] It is almost certain that, apart from Drumm, this group was in fact the seven-man Army Council of the Provisional IRA at the time.[133] As Ó Brádaigh would later remark of its composition, 'so much for the so-called "Southern Leadership" of which we have heard so much'; all but himself and Ó Conaill were from the North.[134] While progress was made towards a peace agreement, the talks had to be hurriedly broken up when the delegates were informed that Garda Special Branch were en route to arrest the republican contingent. In fact, a combined force of 180 Gardaí, soldiers and members of the Special Branch arrived at the venue to find only the Protestant clergymen remaining. The tip-off about the raid had come from a serving member of the Gardaí.[135] Despite the interruption, the meeting lay foundations for what would become the 1975 ceasefire, with an initial unilateral IRA Christmas ceasefire between 22 December and 2 January. The ceasefire did not equate to a total cessation of IRA activity, however. In the South, the organisation continued to arm and train, as well as raise funds through armed robberies and other tactics. The next chapter will focus on IRA activities during the ceasefire period and subsequent year.

6

The Truce and Restructure, 1975–7

The IRA declared a truce, beginning on 9 February 1975. They had suffered several losses in the first weeks of the new year prior to this. On 21 January, two volunteers in Belfast were killed when explosives they were transporting exploded in transit. Eleven days earlier, one of the more contentious killings of the 'Troubles' took place over the border in the Republic of Ireland, that of John Francis Green, an IRA volunteer and native of north Armagh. Green was on the run at the time, staying in a safe house in County Monaghan. According to one version of events, a squad of the loyalist paramilitary Ulster Volunteer Force forcibly entered the house and shot him dead. Former British soldiers have alleged that the squad included members of the British security forces.[1] Shortly after this, Southern IRA volunteer Kevin Coen was shot dead by British soldiers at Kinawley, County Fermanagh. This shooting also took place in disputed circumstances. On the morning of 18 January, Coen and several Leitrim-based IRA volunteers had left Kiltyclogher to take part in a military operation. Accounts differ as to whether their unit came under attack from a fortuitously positioned British Army patrol while attempting to hijack a CIE bus coming from the Republic of Ireland, or whether an IRA roadblock manned by Coen and others was shot at by a civilian car containing British soldiers.[2] A republican account of the killing asserts the latter.[3] Kevin Coen, a native of County Sligo, was the third IRA volunteer from what would later be termed 'Southern Command' to be killed on active service. He first came to the attention of the authorities in November 1972, when he and several other young men from Sligo were stopped by Gardaí in County Leitrim. The car they were traveling in was found to contain a crate of petrol bombs. Taking full responsibility for the cache, Coen was sentenced to six months' imprisonment. All the other occupants of the car were acquitted.[4] At his funeral in Riverstown, County Sligo, the local priest willingly officiated despite a volley of shots being fired over the coffin.[5] A similar incident occurred at Dermot Crowley's funeral in 1973.[6] The South remained particularly active in 1975 and into 1976. The coalition government in turn became increasingly authoritarian in its bid to stamp out republican support and activity. IRA attacks on Gardaí and British diplomats galvanised government attitudes. The coalition continued to improve communication and cooperation with their British counterparts, as documented in this chapter. In tandem with the situation in the North, prisons became a major battleground between Southern authorities and the IRA. By the time the coalition government was voted out of power in 1977, a tense stalemate had emerged.

Continued IRA Activity in the South

Elements of the Southern leadership of the IRA maintained internally that the ceasefire applied only to actions within the 'warzone' i.e. Northern Ireland. This was not publicly declared, nor was it a discussion among the leadership. It was, however, implicitly accepted in certain circles. Unbeknownst to GHQ, fertiliser-boiling for the manufacture of homemade explosives continued in Munster at the same level as previous years.[7] The very month the ceasefire ended, a tanker was discovered outside Newry which had come from south of the border. Its contents indicate the degree to which the activity had continued: two and a half tons (ninety-six bags) of homemade explosives were found within. It was estimated that this was enough for sixty car bombs. Along with these explosives were found numerous detonators, more than twenty live incendiary bombs and 220lbs of gelignite. The latter had been stolen from the Irish Industrial Explosives base at Enfield, County Meath.[8] Several months later, Gardaí scored a major success when they raided a house in a Cork city suburb and discovered what the media described as a 'bomb-making school'.[9] Of the seven arrested in the raid, all but one was from Northern Ireland. Another major discovery post-ceasefire was in County Offaly where two men were caught with four tons of fertiliser and bomb-making equipment.[10] A find at a farmhouse between Clara and Athlone some months later was described as follows:

> Garda inspector Peter Fitzpatrick ... saw a number of plastic fertiliser bags ... each bag contained three stones of ammonia nitrate and there were 140 bags in all. Also found were seven fibre glass water tanks, two of which contained a white crystal material floating on top. There were 25 fibre glass tanks in addition to seven 85-lb glass cylinders and a number of 40 gallon steel barrels. There was crude firing equipment for heating the tanks.[11]

Perhaps due to the relative quiet in terms of operations, the ceasefire period marked a notable increase in the level of expertise within the IRA's engineering department.[12] Other factors include an influx of young men into the IRA post-internment with electrician or technical backgrounds. The institutionalisation of production, the repetition and specialisation in subsequent years peaked efficiency by the mid-1970s.[13] IRA fatalities from premature explosions dropped from thirty-one in 1973 to two or fewer by 1978.[14]

The previous chapter detailed the rise in armed robberies from the early 1970s. This activity peaked in the middle of the decade. The IRA's General Standing Order Number Eight expressly forbid members from carrying out attacks on members of the security forces of the Republic.[15] This order did not therefore rule out armed activity in the South, merely restricted it. Even then only marginally, given the paucity of resources available to the Gardaí in dealing with the huge increase of armed robberies. As one detective remarked later in the decade: 'Let's face it, if the Provisionals decide to have a big bank robbing spree we can't really stop them. We may catch a few while they're at it but for every one we get, three will be away and running.'[16] Taking the organisation as a whole, there is common consensus that by 1975 their financial situation was bleak. As a result, the IRA in the South were increasingly tasked with fundraising responsibilities, something they appear to have taken up with aplomb. The IRA in Munster alone provided the organisation with £1.5m from armed robberies in a six-year period beginning in 1974.[17] These robberies include the hijacking of a postal van in Kerry containing £74,000 and the theft of the takings from the 1977 Munster

Senior Hurling final in Thurles worth £24,000.[18] Both the Kerry and Thurles robberies were reportedly carried out by provincially local units; witnesses to the robbery in Thurles described the thieves as having 'Cork accents'.[19] The Provisional IRA was not the only group to be involved in this activity. To contextualise the scale of this activity, in the first ten.months of 1977, there were 260 armed robberies in the South, averaging far more than one every second day. Only one-third of these resulted in criminal proceedings.[20] One former IRA Volunteer spoke of the advantages of armed robberies as against alternative methods of financing the IRA's campaign:

> The advantage of a bank robbery is that it's over and done with immediately and the movement gets what it needs. Whereas, if you have to appoint someone to run a fruit machine, well the Inland Revenue will start asking the pubs where is it going, so you have to set up a company to do it, and if you've a company to do it you have to have somebody to manage it. And if you've a manager, you can't have the manager compromised so the manager and his staff or her staff are then effectively paid employees. If you've people buying and selling diesel … laundering diesel, what tends to happen is that, because … there are people you don't necessarily want to be seen doing it so you have to have an unhealthy relationship to the underworld, with the criminal fraternity. You have to allow them … you obviously don't want the person who's known as the local O/C to be caught driving a lorry load of bleached diesel so you have to come to a compromised understanding with somebody else. But, bit by bit it tends to undermine … If the purpose of the organisation is to fight an insurrection, if a percentage of it starts to look to make a profit, it undermines the morale, the outlook, the ethos.[21]

For a time, the kidnapping of wealthy businessmen seemed to promise lucrative dividends and followed on from the move away from post office and bank raids.[22] Kidnapping entailed substantial risks from a public relations perspective, however. An early example of this practice was the abduction of Lord and Lady Donoughmore in County Tipperary in 1974 (linked to an attempt to secure the release of republican prisoners) which backfired badly on the Provisionals.[23] The elderly couple appeared on television soon after their release, with Lord Donoughmore sporting visible head wounds from a pistol-whipping. Their plucky nature and apparent *joie de vivre*, in spite of their experiences, did much to capture viewer sympathy.[24] A more prolonged and publicly damaging kidnapping occurred the following year. On 3 October 1975, Dutch industrialist Tiede Herrema was kidnapped near to his Limerick home by an independent republican group.[25] Herrema worked for the Ferenka steel cord manufacturing plant, which employed 1,200 workers in the region, investing almost £5m into the local economy annually. There was considerable outrage, particularly in Limerick city, over the kidnapping. Six thousand workers marched through that city in a protest demonstration demanding Herrema's release.[26] The kidnapping led to a major state-wide search operation, and the Gardaí were not the only pursuers. The IRA leadership was furious at the activity of what was already a distrusted and fringe element of the organisation, led by Eddie Gallagher. IRA volunteers searched the homes of republican sympathisers in the midlands and Munster in the hunt for the kidnappers.[27] Members of the Gardaí got there first, having been given carte blanche by government ministers to beat information out of suspects. After more than two weeks, Herrema and his captors were tracked down to a house in Monasterevin, County Kildare. A major standoff ensued, with large numbers of Gardaí, Irish Defence Forces and international media descending on the midlands town. In addition, four members of the British police travelled over from London to provide advice and assistance. This was the result of secret talks between the Dublin and London governments and was not publicised at the time.[28] The siege ended after two weeks with Herrema's release and the arrest of his kidnappers. The principal mediator during the siege was trade unionist activist and Sinn Féin member, Phil Flynn.

Given the unsanctioned nature of the kidnapping, there was speculation about whether those involved would be accepted into the IRA structures in Portlaoise prison. Security sources were particularly sceptical that Eddie Gallagher would be allowed. He was already suspected of holding back £30,000 from bank robberies undertaken as an IRA volunteer. During his trial, he had also accused leading republicans, Gerry O'Hare and Joe Cahill, of being informers.[29] Gallagher eventually served his sentence on a non-aligned republic wing reportedly titled the Socialist Republican Alliance.[30] During the siege itself, it was reported that locally Gallagher and his gang were regarded with folk hero status, including among off-duty soldiers. The Ferenka plant, long the scene of bitter strikes, closed shortly after the kidnapping trial with the loss of all jobs. However, as Coogan noted: 'This was largely due to labour relations and the fact that ... the factory had been rendered near obsolete by newer technology, but the kidnapping will always linger on in some people's minds as the main causative factor.'[31] While neither of the kidnappings discussed here was sanctioned – they were, in fact, carried out by men and women on the margins of the IRA – it inevitably reflected badly on the organisation. Kidnapping as a fundraising tactic was banned in the South for some years.

Post-Ceasefire Restructure of the Republican Movement

The effectiveness of the IRA's 1975 ceasefire was always limited by geography and events on the ground. Some areas such as South Armagh arguably paid little more than lip service to the agreement.[32] In areas such as Belfast, sporadic breaches followed a pattern of loyalist attacks on Catholic civilians, a tactic which increased significantly during the ceasefire. A Provisional–Official feud in the city at this time also led to several killings. Officially, however, the ceasefire continued until 23 January 1976. Among historians, it is commonly accepted that the ceasefire was a disaster for the IRA. Dominant elements of the republican leadership assumed that ongoing discussions with the British government were undertaken with mutual sincerity, with a view to eventual British withdrawal from Northern Ireland. The British deliberately drew out the discussions to divide the republican movement and build up strong intelligence on its members before the ceasefire's inevitable breakdown. Records of the discussions available in the Brendan Duddy Collection at the National University of Galway library support the basis for the then-republican leadership trusting to British sincerity. Regardless, large sections of the IRA were sceptical – even hostile – to the ceasefire from its outset. The incident centres which were established in the North as part of the ceasefire terms were an early target for militants. These centres were manned by Sinn Féin volunteers and were ostensibly used to observe and continually assess the ceasefire. Their use as community information offices did much to strengthen the party's credibility in some nationalist areas. In others, they were the subject of neglect or attack. An incident centre in

Newry, which was largely under the operational remit of the IRA's South Armagh Brigade, was never actually manned. It was in fact blown up by the IRA while the ceasefire was still officially in place. The incident centre in Derry city was also blown up by the local brigade there.

The breakdown of the ceasefire was quickly followed by the removal of Special Category status in Northern Ireland. There was also an increase in successful British military operations. The dip in IRA operational efficiency was apparent in the early months of 1976. To reverse this trend, the leadership implemented a structural division in the IRA. Henceforth, there were to be two separate logistical and operational commands. This was perhaps the single most significant change within the republican movement between the foundation of the Provisional IRA and the abandonment of abstentionism in 1986. Orthodox accounts of the 'Troubles' maintain that this division allowed for Northern Command to assert its primacy in the campaign and ultimately dominate the republican movement. Other commentators downplay the degree to which it was to be used as a vehicle for dominating the movement by an inner circle. J.B. Bell, for example, noted that precedent existed from decades earlier for a distinct Northern Command.[33] While one can certainly understand the need for such demarcation, Bell downplays or misunderstands the degree to which it was to be used as a vehicle for dominating the movement.[34] Due to Northern Command operating in the 'warzone', it was always going to carry much more clout in the organisation regardless of existing hierarchy.[35] The extent to which the Army Council eventually became almost an appendage to this command is undoubtedly significant. In the first five years of the Provisional IRA's existence, two of their four Chiefs-of-Staff had been Southerners or Southern-based. In contrast, from 1977 until the disbandment of the Provisionals in 2005, not one Chief-of-Staff was a Southerner.[36] There was certainly a logical justification for this. Many of those who lived south of the border were ignorant of the conflict's many facets and nuances. Furthermore, an inevitable frustration arose on the part of many Northern volunteers towards their Southern counterparts as noted in an earlier chapter.[37] As one interviewee stated:

[T]he accusation was frequently made that [Southerners], while willing to support an armed campaign, they had the privilege of doing so from a distance and practically cost-free … Which… it might be too harsh of a criticism, and I don't think it's perfectly fair to say about them. I don't think they were callous. But, having said that, there was some resonance in the accusation.[38]

Tensions undoubtedly existed within the Provisional republican movement along a broadly North–South divide.[39] Although units and volunteers from the Republic played a frontline role in the conflict from the outset, as time passed this was less and less so in terms of offensive operations. A greater focus on secondary roles came to define Southern involvement.[40] This exacerbated Northern elitism.

During much of the 1970s, Belfast served as the cockpit for the IRA's campaign. Volunteers from that city account for over 40 per cent of those named on the Provisional IRA's roll of honour.[41] An awareness of the primacy of their role in the campaign perhaps led to an arrogance in approach. On one occasion, several Belfast volunteers left their training camp in County Clare to go down to a shop in the local village for cigarettes and chocolate while armed. Nothing was reported to the Gardaí and the training officer was dismissed. That the men insisted their superiors had over-reacted to the misadventure exacerbated tensions locally.[42] One interviewee stated: 'It's a known fact that Belfast didn't really understand how the South operated, you know, and they said "oh, we can do things down here." And you couldn't do things down here.'[43] Youth was another possible factor in terms of attitudes; the vast majority of Northern volunteers during the 1970s were under twenty-five years of age.[44] 'Acting as though it was a holiday camp', was how one interviewee saw it; 'their main concern was that they might miss their dole'.[45] Several armed volunteers from Derry allegedly absconded from a midlands training camp only to get lost in the surrounding countryside. Martin McGuinness refused to court-martial the men despite the need for a search conducted by locals, leading to mutual enmity. A gross under-appreciation of the risks daily taken by Southern republicans – and the modest demands they might make – was demonstrated by Seamus Twomey. A midlands farmer whose land was being used for training camps asked that no fires be lit at night and that food instead be cooked using small gas ranges so as not to draw any suspicion. One group from Belfast ignored this request, following which the farmer made a complaint. This was passed up the line to Twomey who allegedly replied, 'Fuck it, you can get another camp.'[46] In their study of the Official IRA, Hanley and Millar wrote of similar tensions.[47] Following the split in the Officials and the emergence of the INLA, such differences remained. In particular, the Dublin-based INLA leadership found it impossible to control and direct units in Belfast.[48] A former Southern member of the INLA stated simply that 'Belfast could not be controlled.'[49]

Clashes with the State

The Irish Defence Forces underwent a personnel increase of 40 per cent during the first half of the 1970s. By 1976, its strength was the highest it had been since the Second World War. At the close of 1975, nearly 700 people had been convicted in the Special Criminal Court for crimes ranging from firearms and explosives possession to armed robbery to IRA membership.[50] Nobody could claim that the coalition government was soft on militant republicanism. A major test came in February 1976 when Frank Stagg, an IRA volunteer in Britain, died on hunger strike in Wakefield prison. Stagg was from Mayo, the same county as Michael Gaughan, and had requested to be buried in the same republican plot at Ballina.[51] The government, fearing a repeat of the public sympathy and support which Michael Gaughan's cortège engendered, was determined to prevent this. Stagg's grieving widow and family were pressured to publicly call for a non-republican funeral. Simultaneously, the plane carrying Stagg's coffin to Dublin was quickly and quietly rerouted to Shannon airport. From there, it was spirited to Mayo by helicopter. A heavy Garda presence at the Shannon mortuary prevented anybody from paying their respects to the body. Frank Stagg was buried in his family's plot, the grave being covered in concrete by order of the government and an armed guard placed onsite to prevent re-interment. There was a full-scale riot on the day of the burial outside Ballina. Gardaí and members of the Irish Defence Forces clashed with republican supporters, including a large contingent from the North. In Dublin that night, several British-owned stores as well as the Shelbourne Hotel were attacked with firebombs.[52] Of his immediate family, only Stagg's widow and one brother – Labour TD, Emmet Stagg – supported the government's actions. Emmet Stagg also aided in the burial of his brother, although it has been reported that Frank requested in his will that Emmet not attend the funeral.[53] Their mother and the rest of Frank Stagg's other eleven siblings were vocally opposed to the government's actions. The Provisional IRA simply waited for budget cuts and government restrictions to cancel the guard. When this occurred several months later, an IRA unit removed the coffin one night by digging down parallel to the grave, past the eighteen-inch layer of concrete. Stagg was re-interred in the republican plot next to Michael Gaughan in a nocturnal ceremony overseen by a Catholic priest, who recited prayers as the work was carried out. A volley of shots was then fired over the grave.[54]

In its desecration of funerary rites and the denial of a dying man's last wishes, the coalition government demonstrated its commitment to preventing outward displays of support for militant republicanism. Even supporters of the government were appalled at the callous act. Taoiseach Liam Cosgrave received letters from Fine Gael voters across the country noting their shock.[55] It was no surprise when the coalition government declared that same year that any civil servant attending the Provisional Sinn Féin Easter commemoration would lose their jobs and pension rights. Although an opponent of IRA violence, Labour TD David Thornley, defied this ban to demonstrate his abhorrence at the stripping of civil liberties. He attended the Dublin rally and was expelled from the Labour parliamentary party. Thornley also received a fine in court.[56] He compounded his transgression by declaring on RTÉ radio in advance of the Easter appearance that if charged before the Special Criminal Court, he would refuse to recognise it. This marked him out as a dangerous fellow-traveller to the authorities, with the British Embassy referring to it as 'pure Provisional language'.[57] Despite the government's ban, the estimated turnout in Dublin for the Provisional rally was 10,000, a figure the government considered very worrying.[58] The British pondered whether many participants lacked specific sympathies with the Provisional IRA 'but felt it essential to show their patriotic feeling on such an occasion etc'. They remained acutely aware of the alternative, however, in that it could represent 'a substantial body of grass-roots Republican opinion which, in certain circumstances, can be mobilised by the IRA and that no Irish government should forget this'.[59]

The 'Heavy Gang'

Legislation and increased security budgets were but two prongs of the government's strategy for defeating the IRA. As noted at the beginning of the chapter, the mid-1970s witnessed an escalation in the number of alleged cases of Garda brutality, as well as in accounts of their ferocity. In 1976, repression and Garda brutality arguably peaked. Of course, such repression cannot be viewed in isolation. Three particular killings in the Republic of Ireland during this period, of two Gardaí and a British ambassador, undoubtedly contributed to a tolerance of such practices within the force. A 1978 satirical book titled *The Comic History of Irish Politics* described the Special Branch as 'Ireland's version of courtesy cops. They are specially trained in the arts of good manners, kindness, gentleness and soft handling. They never, never beat up prisoners to get information out of them.'[60] By the time of the book's publication, the nod-and-wink implications were clear to contemporary Irish readers. A year prior to this, a young Tipperary man had jumped from the second-floor window of Cahir Garda station to escape the police beatings he was being subjected to. He broke his pelvis and nose and suffered lacerations to his legs and arms.[61] That man and three others – two of whom were members of Sinn Féin – had been held under new legislation by which suspects could be kept for seven days of questioning. According to the men, they were subject to regular beatings, deprived of sleep and water, and were forced to sit next to a large fire for extended periods. Their Garda interrogators allegedly told them: 'We'll break you mentally and physically on the seventh hour of the seventh day – that's when they all break.'[62] All this so that the men would confess to a list of crimes and sign pre-written confessions.

Thomas Connors, the one who jumped out of the window, later told journalists, 'I was trying to kill myself. I couldn't stand it. I said to myself – it will last seven days and I'll never stand it.'[63] A subsequent investigation by *The Irish Times* confirmed the widely suspected existence of a Garda 'heavy gang', a group composed primarily of members of the Dublin-based murder squad.[64] One interviewee who experienced this group recalled: 'this crew, this gang went around different police stations where republicans were held, and there was some very nasty people in it, very nasty people.'[65] Later in 1977, *Hibernia* was noting with concern the spread of police brutality. In a report on a Sligo farmer who was deprived of sleep for sixty-three hours while under arrest, the newspaper noted: 'The most unusual aspect of his complaint is that the threats and intimidation to him and his family came from members of the Gardai who operate in uniform. The Heavy Gang's example seems to be spreading.'[66]

Following the fatal shooting of Saor Éire member, Larry White, in Cork city in 1975 – part of a local republican feud – one man reportedly had a plank of wood broken across his back in Edward Street Garda station, Limerick city. The detectives told him: 'We're going to break you, and then you're going to talk and name Seán O'Neill and Joe Quinn, and we'll break them too.'[67] Another man in the city was 'interrogated for fifteen hours by relays of branch men, beaten with a block of wood on the chest and arms and punched all over the body.'[68] One of the suspects in the Larry White investigation – the victim's brother, no less – was reportedly beaten so badly that his testicles swelled to alarming proportions, 'the size of grapefruits.'[69] Martin Ferris claims to have received similar treatment from the 'heavy gang': '[they were] beating the living daylights out of us and they damaged the eardrums and, eh, head down the toilet, kept us awake for four days and four nights, constant pushing and shoving, slapping, squeezing your private parts, things like that, all of that was part of it'.[70] Ferris now wears two hearing aids as a result of a detective boxing him on both ears simultaneously from behind. He also recalled the entry into Portlaoise prison of the Irish Republican Socialist Party (IRSP) members, who were beaten into falsely confessing their part in the 1976 Sallins train robbery: 'The Sallins people, in for the Sallins robbery, came in and they had to be helped up the stairs, they were that badly done. The prison officer was walking with them up the stairs. I'd say they had an awful doing on their privates, they were quite bad.'[71]

Section 31 of the Broadcasting Act aided police brutality during this period. By denying a voice to those who were its prime recipients, the state ensured for several years that reports of such outrages remained on the margins of media reporting. Attempts by republican councillors to highlight abuses at a local level were often met with out-of-order rulings by Fianna Fáil and Fine Gael councillors.[72] Government ignorance of such brutal conduct is a misnomer. As a government minister, Garret FitzGerald was well informed. He maintained in his memoir that he withheld such information from the public in the hope that he might be able to influence the issue from within.[73] In that, he failed. Conor Cruise O'Brien appeared to positively revel in his position as arbiter of the rights and physical safety of Irish citizens who found themselves in Garda custody, employing academic semantics in order to place violence on the part of the state in a distinct and acceptable category.[74] In his memoir, he recalled one occasion where Gardaí, transferring a prisoner from Limerick to Dublin, deliberately took backroads in order to 'beat the shit out of him' without fear of disturbance. O'Brien blithely remarked, 'It didn't worry me.'[75] The speed with which mainstream Irish newspapers proceeded to expose Garda brutality following the Cahir incident illustrates how much of an open secret it already was by the spring of 1977. In 1978, a conference was held in Liberty Hall on 'allegations of abuse and torture of prisoners in Ireland and England' which was presided over by three judges: Basque, Belgian and French. The conference organiser, Capuchin monk Piaras Ó Duill asked the audience at the beginning: 'Is there a representative from the *Irish Times* here?' There was no reply. It was the same for a roll call of all other major Irish publications.[76]

Portlaoise Prison I

Conditions within the prisons continued to decline during this period. As discussed, the Mountjoy helicopter escape in 1973 led the government to transfer republican prisoners (including those in the Curragh) to the maximum-security midlands prison at Portlaoise. By 1975, all but a few Provisional IRA prisoners were being held there. On St Patrick's Day of that year, a mass breakout was attempted. As night fell, a metal chain was thrown at an electricity transformer in the vicinity, causing a blackout at the prison. Within minutes, two explosions occurred: one at the recreational hall doorway – where the prisoners were at the time – and another near a compound wall. To divert Gardaí and sow confusion, cars were also set on fire in six areas surrounding the town, while a reinforced truck laden with explosives and driven by four IRA volunteers unsuccessfully tried to ram the gate of the prison. The latter explosion within the prison enabled several prisoners to reach an outer compound area. This was as far as any reached, however. Due to the blackout, the prison guards (including members of the Irish Defence Forces) were on high alert. Warning shots were fired, allegedly followed by direct targeting of prisoners. This prevented them from crossing the prison yard to the compound wall breach. One prisoner was shot dead.[77] The victim was IRA volunteer Thomas Smith, who had been serving a life sentence for his part in the killing of an unarmed man during an armed robbery in Dublin in 1973 (noted in the previous chapter). Republicans maintain that the Irish Defence Forces deliberately targeted prisoners with live rounds, while the official inquest ruled that Smith was killed by a ricocheting bullet.[78] According to a 1972 army ruling, prison escape attempts were one of only several instances where soldiers could open fire with live rounds, the others being 'in protection of soldiers' or others' lives' and 'in the prevention of serious criminal outrage'.[79] Thomas Smith was buried at Glasnevin Cemetery. During the funeral, sections of the 1,000-strong crowd were attacked by baton-wielding Gardaí as attempts were made to fire shots over the coffin.[80]

The escape attempt and shooting came at a time of particularly heightened tensions. The previous month, a female visitor to the prison was found to be attempting to smuggle gelignite in. As a result, random and often violent strip searches began to be carried out on prisoners with increasing regularity.[81] Mesh wire was also installed separating prisoners from their visitors.[82] An ongoing hunger strike within formed the backdrop to the deepening crisis. During the strike, Minister for Justice Patrick Cooney claimed to have received death threats which were made against government ministers in the event of any hunger strikers dying.[83] These threats were repudiated by the Irish Republican Publicity Bureau, who called upon 'Mr Cooney' to publicly identify the 'intermediaries' he claimed to have received the information from.[84] Cooney declined to do so. That hunger strike lasted fifty days and ended in controversial circumstances. According to Gearóid MacCárthaigh, guarantees had been given by the authorities relating to issues such as visiting rights and food parcels, leading to the conclusion of the strike. He claimed that these concessions were quite quickly 'whittled away' and that the number of strip searches actually increased in the aftermath of the strike.[85] Determining the veracity of this latter claim is difficult. Patrick Casey, an IRA prisoner who served a sentence from January 1975 to April 1977, wrote a statement on the day of his release with Father Piaras Ó Duill as witness regarding conditions within the prison. Casey stated that improvements were brought in after the hunger strike but that soon after a grille and thick Perspex went up in the visitor facilities. Further security precautions were introduced – 'many of which were petty' – but that strip searches and solitary confinement were unknown in the prison until after the Green Street escape in 1976.[86] This occurred on 16 July, when several IRA volunteers managed an audacious escape from holding cells beneath the courthouse on Dublin's Green Street. Bombs exploded inside and outside the building to facilitate the escape attempt, the latter being set by a volunteer masquerading as a tourist with a haversack.[87] Among those who escaped was a key IRA engineer. The authorities surmised that the explosives used inside the building must have come, as did the court-bound prisoners, from Portlaoise prison. As a result, cells and their inmates were subjected to additional searches. Particularly embittering, according to Patrick Casey, was the conduct of the Gardaí involved in these searches. All possessions were taken away and letters read aloud by warders and Gardaí 'around the landing and jeered and mocked'.[88] Letters were then thrown on the ground. Regarding the searches, Casey stated:

> If a prisoner resisted the strip searching, as many as 10 to 15 warders would enter the cell and strip the prisoner by force. Men were beaten about their cells and many were injured. I could hear the cries of men as they were being beaten up. I was stripped forcibly every night and every morning during that week.[89]

The Assassination of Christopher Ewart-Biggs

The government's spirit of no-compromise was galvanised when, days after the Green Street escape, the IRA assassinated Christopher Ewart-Biggs, the British Ambassador to the Republic of Ireland. Ewart-Biggs had arrived in Ireland only a fortnight before. A veteran of the Second World War, and a participant in the victory at El-Alamein, he was considered a war hero in Britain. To the IRA, his post-War work in British military intelligence made him a figure of considerable anxiety, as well as a target of prestige.[90] On 21 July 1976, he was travelling in his official car along with his secretary Judith Cook, driver Brian O'Driscoll, and Brian

Cubbon, then the most senior civil servant in Northern Ireland. Less than 200 yards from his Sandymount home, the car struck a landmine, causing a large explosion and throwing the car from the road. The Ambassador and Judith Cook were both killed, while O'Driscoll and Cubbon suffered serious injury. Two men were reportedly seen running from the scene in the moments after the explosion.[91] Three thousand Gardaí were drafted in to assist with the investigation and established several lines of enquiry early on. Four men were arrested, and a jacket and camouflage hat were found near the scene.[92] However, the strength of the Garda leads was dubious. Despite eye-witness descriptions apparently matching one of those linked to the unsolved Whitecross massacre in January of the same year, a Garda Chief Superintendent later ruled out the involvement of the South Armagh IRA.[93] A fingerprint that was discovered on a motorcycle helmet believed to have been used by the assassins was passed to the RUC and Scotland Yard. The print was later revealed to be that of an expert in the Garda Technical Bureau.[94] Garda Commissioner, Ned Garvey, was aware of this misidentification for three months prior to alerting the government. This was one of the primary ostensible reasons Fianna Fáil gave for ousting Garvey when they came to power the following year, Garvey being more aligned politically with the previous coalition government.[95] A report from the British Embassy in Dublin shortly before Garvey's removal noted:

> There are signs that tension between the Garda Commissioner, Edmund Garvey, and the Government may be coming to a head. Garvey had dinner with the Ambassador last week and spoke very frankly about his suspicion of the new Government. He referred nostalgically to Mr Cooney's period as Minister for Justice … He also complained that prison conditions were being made too lenient; that the courts were too generous in releasing known criminals on bail; and that Fianna Fail contained too many Republican sympathisers. The Government, for their part, have lost none of their initial dislike of Garvey. Dunlop, the Government Press Secretary, has told me in confidence that Fianna Fail on coming to power discovered that the *Irish Times* allegations about the existence of a Garda 'heavy gang' were after all substantially true. Dunlop spoke bitterly about Garvey's 'reactionary' views and

blamed him for defending an unnecessarily crude interrogation system and for resisting efforts to investigate Garda abuses.[96]

Nobody was ever convicted for the killing of Christopher Ewart-Biggs and Judith Cook. Two months after the attack, the IRA claimed responsibility in an interview with the *Sunday Independent*, stating: 'We make no apology for it. He was sent here to co-ordinate British intelligence activities, and he was assassinated because of that, and in retaliation for the murder of Peter Cleary in Crossmaglen, and for the activities of the SAS in South-Armagh.'[97] According to Kieran Conway, the single IRA volunteer who carried out this operation was based in England, and the attack was more opportunistic than has previously been attributed.[98] There was considerable public abhorrence at the killings. The Ambassador's age, the fact that civilians were also killed and wounded, and the clear diplomatic transgression this represented served to make it an international story for some time. Very soon after, the coalition government introduced several significant pieces of legislation. The first of these was the Emergency Powers Bill. This extended the period a suspect could be held in custody to seven days. Alongside this was passed the Criminal Law Act. This more than tripled the previous maximum sentence for IRA membership, from two years to seven. The law also made provision for new offences, such as recruitment to subversive organisations.[99]

The British Embassy in Dublin attributed the lack of significant opposition to the legislation to public outrage over the killings as well as the targeted killing of a Garda (discussed below).[100] Another likely contributing factor to the muted opposition was the level of censorship, self- and imposed, which prevailed among much of the Irish media. While Section 31 of the Broadcasting Act has been noted, a more widespread self-censorship took root during the tenure of the coalition government and went in tandem with employment blacklisting. This partly stems from hostility to the Provisional republican movement from elements of the media who maintained strong connections with their ideological rivals, the Official IRA.[101] Overall, the Provisionals considered the *Irish Press* under Tim Pat Coogan's editorship to be the 'least biased in its attitudes' of the southern dailies.[102] That the editorial line in the *Irish Press* was less condemnatory than its competitors was evident to Conor Cruise

O'Brien, whose conduct during his ministerial tenure became increasingly disturbing. Remarkably, Cruise O'Brien would later pen a description of himself as a liberal democrat concerned with rights such as the freedom of expression, which he argued were an important bulwark against internal threats to democracy.[103] Prior to this was the notorious encounter with veteran *Washington Post* journalist, Bernard Rossiter. During a conversation in Cruise O'Brien's office, the government minister declared his intention to introduce new legislation. This would cleanse Ireland of what he saw as the poisonous culture of republican ballads and of schoolteachers who glorified past IRA heroes. Cruise O'Brien opened a desk drawer and produced a collection of cuttings from the 'letters to the editor' section of the *Irish Press*. '[O'Brien] did not propose, he said, to use [Emergency Powers Bill] against the authors of such letters, but against the editor of the paper.'[104] One can only presume he was aiming at a particularly subtle form of irony when, in criticising Soviet practices of dealing with dissenting journalists, he later wrote: 'if you are fired from a given capitalist newspaper … you still have a variety of opportunities within the capitalist market generally'.[105] After losing his seat in the 1977 general election, Cruise O'Brien took up editorship of the *Observer* newspaper in Britain. One of his first actions there was to fire journalist, Mary Holland. He was unhappy at a profile she had written on Mary Nelis, the mother of an IRA prisoner in Northern Ireland. Nelis had travelled Europe clad in a blanket to raise awareness of the dirty strike in which her son was participating for several years. She had once been an SDLP supporter and Holland deftly and sympathetically traced her political odyssey.[106]

Aftermath

The coalition government had intended for some time to introduce legislation similar to the Emergency Powers Bill and Criminal Law Act. They feared a public backlash and evidently felt it prudent to wait until the IRA committed an outrageous act of violence. As Minister Cooney remarked to a Conservative peer, Lord William Harris, following the killing of Christopher Ewart-Biggs and Judith Cook, the legislation could now pass through the Oireachtas with little opposition. During that same meeting, Cooney asked that the British refrain from further 'unfortunate events' such as the Bloody Sunday killings while the legislation was being debated. He did, however, also assure Lord Harris that any such 'political abrasiveness' from the British side would not prevent continued security cooperation between the two governments.[107] Despite British restraint, the Irish President Cearbhall Ó Dálaigh referred the Emergency Powers Bill to the Supreme Court to verify its constitutionality, which it did. The activating of this presidential prerogative led Minister for Defence Paddy Donegan to refer to Ó Dálaigh as a 'thundering disgrace' when addressing troops at a barracks in Mullingar on 18 October. In the fallout that ensued, Ó Dálaigh resigned as President, to be replaced by Patrick Hillery.[108] An interesting addendum to this incident was recounted by veteran republican, Mai Dálaigh, several years later. Her brother, Charlie, was an IRA volunteer executed in Drumboe, County Donegal, during the Civil War. She recounted how her sister met Cearbhall at a social function shortly after his resignation and said to him: 'As one Dálaigh to another, I am to congratulate you on the stand you took.' Cearbhall Ó Dálaigh immediately responded: 'I did it for Charlie and his brothers; you can't beat Kerry.'[109]

The British government was no less sensitive to the potential exploitation of public abhorrence and subsequent embarrassment of the coalition government. It pushed for action in two ways. The first was to secure the release of British soldiers arrested in the Republic of Ireland. On the night of 5 May 1976, eight SAS troops in two vehicles had been arrested by Gardaí manning a roadblock, with military support. The elite British soldiers attributed their presence in the wrong state to a map-reading error. Concerns were raised by Gardaí due to the unorthodox weaponry the men possessed. These included a shotgun and dagger. Several months prior, IRA volunteer Sean McKenna was snatched from the Republic side of the border by SAS troops and brought to Northern Ireland. There, he was promptly arrested and sentenced to a lengthy spell in prison by a juryless court. As noted at the beginning of this chapter, the previous year a local IRA leader, John Francis Green, was assassinated in County Monaghan by a purported loyalist squad. For the coalition government, the arrest of the SAS men put them in a difficult political situation. They could not so blatantly abrogate sovereign responsibility by releasing the men without charge. Yet they had no desire to imprison them. The assassination of Ewart-Biggs provided the British government with leverage to release them and the Irish government with an excuse for leniency. A confidential British memo discussing this request contained the hand-written note: 'I find all this letter squalid, but in the language of realpolitik I supposed you always draw up a shopping list when something like this happens.'[110] The British also sought to pressure the Irish government into dropping the case it had brought to the European Court of Human Rights at Strasbourg, concerning the torture of internees in Northern Ireland. A memo noted:

> Even if the traumatic effects of the assassination on Irish opinion fades or proves temporary, I cannot imagine a better time than the present for the Irish government to bring itself to make some specific gesture of goodwill towards Britain. In my view, the single benefit which we could expect to derive from the Irish people's sense of shame and responsibility for the murder of a British Ambassador would be a decision not to pursue the state case of Strasbourg.[111]

The British government also considered requesting fly-by rights in Irish airspace, though this was not pursued as the Irish government flatly turned it down.[112] While the case at Strasbourg continued, a concession was given on the first request. The eight SAS men were charged with unlawful arms possession, fined £100 each and released over the border whence they came.

The introduction of the Emergency Powers Bill paved the way for a fundamental change in IRA policy. As a result of measures contained in the new legislation, IRA volunteers faced the stark reality of several years in jail simply on the attestation of a Garda superintendent. The IRA leadership therefore began to reconsider the prohibition on volunteers recognising the courts – specifically, the Republic of Ireland's Special Criminal Court – without facing censure by the organisation.[113] Originally floated as a policy for change by the reformist leadership of the 1960s (see Chapter 1), the ban on court recognition continued up to the split whence it was maintained only by the Provisionals.[114] The policy was originally introduced as a standing order in 1925 by then Chief-of-Staff, Frank Aiken, shortly before he left the IRA. It was a policy that, in the words of one republican commentator, held the movement 'in a strait jacket for decades'.[115] Non-recognition stemmed from the basic republican position of denying legitimacy to British-imposed political institutions and their legal appendages. Its longevity arguably rested greatly on the strong influence of successive generations of IRA leadership who had experienced the Civil War.[116] For members of the Provisional republican movement, recognition of the courts could and often did entail expulsion; as in the case of prominent Belfast volunteer, Anthony 'Dutch' Doherty, when he recognised a court in Dublin.[117] Newspaper reports from the 1970s contain many accounts where persons charged under Section 30 of the Offences against the State Act refused to recognise the court.[118] However, exceptions were occasionally made. Several accounts exist concerning female republicans who were given permission to apply for bail and/or defend themselves in court. Such instances usually arose where children were involved and the father was dead or himself imprisoned.[119] Shane Paul O'Doherty claimed that it was a localised phenomenon, adding: 'it led to anomalies in the prison, where some Belfast people could recognise the courts which were going to try them, while persons from other areas of Northern Ireland could not'.[120] Belfast republican, Richard O'Rawe, while noting that volunteers were ordered to dismiss their legal counsel, wrote of representing himself in 1974, being acquitted and receiving no censure from the republican movement.[121] Similarly Leitrim republican, John Joe McGirl, represented himself in 1972 and was acquitted of the charge of IRA membership.[122] It is perhaps these occasional successes that O'Halpin referred to when explaining the Dublin decision to amend the Offenses against the State Act in November 1972.[123] The problem with the policy of non-recognition was that the action was in itself a proxy declaration of Provisional IRA membership.[124] A former volunteer remarked:

> When I went to jail first, I refused to recognise the court, 1973, seventeen years of age. This was the policy; you went up. You know, if I had gone up and said I wasn't a member of the IRA at the time, I would have been released, because they had nothing on me, they were just going on a Superintendent's word against me. And the fact that I stood up and said 'I'm refusing to recognise this court', I wasn't fighting the case – it was an admission of guilt.[125]

The policy's illogic was noted by another interviewee:

Really you went around and you carried out the Sinn Féin policy of non-recognition. But you were fooling yourself a lot of the time. You know, you knew in your heart and soul it was kind of ridiculous, you'd go to court and they don't recognise you [*sic*]. I remember [name redacted] going to court inside in Limerick one time and he got up and he said he didn't recognise the court. And the judge said to him, I was at that, he says 'Well, you can go outside and see if you can recognise it.' He dismissed the case. But I thought that was a salutary lesson alright.[126]

Non-recognition was arguably a tolerable hindrance in the South at the beginning of the conflict when IRA membership carried a prison sentence of six months. However, it became a millstone as the standard sentence rose, with the burden of proof resting almost entirely on a defendant's ability to repudiate the allegations of senior Gardaí.[127] By pleading 'not guilty' to IRA membership charges, volunteers placed the onus on Gardaí to provide actual proof of membership.[128] The policy change would, it was claimed, 'emasculate' government measures and 'make a laughing stock of the government'; so much so that Sinn Féin sought a change in their own constitution to allow for the same at their 1976 ardfheis.[129] Daithi Ó Conaill was the first leadership figure to recognise the courts and fight a charge, one of assaulting and obstructing a Garda. Apparently, 'O Conaill felt so strongly about it [the charge] that he had recognised the court and taken advice of counsel in regard to the charges. He was incensed at being accused of behaving like a corner boy.'[130] It is surely no coincidence that this occurred less than a fortnight before the Army Council, which included Ó Conaill, rescinded the policy of non-recognition. What is most likely is that this was the litmus test for court recognition. This policy was shortly extended to the North also.[131] Its success was such that Coogan would later write: 'many senior IRA men now recognise the courts, plead their case and get off to fight another day, much to the chagrin of the security forces on both sides of the border'.[132] In a cable from the British Embassy in Dublin in June 1978, a frustrated note was added to a short newspaper report on the acquittal of two young men charged with membership of the IRA:

This led to a comment by the judge which I think is the closest statement I have seen of the reason why denials of membership by an accused person tends to lead to automatic acquittal on this charge. The court ruled that the men were entitled to be acquitted, because the court preferred sworn testimony to a statement of belief.[133]

Portlaoise Prison II

In the spring of 1976, as the coalition government entered its final year of existence, conditions for prisoners at Portlaoise continued to deteriorate:

> Solitary confinement is a term the prison authorities don't like you to use. They talk of the segregation area … [republican prisoners] are allowed only a ½ hour of daily exercise … For the remaining 23 ½ hours he is detained in his bare feet in the cement-floored cell which is entirely devoid of any furnishings during the day. At night, a mattress and bedding are brought into the cell.[134]

Martin Ferris maintains that the coalition government sought to rapidly align their incarceration policies with those introduced in Northern Ireland in March 1976 as part of that regime's 'criminalisation' policy:

> From the first of March 1976 in the North you had Roy Mason depoliticising the whole thing within the prisons, trying to impose criminal status … the same thing happened within the Twenty-six Counties, but it was never said … there was a deliberate attempt by the authorities within the prison, directed and orchestrated by the minister, the Department of Justice and the minister – and supported by the government – to depoliticise the prison. I think they thought along with the Brits that if you can break the spirit and resistance of the prisoners, you will break the struggle. That was their strategy. And they tried to do the very same thing in Portlaoise.[135]

Solitary confinement was one of the principal methods used to break the will of prisoners, with one sworn testimony listing the following examples:

(1) Martin Ferris, one month: 'telling lag not to sweep the water into his cell' (2) Arthur Burns, one week: putting out light (3) John Little, one week: 'Telling the prison warder on visit who got the visit you r me [*sic*] when he told me to speak up'.[136]

The treatment of visitors by prison staff caused considerable resentment. Coogan wrote of families being kept waiting in the rain for long periods and even denied pre-approved visits. One visit was cut short within seconds because the prisoner's mother greeted her son in Irish. The woman was a native of the Donegal Gaeltacht, who had travelled nearly 200 miles on a round trip that day to visit her son.[137] The mother of another prisoner travelled almost the same distance to see her son, only to be refused access altogether. Her daughter, the prisoner's sister, waited outside the prison in 'biting cold and frost' from half-nine in the morning and only got to see him at half-two that afternoon.[138] The mother of another, James Kavanagh, similarly wrote of standing outside the prison gates for two and a half hours in the rain, about her son not receiving his twenty-first birthday cards, about not being allowed in to see him after receiving a letter of permission from the governor and about her daughter receiving a letter of permission from the governor after the appointed date.[139] Where family members did get to visit prisoners, the same adjectives appear time and time again in depositions made to a local parish priest: 'unshaven', 'distressed', 'haggard'.[140]

The brutality of the regime within Portlaoise prison during this period was largely confirmed by the Prison Officers Association several years later.[141] Repeated and often violent strip searches were carried out on prisoners, as well as regular beatings. The deposition of one prisoner noted the names of those who were beaten in July 1976 for refusing to strip:

Arthur Burns (himself), Eamonn Murphy and Michael McDonagh (all from Dundalk); Joe Ennis and Pat Rehill (Cavan – Pat was OC by late 1976); Donal de Barra (Fermanagh); Martin Ferris and Bobby Mc; Michael 'Sinbad' Healy (Galway); Seamus Rafferty (Dundalk); Brendan McGill (Dublin) and George McDermott (Clones).[142]

Tom Sullivan, an IRA prisoner from Limerick, stated that Clareman Michael McNamara was strip searched twice in less than twenty minutes. Bundoran Sinn Féin councillor, Joe O'Neill, swore to being strip searched six times in twenty-four-hours. Prison warder conduct during these strip searches was not unlike that occurring contemporaneously in the H-Blocks, though with the absence of the hated mirror search: 'There's the other element, a minority, who enjoy it. They jeer at you. After they have examined your back passage they will turn you over, holding you down on the floor, and lift up your private parts to look beneath, and pull back your foreskin roughly with their bare hands.'[143] One prisoner sought a meeting with his solicitor, but was discouraged from requesting more by the set-up in the meeting room. Four foot of table separated the two men and prison warders stood on either side.[144] A visit by one mother to her incarcerated teenage son was conducted side by side with a warder who took notes throughout. Following this, she was denied visits 'for some time'. When next she saw her son, he was 'jumpy and distressed … his hair pulled from the roots … his eyes were swollen … I asked him who plucked him … He didn't dare answer that.' One visit was cut short after a few seconds 'with no explanation. Kevin was roughly dragged away severly [sic] beaten and God only knows what they did to him.'[145] Similarly, the mother of John Hay wrote: 'my son appeared and was staggering; his speech was slurred; his left eye and the left side of his nose were black and blue; the hair on the back of his head was gone leaving a large bald spot'. Her son informed her that at eight o'clock that morning a Garda riot squad of ten had stripped him, pulled him up by the hair and beat him with batons. With some exceptions, such as Father Kearney from Cavan – a family friend of one of the prisoners who wrote a condemnatory letter regarding prison abuses – the clergy did not speak out against this brutality. Frustration over this was noted in a statement by one released prisoner who declared that only three groups were aware of the abuse in the prison: warders, prisoners and priests: 'when I asked one of them [priest] did he agree with what was being done, he replied "God said 'Be good to your slaves'", whatever that meant. They say if they spoke out they would be stopped coming in at all. But if they did speak out people might listen.'[146]

The Chief Prison Officer during this period was Brian Stack. In his biography, Martin Ferris said of him:

Whereas [another man] was a recognised bully boy and heavy, Stack, in contrast, usually directed. Stack was a particularly vindictive individual. He would never forget a previous incident, and if he took a dislike to a certain prisoner, he would wait until a suitable opportunity arose to punish the man in some way or other. He thought nothing of having officers hold a prisoner while he struck him with his baton during a strip-search.[147]

According to Ferris, Stack was despised not just by republicans, but also by many prison officers and ordinary prisoners. A contemporary deposition by a newly released prisoner similarly stated that 'about fifty-five to sixty-five percent of the warders don't agree with what's going on, but they are being watched all the time too'.[148] This was one of the principal grievances at the Prison Officers Association conference some years later:

Portlaoise delegates claimed that staff who had tried to restrain colleagues from beating prisoners had been threatened with physical violence and subjected to verbal abuse by the management. They demanded an end to 'harassment and jackboot tactics' by management and said they must make it clear they did not condone the abuse of prisoners.[149]

Former prisoner John Hickey claimed that some of the principal culprits were the Gardaí stationed in the prison 'with nothing to do … They are sitting on the landings all the time, completely bored. One of them will trip you as you go past. It's not much, but you react. That's the way the trouble begins.'[150]

This period of extreme tension within the prison, as well as the broader escalation in coercive Garda practices outside, precipitated the horrific incident near Portarlington on 15 October 1976. Responding to an anonymous phone call to Portlaoise Garda station, which warned of several men acting suspiciously around a disused house at Garryhinch, several Gardaí left Portlaoise and Portarlington stations to investigate. Attempting to enter the abandoned building, they triggered a booby-trap bomb which had been hooked up to the front door.[151] Garda Michael Clerkin was killed and his four colleagues were severely wounded; one of them, Detective Garda Tom Peters, was left blind and deaf. While the British erroneously referred to the killing as 'the first deliberate murder of a member of An Garda Siochana since the [civil] war', they accurately summarised the ensuing 'public revulsion' and 'ground-swell of hostility towards terrorism'.[152] Although this incident coincided with the introduction of the new Emergency Powers Bill – to be introduced at midnight that same night – it is likely that the context for the attack was more local. Minister Cooney had previously used words which seemed to justify the town of Portlaoise being held hostage by the government so long as the IRA continued its campaign:

> I can understand that the people of Portlaoise are upset and alarmed ... so long as the IRA maintain their campaign, the community will be upset ... until such time as the community as a whole shakes off its complacency about the IRA ... parts of the country will be discommoded – particularly Portlaoise.[153]

One theory posited by the *Irish Independent* in the aftermath of the bombing was that the recent arrest of three local IRA volunteers in the area provided the motive for the attack.[154] Certainly, those members of the Provisional IRA who operated in this part of the midlands had a wildcard reputation, as evinced by their involvement in the unsanctioned Herrema kidnapping the previous year. Liz Walsh wrote that the attack occurred against a backdrop of heightened tension between republicans and the Gardaí in Portlaoise. She noted several incidents between republicans and the Special Branch in the town in the days prior to the explosion and claimed that the bomb was intended for another plain-clothes officer in Portlaoise against whom local republicans had a grudge.[155] One of the officers who had been stationed with Garda Clerkin similarly stated: 'we know who did it. We think it was a maverick group.'[156] Contemporary press reports also asserted the independent nature of the 'gang' who were believed to have carried out the attack. Nobody was ever convicted for this attack although a prime suspect was subsequently charged with IRA membership.[157]

Increased British–Irish Security Cooperation

Referring to an IRA arms find in County Meath in 1976, the British Embassy in Dublin noted that the Irish Defence Forces could not provide information directly, instead referring them to the RUC. However, in an addendum, it was noted:

> I feel pretty sure that the RUC will get from the Garda more details than the Garda are prepared to reveal to the Department of Foreign Affairs or the latter to us. However, the Department of Foreign Affairs [DFA] added that if the British authorities were not able through police channels to obtain specific information which they needed, we should ask for it through diplomatic channels (this is a ritual point the DFA always make on such occasions).[158]

The latter period of the coalition government's tenure witnessed a considerably greater level of security cooperation than had hitherto existed. Information was shared more readily and the security forces along the border proved far more cooperative. The British were particularly satisfied with the conduct of the Gardaí along the border, noting that they 'have defused several potentially tiresome incidents recently, with relaxed good sense'.[159] The issue of British soldiers crossing the border, intentionally or otherwise, was still something of a sensitive one. The British government was, however, beginning to allow that decisions on this were the prerogative of the Irish authorities: 'There seems no advantage in pressing harder to obtain complete agreement with the Irish on the treatment of soldiers crossing the border, especially in plain clothes; we are left with a small area of uncertainty, but will do better to rely on Garda understanding than to force the issue.'[160]

The British had also begun to compile detailed reports of IRA border activity to present to their Irish government counterparts as part of joint consultative committees. In one cross-border study undertaken by the RUC and British Army between March 1976 and May 1977, the IRA reportedly mounted 164 attacks against targets within two miles of the border. The report emphasised that the cross-border connection was beyond dispute in fifty-one cases, with 'merely strong indications in the remaining 113'.[161] While border activity accounted for 10 per cent of all IRA actions, it was responsible for 20 per cent of security force killings and 2 per cent of civilian deaths. Thus, despite the increased cooperation, the British government felt that the Irish security forces could yet be doing more. In a draft document in advance of a meeting between the British Ambassador and Jack Lynch in 1977 (he having replaced Liam Cosgrave as Taoiseach following a general election at the beginning of the year), the use of the border to evade arrest was a particular point of emphasis. The document noted:

> Moreover, and of central importance, it is beyond doubt that virtually all the Provisionals' firearms and probably all their explosives come into Northern Ireland across the land border ... This is an argument which the Republic's authorities have been very reluctant to concede; they tend to argue that the only sort of cross border terrorism which they have any responsibility for helping to prevent is activity in the immediate vicinity of the boundary which can be conclusively shown to have originated from their side in the immediate sense. This attitude is not justified by the facts ... We accept – as Ministers have publicly acknowledged on many occasions – that security cooperations between the two governments has [sic] improved steadily ... Most members of the Garda appear genuinely keen to cooperate with the RUC and to crack down on the IRA on their side of the border – though even those who are keen are fairly slow to adapt their techniques to accord with modern police methods.[162]

As previously noted, the one potential concession on which the Irish government remained intransigent was helicopter overflights. Cooperation between the British and Irish engendered by the coalition government scarcely diminished when Fianna Fáil were returned to government in 1977.

Portlaoise Prison III

The Fine Gael–Labour coalition was to face one final major challenge from the Provisional republican movement before that change of power. From 1 March 1976, the revoking of Special Category status for prisoners in Northern Ireland led to an escalating sequence of prison protests culminating in the 1981 hunger strike. As a focus point, the British government was aware from early 1977 that prisons in the South as well as the North of Ireland would factor into republican campaigning. Indeed, this would become a major point of protest and propaganda. The British noted that the IRA would be aided by the 'general assumption that conditions in Portlaoise are pretty grisly'.[163] On 6 March 1977, twenty IRA prisoners in Portlaoise prison led by Daithí Ó Conaill, Dan Hoban and Belfastman Leo Martin, began refusing food in a campaign for improved conditions.[164] This second hunger strike in two years lasted forty-seven days and ended in apparent failure.[165] During the course of the strike, two Labour TDs were punched and kicked by republican supporters during a rally, as well as verbally abused.[166] Attempts were made to publicly highlight the prison issue, notably in an illegal demonstration on the pitch at Croke Park prior to the football league final between Kerry and Dublin.[167] An editorial in *Hibernia* following the cessation of the hunger strike hit at the failure to gauge popular opinion prior to its launch though also demonstrating a lack of prescience in its closing remark:

> The Provisional organisation was left in no doubt that their measure of public support in the south has declined appreciably even over the past couple of years. Their protest demonstrations were poorly attended; the media, both editorially and in selective presentation of news and letters, was almost universally against them … The failure of the Portlaoise hungerstrike was a failure to gain popular support for what were, after all, quite reasonable demands … The republican movement will be slower to employ the hunger-strike tactic in future.[168]

As with the 1975 hunger strike, those prisoners who were rushed to hospital as a result of their protest spoke of receiving excellent treatment from staff. The cheering crowds that flanked the ambulances leaving the prison en route to the hospital during the earlier hunger strike would seem to indicate that Minister Cooney was not entirely wrong in his earlier claims that the Portlaoise area contained considerable local support for the Provisionals.[169]

✳✳✳

The general election of 16 June 1977 returned Fianna Fáil to power with the largest parliamentary majority in the history of the state.[170] Significantly, of those coalition cabinet ministers who lost their seats in that election,

two – Paddy Cooney and Conor Cruise O'Brien – were most identified
with the creation of a repressive society during the tenure of the coalition
government. A later study of the election found that security was a major
issue for only one-fifth of voters.[171] *Hibernia* provided a more nuanced
analysis of the results, however:

> The unspoken resentment against the coalition, in particular against
> Fine Gael, was largely unspeakable. It could not be labelled and
> categorised. *It is not the same thing as an 'issue'* ... We have heard
> the allegations of Garda brutality spelt out, we have seen the Minister
> for Justice stonewall simple demands for information about prison
> conditions while prisoners approached death on hunger-strike ... The
> coalition government had built up an atmosphere of intimidation in
> which it became subversive to seek information.[172]

Following Fianna Fáil's return to government, all those concessions that
had been lost to prisoners which might be construed as bestowing political
status were quietly and incrementally returned.[173] The IRA that emerged
from this period was a smaller, more professional organisation than that
of the early years of the conflict. Despite prison concessions, the policies of
police brutality, censorship and blacklisting introduced during the tenure
of the coalition government were continued by and large by successive
administrations, regardless of party. Republicanism in the South entered
a state of subterfuge and discretion. Mass meetings and public campaigns
became a rarer tactic, restricted in the main to major episodes of public
concern or outrage such as the later hunger strikes. IRA activity did not
diminish, however, but merely continued in a less overt fashion. The focus
of fundraising altered, and alternative channels for arms importations were
introduced.

Assassination. Escalation?
1978–80

The year 1978 opened rather well for the Provisionals. In a speech on 8 January, Fianna Fáil Taoiseach Jack Lynch called for a British declaration of intent to withdraw from Northern Ireland. Politicking as this may have been, it was followed by a similar call from Cardinal Ó Fiach on 16 January. The British newspaper, the *Daily Mail* added its voice in August.[1] From a public relations perspective, the British were on the ropes. The European Court of Human Rights deemed that British Army activities during the implementation of internment in 1971 amounted to torture, while a damning Amnesty International report on similar treatment of contemporary prisoners was published later in the year. Politically, the republican movement was becoming more astute and overtly revolutionary following the leadership changes post-ceasefire. Sinn Féin would continue to move towards a more vocally socialist position, aligning itself with various anti-colonial movements across the globe. This caused concern in British governmental circles. Meanwhile, the IRA continued to seek modern weaponry as well as hone its homemade capabilities. Domestic financing of its campaign continued, and the latter part of the decade more generally saw a move towards more specialised training of volunteers. The Easter commemorations in 1978 promised military escalation and indeed there was a surge of activity in the closing months of the year. The increase in the number of British security forces personnel killed since the immediate post-ceasefire period, and the decrease in the proportion of civilian casualties during the late 1970s, seemed to have borne out the success of the post-ceasefire restructure. This chapter examines the increasing sophistication of the IRA's military capabilities, albeit against a backdrop of general decline in British casualties when compared to the high-water mark of 1972. The increasing political awareness of the republican movement was handicapped by several major IRA attacks which alienated potential supporters in the South. This is borne out by the relative lack of support shown for prisoners in Portlaoise at a time of continued hardship in the prison. This is another area of focus for this chapter. The focus of the prison campaign shifted to the H-Blocks in Northern Ireland at the end of the decade. The escalating humanitarian crisis there brought Southerners onto the streets in numbers not witnessed in years.

Increased IRA Military Sophistication and Setbacks

As noted, the restructure of the Provisionals post-ceasefire saw immediate positive effects for the movement. A demonstration of the outward confidence of the IRA during this period took place at the Bloody Sunday commemoration in Derry in January 1978. At this large public rally, several IRA volunteers revealed the organisation's recent acquisition of M60 general-purpose machine guns. This staged demonstration was met with cheering and applause from the crowds. The headline of the next issue of An Phoblacht read: 'IRA steps up the offensive.'[2] Shortly after this, Conservative MP Airey Neave declared that specialised IRA weapons training for the M60 was taking place in the Republic of Ireland. This soured relations between the British and Irish governments.[3] Tensions flared again a fortnight after Neave's declaration, in the aftermath of the first British fatality from this weapon. Gunner Paul Sheppard was killed in an IRA ambush on Cliftonpark Avenue, Belfast. Despite public outrage and disavowals from the Irish government, privately there were serious concerns regarding the IRA acquisition of M60s and potential training in the South. Specialised training camps had indeed been established in the west of Ireland since the acquisition of this weapon. They were led by no less than a former officer of the Irish Defence Forces. Select Northern IRA volunteers had been ferried South in small groups to avail of this training.[4] The M60s were used in numerous attacks by the IRA throughout Northern Ireland. In 1980, a Belfast unit equipped with one of the machine guns was lured to a house in Belfast where they were surrounded by the British

Army and SAS. Following a gun battle in which an officer of the SAS was killed, the IRA unit surrendered. The composition of the media-nicknamed 'M60 gang' indicates the class of volunteer who had been selected to use the weapon. Of those men, Paul Magee and Joe Doherty were particularly highly experienced IRA volunteers.

The year prior to the acquisition of the M60s, the IRA also obtained several Browning machine guns. These were a general-purpose machine gun and saw widespread use by the US Army during the Second World War and Korean War. Despite their vintage, they were capable of shooting down a helicopter if used with accuracy. As with the M60s, these weapons also sparked concern and speculation as to their origin. According to one account, following the Carnation Revolution in Portugal, the extremist wing of the Portuguese Communist Party – then in power – had approached the IRA through intermediaries. They invited the IRA to produce a 'shopping list' that elements of the Portuguese government and military would seek to accommodate. A first approach was allegedly rejected outright by Seamus Twomey, as Chief-of-Staff, and Joe Cahill, in his capacity as treasurer, as they did not want to deal with communists.[5] However, in April 1977, *The Irish Times* reported on the visit to Belfast of a 'respectable figure from a prominent Portuguese political party'.[6] The article alluded to the fact that his appearance may have had something to do with the Provisionals' recent acquisition of Browning automatic rifles. A 1978 issue of the current affairs magazine *Magill* carried a statement from the Provisional IRA which read: 'We have received at no stage any help from the Soviet Union or any east European country. They are not interested in struggles in wars for national liberation.'[7] Of course, this statement makes no reference to a potential Portuguese offer.

It is also worth noting that over sixty members of Portugal's parliament signed a petition of support for Bobby Sands during his hunger strike declaring him to be 'a patriot and a fighter for human and civil rights'.[8] The deadly efficiency of the Browning was evident in South Armagh on 17 February 1978. That day, an IRA unit shot down a Gazelle British military helicopter, killing one soldier and injuring several others. The British vehemently rejected IRA claims of responsibility for shooting down the helicopter, attributing the crash to evasive action taken by the pilot to avoid gunfire, which went awry. In fact, a contemporary British internal report acknowledged that IRA gunfire was responsible, but this was not publicly acknowledged until 2015.[9] IRA elation and indeed media coverage of this military success was overshadowed by an attack elsewhere that same day. A totally inadequate bomb warning by an IRA unit at the La Mon hotel in County Down resulted in an incomplete evacuation of the premises. In the ensuing explosion and fire, twelve civilians were incinerated, including three married couples.[10] There was considerable public outrage in the South in the aftermath of this bombing. The largely defunct Peace People held a rally in Dublin city centre which was attended by approximately 1,000 people. Gardaí clashed with thirty or so republican supporters who heckled the crowd as it passed near the Sinn Féin offices in the city.[11]

The incendiary weapon used in the La Mon attack was colloquially referred to as a 'box bomb' and was manufactured in great numbers in the South post-ceasefire. While very simple to produce, they were exceptionally damaging. During the early 1970s, the Provisional IRA's Derry Brigade had effectively employed small, crude incendiaries to make that city look, in the words of Eamonn McCann, 'as if it had been hit from the air'.[12] The box bomb was slightly different. It consisted of a wooden box perhaps a foot long filled with detonating cord (Cordtex), with a memo-park timer attached, referred to internally as 'GHQ timers'. In their most ubiquitous form, these timers were present as parking meter timers. They were stolen from such meters all over the island. Dervla Murphy, in her travels in Northern Ireland during 1976, remarked that all the parking meters in Belfast had had their timers torn out.[13] Petrol-filled containers were usually placed on either side of the Cordtex-packed wooden box. A small detonator would ignite the Cordtex when the timer ran out. Cordtex explodes at a rate of four miles per second, effectively igniting the petrol instantly, the force of the explosive blast then pushing the burning liquid outwards. A typical contemporary newspaper report on the use of these bombs reads thus: 'The electricity board showroom was destroyed by a 200lb explosion followed by a fire.'[14] Box bombs were not intended as anti-personnel devices, but rather to destroy businesses and buildings as part of the IRA's renewed economic bombing campaign. This was an integral part of the organisation's post-ceasefire strategy to demonstrate renewed efficiency and determination. Their offensive appeal was cemented by operations such as that at another hotel in County Down in October 1977. On that occasion, one such easily produced device destroyed the entire building at a cost of more than £250,000 with no casualties.[15] The proliferation of box bombs was further spurred by the need to dismiss British claims of a decrease in IRA activity at this time.[16] Following the La Mon atrocity, the Army Council banned the use of box bombs.[17]

As the decade progressed, the efficacy of IRA mortar training in the South continued to show results during engagements in the North. The same British Army regiment targeted during the Gazelle helicopter attack suffered serious casualties three weeks earlier when the Forkhill RUC barracks was struck by several mortar shells fired from the back of a truck. Despite the launch area having no line of sight to the complex, shells reportedly hit the barracks washroom and accommodation block. Three RUC officers were subsequently injured when investigating the booby-trapped launch vehicle.[18] The following year, the RUC barracks at Newtownhamilton in County Armagh came under sustained mortar and rifle fire. One British soldier was killed and eight others (including two civilian contractors) wounded.[19] The IRA also began to move towards larger, more sophisticated bombs during this period. Technologically, republicans were also making advances. Two British soldiers were killed in remote-controlled bomb attacks in July 1978 in Tyrone and Armagh, respectively. In both cases, homemade explosives were used that almost certainly originated South of the border. The devastating attack on the British Army at Warrenpoint on 27 August 1979 was the culmination of incremental advances in IRA tactics and logistics. An IRA unit positioned on the Republic side of the border detonated two huge loads of homemade explosives, striking an army convoy and its relief party. The deliberate and accurate targeting of the relief party demonstrated the outcome of IRA analysis of how the British military reacted in the aftermath of conventional bomb attacks. In the panicked aftermath of the first explosion, British soldiers fired across the border killing an English tourist who had been fishing in the area. Contemporary British Army claims of the survivors coming under fire after the explosions likely referred to ammunition from their own convoy exploding due to the heat of the fires caused by the blast. Two IRA volunteers from South Armagh were arrested by Gardaí shortly after the attack while riding a motorcycle. Both were shortly thereafter released due to lack of evidence for prosecution.

Strategically and militarily, the Warrenpoint ambush was a major success for the IRA. As with the Gazelle helicopter–La Mon operations, however, an attack on civilians that same day overshadowed the success. At Mullaghmore in County Sligo, on the far side of the country to Warrenpoint, Louis Mountbatten, former Viceroy of India and second cousin to Elizabeth II, was killed along with his wife, two grandsons and a local boy. The IRA had planted a bomb on their boat which exploded several hundred yards offshore. Mountbatten had been holidaying in the area for many years and was well-known locally. Although Gardaí had cautioned him that he was at risk from militant republicans, he took no added security precautions. Hours prior to the attack, IRA volunteer Thomas McMahon was arrested in County Longford on suspicion of driving a stolen vehicle. He was being held for questioning when reports of the explosion filtered in. Forensic testing subsequently linked him to the destroyed boat. McMahon was sentenced to life imprisonment later that same year. He served his sentence in Portlaoise prison and was released in 1998 as part of the Belfast Agreement. Among much of the Southern public, news of the attack at Mullaghmore was received with horror. Letters to newspapers following the attack ranged from the moderate – the still-afloat Peace People called for a 'day of mourning' – to the worryingly hysterical: 'Eire should repent in sackcloth and ashes'; 'we are all stained by the events that occurred'; 'the world must think us beyond redemption.'[20] Arguably, this episode like no other led to a hardening of attitudes towards the Provisionals' militant republicanism, even arguably affecting the limits of support given to the hunger strikes of 1980–1.

A papal visit to Ireland took place shortly after these two IRA operations. This was the first papal visit to Ireland, and a long-anticipated event. Although there were plans for the Pope to visit Northern Ireland, the heightened tension and security risk following the attacks made this impossible. Speaking in County Louth, the Pope addressed the IRA, the 'men of violence', imploring them: 'On my knees I beg you to turn away from the paths of violence and return to the ways of peace.'[21] In response, the IRA published a five-page booklet entitled 'The Road to Peace in Ireland'. In the booklet, their response to the Pope's appeal was subdued but resolute, noting that nobody could speak of 'men of violence' in Ireland without reference to the 33,000 British soldiers and police, repressive laws and torture. The IRA's firm message was that, in all conscience, 'we believe that force is by far the only means of removing the evil of British presence in Ireland'.[22]

Several months prior to the Mullaghmore and Warrenpoint attacks, a top-secret British Army intelligence report written by James Glover, Commander of the British Land Forces in Northern Ireland, was leaked to the press. Contained within this report were evaluations of the various membership sections of the Provisional IRA. On the leadership, it noted that: 'PIRA [sic] is essentially a working class organisation based in the ghetto areas of the cities and in the poorer rural areas ... there is a strata of intelligent, astute and experienced terrorists who provide the backbone of the organisation.' On the engineering department: 'PIRA [sic] has an adequate supply of members who are skilled in the production of explosive devices.' Most revealing is what the report had to say about 'rank and file terrorists': 'our evidence ... does not support the view that they are merely mindless hooligans drawn from the unemployed and unemployable'.[23] Following the leaking of this report to the press, British Permanent Undersecretary to the Minister of Defence Frank Cooper wrote to another senior civil servant:

> I have no doubt that the Dublin Government will be embarrassed by the passages about the use of the South by terrorists. So they should be. They are only too readily disposed to play down the extent to which terrorists use the South as a base from which to mount their attacks. But the South is freely used for that purpose; and in light of the recent casualties among members of the Security Forces it seems to me no bad thing that Dublin should be reminded about it.[24]

Cooper was eager to make the most of the leaking of the report, insisting that it also damaged the Irish government. He added: 'Whenever the Irish authorities have asked us for specific cases of lack of security cooperation, we have failed to come up with a single instance.'[25] It was alleged in some corners that the report had in fact been leaked by elements of the British security services for budgetary and electoral reasons. The Provisionals never revealed in detail how they obtained a copy.[26] Among the consequences of the report's leak was an increased British push for army-to-army communications along the border; a stonewalling identified by the British as being 'primarily political'.[27] According to a British account of a meeting between Gerry Collins, Minister for Justice in the Fianna Fáil government, and Conservative MP, Robert Atkins:

> Mr Gerry Collins ... went on to reveal the usual Irish hypersensitivity towards criticism, implied or otherwise, by referring to press reports suggesting that Irish security forces were not pulling their weight and to the leaked British Army document ... he reverted to the idea that more British Army involvement was needed, admitting at the same time that the Irish Army was not being fired at as was the case with our security forces.[28]

Mr Collins' feelings were that the authorities in the South where damned no matter their actions. To him, it had reached a point where the Gardaí were criticised for discovery of IRA bomb factories as it demonstrated that they allowed terrorists to operate in the Republic at all. The report concluded that any discussions with government ministers of the Republic fell down upon difficulties in telling the Irish how and to what end their troops should be deployed. The British continued to press for greater cooperation on security during the late 1970s, particularly on the military communications aspect noted above. Previous reports had identified the Irish Defence Forces as being more recalcitrant than the Garda in this respect. Two exceptions to general British experiences with the Gardaí were those in the Monaghan salient area – who reportedly provided the RUC with enough minor titbits of information to head off claims of non-co-operation – and those in County Donegal who were pleasingly cooperative in the flow of information. Overall, however, British military intelligence on the ground continued to be severely lacking in many areas. It was during this period that the British Army rejected RUC requests for increased vehicle patrolling in South Armagh as achieving nothing other than increased casualties, concluding: 'The Army rejects cosmetic operations.'[29]

IRA Military Stagnation and Frustration

Although the IRA acquired general-purpose machine guns during this period and improved their engineering capabilities, the latter half of the

1970s witnessed a relative decline in activity. In 1977, violence was down to its lowest level since 1970 and deaths had more than halved from the previous year. The trend continued; a later *An Phoblacht* article bluntly stated: '1978 was a bad year for republicans.'[30] A relative shortage of arms and explosives North and South of the border was a critical factor. This was in large part due to improved intelligence on the part of the respective security sources. Garda seizures in particular, such as the discovery of nearly two tons of explosives near Athlone, caused real damage to the Provisional IRA.[31] In 1977, another arms importation attempt went disastrously wrong. The planned transportation of small arms (including rocket-launchers), ammunition and explosives from Antwerp to Dublin was a failure, with the weapons being seized in Belgium. According to British Intelligence, the weaponry originated in the Middle East and came to Antwerp via West Germany.[32] A middle-aged IRA volunteer was arrested in Dublin during the security operation following the arms discovery. He was subsequently charged with conspiring to import arms into the state and with IRA membership. During his trial, it emerged that he ran a 'front' electrical business in Dublin city centre.[33] Information provided by the man during his interrogation led to the capture of IRA Chief-of-Staff, Seamus Twomey, in Dublin later that year. Another major consequence of the seizure was the IRA assassination of Richard Sykes, British Ambassador to the Netherlands in March 1979. The Ambassador's Dutch chauffeur was also shot dead in this attack. An alleged IRA statement shortly after the killing simply stated, 'We are responsible. This is only the beginning of the war.'[34] The IRA had long suspected that Sykes was responsible for coordinating a major European intelligence operation against them. The Antwerp arms seizure was but one of his successes against the IRA in this regard. Sykes had undoubtedly been dispatched to the Hague at least in part to coordinate intelligence. According to an internal British memo from the Hague Embassy to the Foreign Office:

The Irish authorities asked the British Government to put an end through its channels to arms traffic [referring to Antwerp] of this kind. The obvious person for this was Sir Richard, who had already been involved in anti-IRA activity. The staff of the British delegation to NATO was augmented by 'a special agent in diplomatic service'.

This was Mr Holmer, who through NATO channels could also 'keep a watch on west Germany'.[35]

During the tenure of the coalition government, Richard Sykes had served as Deputy Under-Secretary in the Foreign and Commonwealth Office. Part of his function in this role was to liaise with Minister for Foreign Affairs Garret FitzGerald. In that role, his aim was to help FitzGerald understand that public outrage at IRA atrocities could be leveraged to develop greater British–Irish security cooperation. Particularly in areas 'where the constraints of public opinion had hitherto caused them difficulties'.[36]

Several months prior to the Antwerp seizure, the IRA shot dead an alleged informer in a public house in the Liberties area of Dublin. The victim, John Lawlor, was a haulage operator who was suspected of breaking under interrogation and providing valuable information to the Gardaí regarding IRA personnel. The arrest and interrogation of Lawlor followed on from the discovery of a significant quantity of arms destined for IRA units operating in Britain on 27 August 1977. The arms cache included 230lbs of gelignite, 200 feet of Cordtex, nearly 100 incendiary devices, two assault rifles, five handguns and dozens of detonators and other complex explosives paraphernalia. According to British intelligence:

> A haulier who travels regularly from Dublin to Liverpool was approached in Dublin and offered money to transport an empty container from an address in Dublin to the Toddington service station, 37 miles north of Hendon on the M1 motorway. Since the container turned out, on arrival at the docks, to be too large for the ferry, the haulier exchanged it (on his own authority) for what he knew to be another empty container. On delivering the substitute container to contacts at Toddington, he was so taken aback by their anger and annoyance that he arranged for the Gardai to be informed. They examined the original container (which had remained in a yard in Dublin) and found it to have a hidden compartment (behind a plywood board) in which were five holdalls containing the cache.[37]

The haulier subsequently identified Lawlor as being his contact – both in Dublin and Toddington – after which he was arrested and interrogated by

Gardaí. On the night of his killing, according to witnesses, Lawlor sat with another man for a time at the counter of the public house. The two had a drink together before the unidentified man produced a gun, shot Lawlor and walked out of the public house. There were no arrests in the aftermath. Shortly afterwards, the IRA released a statement accusing the victim of having 'gratuitously given important information to the authorities'.[38]

Despite the potential for negative publicity, the IRA continued to target members of the British armed forces in the Republic. Two notable incidents were the shooting of an off-duty British soldier at his wedding in County Meath in 1978 and the killing of an off-duty RUC member in County Monaghan in 1979. In the case of the former, Lieutenant Gary Cass was married in Trim on 26 August 1978. As he and his new bride walked down a red carpet at the church gate, three men armed with a pistol, shotgun and rifle attacked. Cass was hit by several pistol bullets. Having fallen to the ground, the IRA volunteer armed with the shotgun stepped forward and fired into Cass' prone body. Amazingly, he survived. The IRA unit got into a white Mercedes car and drove off in the direction of Dublin.[39] The car had been stolen from outside a public house in County Cavan several nights earlier and was found burned out near Navan several hours after the shooting.[40] Two men, Desmond O'Hare and Peadar McElvenna, both with Dublin addresses, were later arrested and charged with armed murder. British Army witnesses to the shooting were subject to delicate security arrangements when travelling to and from the trial to testify. The men were accommodated at the British Army Headquarters in Lisburn and travelled to Dublin daily by army aircraft. At the point of landing, the Gardaí assumed responsibility and transported them to and from the courts.

Following a fifteen-day trial, both O'Hare and McElvenna were acquitted as the juryless Special Criminal Court was unwilling to make a judgement 'beyond all reasonable doubt' that the accused were guilty.[41] During the trial, O'Hare had lodged a complaint about the identity parade from which he was picked out by witnesses. He had been put in the parade wearing his dirty work clothes after two days in a prison cell. All the other men in the parade were soldiers from Collins Barracks in Dublin, clean-shaven and in neat civilian clothing.[42] O'Hare would later achieve notoriety as a member of the INLA for the kidnapping and brutal torture of dentist, John O'Grady.

The latter attack in the South was the fatal shooting of Stanley Hazelton, an RUC reservist based in Moy, County Tyrone. Crossing the border into Monaghan on 23 December 1979, to collect the Christmas turkey for his family, his car was struck by over twenty bullets fired by IRA volunteers. SDLP politician, Austin Currie, and Fr Denis Faul both condemned the killing.[43]

Financing the Provisional IRA during the Late 1970s

The IRA's ferocious, if delayed, response to the Antwerp arms seizure stemmed in part from the financial loss it represented. Contemporary sources posit that an entire year's budget was spent on this purchase.[44] According to the leaked Glover Report, at this time, the IRA's annual income was approximately £950,000 (Stg).[45] Payment to full-time IRA volunteers and Sinn Féin members was estimated to account for £400,000 (just over £7,500 a week) with newspapers, leaflets etc. costing £150,000, the prisoner dependents' fund amounting to £180,000 and £50,000 going to transport and travel costs. If this report can be taken as relatively accurate, the Provisional IRA was left with an average of £170,000 to spend on arms annually.[46] Methodologically, financing the republican movement during this period remained much the same as previous years, albeit escalated. At the beginning of 1978, the number of armed robberies occurring in the Republic appeared to be on the decline. The Irish Times even ran an article entitled 'Where have all the robbers gone?'[47] If this was representative of wishful optimism, it was soon to be rudely dispelled. By the mid-point of that year there had been 106 armed robberies in the South.[48] While this figure was down from the previous year, there was increased sophistication in targeting. In 1978, more than double the amount of money was taken from robberies than had been the previous year: £2,196,508 as opposed to £919,521 in 1977.[49] In 1977, no charges were brought in 63 per cent of the recorded armed robberies.[50] A contemporary editorial in The Irish Times stated frankly: 'the Friday robbery is becoming almost as prevalent as the Sunday church attendance … The robbers, as it were, are thumbing their noses right in the [justice] minister's constituency … [they] are clearly running rings around the Gardaí.'[51] One Garda was willing to admit the service's shortcomings, saying 'the robbers have us outclassed.'[52] The INLA's theft of £400,000 from a security van in County Limerick in 1978 and the Provisional IRA's £250,000 from a train robbery near Sallins, County Kildare, two years previously (for which members of the IRSP were blamed) represent two examples of major armed robberies during this period. There were many more, smaller such robberies taking place.[53] Such was the number of armed robberies that the IRA's cell system began to be impacted. As one interviewee recalled:

> Very often a robbery would happen, you know, and right in the same area a camp could be going ahead. People had been caught because the guards had been everywhere and you'd be there 'What the hell happened?' and somebody would hear on the radio that there'd been a robbery so it'd be 'Why didn't they tell us about it?' … there'd be certain units specifically for fundraising we'll say and others for different operations … But the problem with that system, that's fine, but somehow or other there could be two operations going side by side. One goes wrong then the rest get caught. So, there was a few close calls.[54]

In October 1980, such an event occurred with tragic consequences. Following a bank robbery in County Kilkenny, Gardaí in neighbouring County Wexford were tasked with checking on the movements of local republicans. One of these was Peter Rogers. Rogers was originally from Belfast but had settled and married in the South after an audacious escape from the prison ship, *HMS Maidstone*, along with several other IRA volunteers in January 1972. Unconnected with the bank robbery, Rogers was in the process of moving weapons in his van when two Gardaí, Detectives Garda Seamus Quaid and Donal Lyttleton, recognised the vehicle near a quarry. Ordered out of the van, Rogers pulled a concealed weapon out and demanded to be allowed to pass. Accounts differ as to the following sequence of events. What is clear is that a shootout ensued in which Rogers was shot in the leg and Detective Garda Quaid was killed.[55] Rogers surrendered to authorities the following morning and was sentenced to life imprisonment in Portlaoise prison.

As the decade drew to a close, there appeared to be no end to the proliferation of armed robberies. In 1979 alone, almost £2.5m was stolen in the South.[56] The following year, Minister for Justice Gerry Collins could declare that the amount taken in 1980 was down 40 per cent from the previous year; though this was something of an empty boast given the unlikelihood of that year's figure ever being reached again.[57] In 1980, *Magill* stated that nearly £5m had been stolen in the South in the prior three years; 'reliable sources' claimed that the Provisionals benefited from at least a third of that money.[58]

Armed robberies carried a serious risk of violence, escalation in probability obviously increasing to scale. In 1979, six people including a Garda were wounded during such robberies.[59] This significantly damaged residual 'Robin Hood' perceptions of the perpetrators. In August of that year, 32-year-old Eamon Ryan was shot dead by an IRA unit during a raid on a bank in Tramore, County Waterford. The victim, a civil servant living in Dublin with his family, had been in the bank with his infant child when the raid took place. Although Gardaí established a roadblock with their cars, the raiders broke through and escaped. Their car was found at Coolnacapogue, a few miles from the town. There, the IRA men switched to another car which drove through a second roadblock at Dunmore East. The weapons, four handguns and an Armalite rifle, as well as the cash – just £5,500 – were later recovered in a plastic sack hidden in a field, the location of which the Gardaí refused to disclose. They did, however, state their awareness of those houses which were used by the IRA in the area as safehouses. Three people were subsequently charged in connection with this botched operation. Two men served life sentences for murder, while a third was convicted for his part as the getaway driver.[60] Eamon Ryan was not the only fatality arising out of IRA armed robberies in the Republic during this period. The previous year, on 3 February 1978, Tyrone publican Bernard Browne was shot and killed during a raid on a supermarket at Killygordon, County Donegal. According to a contemporary news report:

> A raid took place on the grocery and hardware at McCreery and Co., Killygordon. A number of people were ordered there to go into the post office, but one of the customers, Mr. Bernard Browne, attempted to get a grip on the raiders, and as he did so the gunman fired and one shot struck him on the chest. He was removed to Letterkenny General Hospital, where he died on Friday last, 3rd February.[61]

The following year, two young men from Donegal and Tyrone respectively were charged with Browne's murder. They admitted IRA membership while denying the murder charge. One was found guilty of murder and sentenced to a life sentence of penal servitude while the other received a three-year sentence on a reduced manslaughter charge.[62] Incidents such as these shocked and sickened large sections of the public. It is likely that support declined, and doors closed to volunteers. However, it was primarily increased security measures introduced in the subsequent years which led to a decline in this fundraising tactic for the Provisional IRA.

Political Sophistication?

The republican movement that emerged from the post-ceasefire restructure was one geared for a long struggle. Had anybody been in doubt of that, Jimmy Drumm's 'long war' speech at the 1977 Bodenstown commemoration made it clear. It was noted by the Northern Ireland Office that this speech was shortly followed by an article in *Republican News* advocating the spread of the 'struggle' to the South.[63] The primary focus of the Provisionals' restructure during this period was military. However, a document outlining this restructure found on Seamus Twomey after his arrest in 1977 also sought to maximise satellite organisations in the 'struggle'. Within the republican movement, there was scepticism about just how ascendant or respected the political aspect was during the conflict. The increasing sophistication of Sinn Féin was noted by a concerned British Embassy in Dublin, which was eager to receive regular updates from the Irish Republican Information Service, noting in October 1978 that a recent issue contained a 'surprisingly rational discussion of what would be involved in a British withdrawal.'[64] Unfortunately, for the Embassy, as it noted in a memo: 'We are at a loss however to suggest a way of putting ourselves on the mailing list without either giving the PIRA a propaganda stick ("Brits beg for PSF information") or attracting attention to an individual member of the staff. We could not rely on any of these local journalists to supply us on a regular basis.'[65]

It was during this period that a very real power and dynamic shift occurred within the publicity organs of the Provisionals. *An Phoblacht* and *Republican News*, the Southern and Northern newspapers respectively, merged at the beginning of 1978, ostensibly to present a unified façade.[66] Editorship of this 'new' paper, *An Phoblacht-Republican News (AP/RN)*, devolved to a young leftist republican from Belfast called Danny Morrison. Morrison had been interned for several years in the early 1970s and had some minor previous experience as editor of a student newspaper.[67] His talent for propaganda was spotted by Belfast O/C Billy McKee in the mid-1970s which brought him editorship of *Republican News*. Around this same period, Morrison was apparently converted to the 'new departure' being propagated by Gerry Adams, Brendan Hughes and Ivor Bell.[68] A brief piece in *Hibernia* on the merging of the two newspapers stated bluntly:

> Although its first lead article opened defiantly with the line: 'Not such a big surprise...' the newly merged *An Phoblacht/Republican News* may come as a shock to southern republicans weaned on years of *An Phoblacht* ... The new paper confirms predictions that the new organ would mirror the more militant and socialist line of the Belfast Provisionals ... to outflank southern 'moderates' such as Daithi O'Conaill and Ruairi O'Bradaigh.[69]

Morrison certainly brought panache to the newspaper and was a very skilled propagandist. Under his editorship, *AP/RN* combined militancy on the Northern situation with broader leftist politics incorporating coverage of other struggles across the world.[70] However, by 1980 the newspaper had little of the influence of *An Phoblacht* remaining and was very much considered the newspaper of the new leadership, with its articles demonstrating fluency in revolutionary rhetoric.[71]

Republican propaganda also improved in other areas. A sloganeering campaign began to be noted with unease by British and Irish authorities due to its increasingly widespread, on-message and systematic presence. The British had earlier paid veiled compliments to another island-wide slogan campaign of 'Brits Out – Peace In'. A report from their Dublin embassy dryly noted that the seriousness of the sloganeers' efforts was 'already apparent in the unusual accuracy of the spelling employed'.[72] On one thirty-mile stretch of road in County Roscommon, various forms of the slogan were painted twenty-seven times.[73] Prominent locations were chosen for these slogans to maximise visibility and publicity, including large gable-ended homes and historical landmarks such as castles. A more ambitious group in County Sligo took it upon themselves to burn 'Brits Out' into the side of Benbulbin mountain. The mountain, an iconic landmark in the area, was scaled by a group bearing sacks of lime. Letters twenty-five feet high were burned into its side.[74] The operation would have required considerable logistical planning. As well as its propaganda affect, these sloganeering campaigns were deeply concerning to the Irish government due to their effects on tourism from Britain. There were threats from British businessmen to mount a 'Boycott Ireland' campaign. This would be accompanied by paid advertisements in British newspapers, including polaroid photographs of various slogans to urge British tourists not to consider Ireland for their holidays.[75] There were active county council efforts to wash away all such slogans from public walls throughout the latter part of the 1970s. The Provisionals changed their message in 1978, to focus on the prison situation in Northern Ireland. While the British referred to this as a 'desultory campaign', that the change systematically went island-wide – including a new message burned into the side of Benbulbin – indicates a degree of planning and discipline concomitant with the increasing republican intention to professionalise conduct in all facets of their campaign.

Prison Clashes and Campaigns

By the time the slogan campaign began to focus on the prison crisis in Northern Ireland, republican prisoners in the H-Blocks who had refused to wear prison uniforms had been 'on the blanket' for up to two years. In 1978, due to increasing prison warder brutality directed at prisoners leaving their cells to shower or slop out, the dirty protest began. Republican prisoners, wearing nothing but a small prison blanket, refused to leave their cells and instead disposed of human waste by smearing it on the cell walls and attempting to pour it out under the door into the corridor. As the campaign escalated, the IRA began to target prison officers in the North for assassination in earnest.[76] Efforts to draw greater public attention to the humanitarian crisis taking place within the prisons were made through protest marches and even participation, albeit contested, in more inclusive events. Such events took place north and south of the border. In August

1978, *An Phoblacht* reported, 'several thousand people watched and cheered the H-Block protest, staged by Wexford Sinn Féin at the annual Mardi Gras Festival in Taghmon village'.[77] Demonstrations with a different scope were not so well attended. A British report of a protest at their embassy on the second anniversary of the death of Frank Stagg noted that Gardaí expected a large crowd: 'In the event, about eighteen demonstrators turned up, stood around for 40 minutes and then drifted away after burning a Union Jack and tossing it into the Embassy grounds … The poor turnout was not surprising in view of the wintry weather. It must be a cause for concern in PSF [Provisional Sinn Féin] that they have not been able to mount a decent demonstration in Dublin for many months'.[78]

It was noted in the previous chapter that the Provisionals were disappointed by the response in the South to the 1977 hunger strike in Portlaoise prison. The treatment of prisoners there continued to deteriorate in parallel, if not in the scale of intensity, with the Northern prison situation.[79] Although the Fianna Fáil government had restored some of the lost privileges for republican prisoners following their elevation to power, warder brutality was still endemic. This, and continued routine Garda brutality, made the British government tetchy when their Irish counterparts questioned events in the North, as they regularly did. An internal British government memo mused whether it was 'appropriate to remind Mr O'Kennedy [Michael, Fianna Fáil Minister for Foreign Affairs] that his own house is not in the best possible order' following remarks he made on the H-Block crisis.[80] A report published by Amnesty International on Garda abuses during this period noted that 'suspects had not been allowed access to solicitors until an incriminating statement had been signed, that the Garda had prolonged the detention of some suspects in order to conceal from the courts injuries sustained in police custody, and that the courts had failed to scrutinize allegations of ill-treatment'.[81]

In the wake of revelations about the heavy gang, the Irish government established a commission to examine allegations of abuse, headed up by Justice Barra O Briain. The results of that report were wide-ranging, and twenty-two recommendations were made to the government with respect to Garda conduct during arrest and interrogation of suspected subversives. The government rejected one-third of these recommendations, including ending the policy of bringing people to police barracks to 'assist with enquiries'. Another third was 'set aside for further study'.[82] In April 1978, *An Phoblacht* was reporting the return of the heavy gang with a headline 'Garda torture begins again'. The newspaper alleged that a man from Arigna, County Leitrim, had been held by Gardaí for days, suffering many beatings, and that all the while his family did not know where he was.[83] Within Portlaoise prison, however, there were also reports of IRA prisoners engaging in violence against dissidents within their own movement. Several newspapers reported allegations made by Joe Stagg of the Irish Civil Rights Association, a brother of Frank Stagg and the father of a serving IRA prisoner. He claimed that thirteen IRA prisoners were 'beaten up for questioning the socialist and autocratic line taken by their leaders in the prison'.[84] Perhaps the biggest boon for the Provisionals by the close of the decade was the increasing public support for the five demands of H-Block prisoners.[85] This was a level of popular support that had been dominant in the South for some years. As with the response to Bloody Sunday, many participants in demonstrations and protests were motivated by humanitarianism. Others, however, were part of that section of society moving nebulously between tolerance, support and perhaps subsequent participation in militant republicanism.

***

Reporting on the 1978 Sinn Féin ardfheis, an official from the British embassy in Dublin wrote:

> [Philip] Whitfield [who attended the open sessions] said that the most striking feature of the conference was the extent to which it was dominated by Gerry Adams. He said that Adams was not in any way impressive either personally or intellectually: he was 'no Maire Drumm'. But he set the tone for the conference and determined the outcome on all major issues. Cahill by contrast seemed to carry little influence and his constant appeals for money were ill-received. O'Connell spoke only briefly but seemed to be active in the corridors.[86]

Adams was beginning to be recognised as a doyen of the republican movement by the close of the decade. He had long been such in Belfast and, subsequently, Northern Ireland. This was occasionally met with bemusement when Northerners travelled South:

> There was a guy down, I met him, he wasn't on the run or anything like that, he was just down on a break. But he was down in the pub one night in Ennis and you could hear him all over the place, you know, 'Ah, big Gerry will do this' and 'big Gerry will do that'. 'They're going to sort out the North and then sort out the South' and I goes 'I'm getting out of here.' You can't deal with that kind of shit.[87]

Militarily, by the end of the 1970s, the conflict had entered a clear stalemate. Unlike the situation preceding the 1975 truce, the number of British Army casualties was now on the level deemed acceptable by the British. The 'Ulsterisation' of the conflict – the replacement of squaddies from Britain with members of the locally raised Ulster Defence Regiment – aided perceptions. Technologically and professionally, the IRA was at its most efficient since the outbreak of the 'Troubles'. Warrenpoint demonstrates this peak IRA professionalism, as acknowledged by British Army officers.[88] However, the popular revolution potential of the early 1970s was gone. War weariness, criminalisation, IRA atrocities and government propaganda all had an effect. The opportunity for such major attacks – urban or rural – were no longer as present as in previous years. This trend would continue throughout the 1980s and 1990s. Reduced and more efficient army patrols, high-level military surveillance techniques and the ability of the British Army to swamp urban areas, particularly with troops at the first sign of IRA activity, contributed. While opportunities were reduced, it is unlikely that the IRA would have attained such a level of efficiency without the South. As a hinterland to the conflict, the IRA could perfect their training and homemade armaments ingenuity here.

Successive Irish governments recognised this and sought to shut down militant republican activities, this despite the fact that the Fianna Fáil administration of 1979 was composed of a number of TDs – even ministers – who had previously voiced support for such republicanism. The IRA in the South mirrored organisational and strategic changes in the North at the end of the decade. It too no longer sought a mass movement, at least on the military side. Potential recruits to the IRA were as likely to be turned away as accepted. If the latter, they were ordered to avoid any republican activity: commemorations, demonstrations, fundraisers. The fast-escalating prison crises in the North and H-Block campaign rendered this next to impossible. The hunger strikes would demonstrate that, yet again, militant Irish republicanism could galvanise the people of the Twenty-Six Counties in vast numbers.

OVERVIEW

Relatively speaking, and considering its proximity to Northern Ireland, the Southern state emerged from the 'Troubles' remarkably unscathed in terms of deaths and casualties. With the exception of loyalist bombs in 1972 and 1974 and several high-profile IRA attacks, violence in the South rarely led to fatalities. As such, the Republic of Ireland could be wrongly viewed as a state where little 'Troubles'-related violence occurred during the periods between such sporadic killings. This book counters such assumptions. Throughout the conflict, the Twenty-Six Counties witnessed considerable activity related to the 'Northern Troubles'. The South was integral to the Provisional IRA's existence and to the longevity of their military campaign. Prior to the outbreak of violence in 1968–9 and independently of their socio-economic campaigns during the previous six years or so, the IRA had been a tangible presence there. Despite severe setbacks in every decade from the 1920s onwards, the organisation was revived by Southerner and Northerner alike, time and time again. This was due to the continued British military presence in Ireland; the concept of a thirty-two-county nation whose sovereignty was perceived as indefeasible by Irish republicans. During the 1960s, a radical, if naïve, strategy was enacted which recognised the failures of previous campaigns and sought to avoid a repeat of Operation Harvest. However, and regardless of the reformist leadership's intentions for the republican movement, sectarian escalation ultimately led to an outbreak of communal violence in the North. Security forces of that state were a party to the violence.[1] The lethargy of the IRA leadership in defending vulnerable nationalists in Belfast during this period precipitated a split in the republican movement. This ensured that supporters of another military campaign – 'finishing off the job once and for all' – had a structure and an organisation for the purpose.[2] Much of this structure existed in the South, ensuring the geographical interlinking of those who supported 'armed struggle' against Britain.

The ferocity of violence in subsequent years was far removed from the relative moribundity of Operation Harvest. This is due to several factors. Firstly, the former campaign had been launched unilaterally by the IRA. That is, there were no immediate provocations: the continued British occupation of Northern Ireland sufficed as motive. Thus, the IRA had to sustain its own momentum. Once this slackened – due to events such as the Edentubber disaster and the introduction of internment on both sides of the border – the campaign was doomed to failure.[3] Conversely, the 'Troubles' were propelled by multiple factors: the context of unionist intransigence during the civil rights campaign, the spirit of '68, British Army brutality and the presence of an IRA 'old guard' who channelled the ire of radicalised and embittered young nationalists. A rejection of genuine and inclusive political solutions by the key protagonists ensured the primacy of the gun.[4] A contempt for or suspicion of politics and politicians was a common theme in several interviews for this study. Similar studies have found the same.[5] During the first fifty years of the Northern state, the vast majority of parliamentary representatives (Stormont and Westminster) had opposed equal rights for its citizens. Furthermore, following the implementation of direct rule in 1972, the British government sought to introduce 'power-sharing' while proscribing the political representatives of one of the key parties to the conflict.[6] Given the above, the momentum for the IRA's own role in the 'Troubles' derived principally from the situation within the North.

The Republic of Ireland never imposed internment during the 'Troubles'. This had been a major obstacle to the momentum of Southern republicanism in previous campaigns. The European Convention on Human Rights stated that any state seeking to introduce such a measure had to be facing an existential crisis at the time of imposition.[7] There was never any such crisis in the South, in large part due to the IRA's General Standing Order Number Eight. Legal restrictions aside, the nature of and context to this IRA campaign deemed it unwise for successive governments to introduce such measures.[8] As was the case in previous campaigns, IRA volunteers were of their communities. The ability of many volunteers to live otherwise ordinary lives divorced from their paramilitary roles was crucial and must be accepted if one is to understand contemporary Irish republicanism. A man jailed for arms possession in 1975 would have had workmates, friends and family who knew him in these roles independent of his IRA activity. Many IRA volunteers were involved in sporting organisations and community initiatives. Thus, although the IRA as a structure may not have been a part of the community in the South, its members as individuals were. One major problem for successive Southern governments was that a large proportion of its citizens distanced the carnage in Northern Ireland from its underpinning IRA activity in the Republic. An additional problem was that many people approved of the Provisional IRA's objectives while perhaps not endorsing all the tactics utilised. There are myriad examples one could draw upon to illustrate this point ranging from muted opposition to the introduction of Section 31 and the Special Criminal Courts to the perceived need for Garda intimidation tactics. Taoiseach Liam Cosgrave received numerous letters in 1973 from Fine Gael supporters urging him to grant political status to hunger-striking republican prisoners.[9] It is through the unorthodox, repressive or outright illegal measures employed by Southern governments and the legal establishment that one can see the threat posed by the Provisional IRA. This was not so much existentially to that state, but in terms of what it represented to its citizens: an armed rebuttal to British claims over a part of Ireland while also being perceived as a defender of the nationalist minority in the North. This occurred at the same time as the Irish Defence Forces were aiding their British counterparts on border duty.

The conflict ultimately highlighted two major issues in North–South relations. Firstly, there was a gulf in perceptions and experiences of people from the two states. An early part of this book questioned the relevancy of the border to the social – and occasionally the economic – life of those living away from its hinterland. However, it cannot be denied that it represented a significant psychological barrier to many. A number of interviewees had never even crossed the border prior to their involvement in republicanism. Padraig O'Malley noted that only 20 per cent of Southerners had travelled to Northern Ireland between 1968 and 1978.[10] The physical demarcation and the relative lack of violence that spilled over it from the North were major issues. As the conflict continued year after year, many Southerners ultimately came to view the North as a more barbaric place. The occasional atrocity in the South merely exacerbated such disdain.[11] The few instances where Southerners sought to take a proactive role in promoting peace invariably ended in failure. This was due in no small part to the inability of such organisations to unequivocally condemn all violence. The short-lived Peace People are but the most well-known example. Such endeavours in the South were also compromised by the distinct anti-Northern attitude among many of its leaders.[12] Ultimately, their actions served to further the gap in understanding between the two jurisdictions. A second issue was the degree to which the border emphasised the unity of Irish republicanism. Despite fifty years of partition, a strong sense of solidarity still existed. Southern republicans actively participated in early episodes of the 'Troubles', such as the Battle of the Bogside, leaving work and family to come to the aid of beleaguered nationalists in the North.[13] A concerted effort to disregard the border can be seen in the reshuffle of the Provisional IRA's Army Council in the first half of 1970. MacStiofáin and others had argued long before the split of 1969–70 that Goulding was ignoring the North. Thus, although the caretaker Army Council was overwhelmingly Southern-based; this reshuffle sought to provide more of an all-Ireland balance to the IRA leadership.[14] The contemporary notion that the Provisionals experienced a bitter power struggle focused solely upon a North–South divide is fallacious. This myth is largely a product of the editorial monopoly of one internal faction. Journalism that unquestionably repeated this angle contributed.[15] In their rise to the position of leadership, 'young guns' – primarily from Belfast – purged and persecuted opponents without prejudice to geography. That their two most senior ideological opponents were middle-aged Southerners who were well-known to the media simply helped foster a narrative of simplistic binaries over the years.

The role of republicanism in the South during the conflict was that of an engine vis à vis its population, both passive and active, as well as its material and location. The sheer number of republican prisoners in Southern jails during the 1970s attests to this.[16] The scale and longevity of the Provisional IRA's campaign emphasises that there was a sizable though ultimately immeasurable body of tolerance if not support for militant republicanism at all levels of the population throughout the Republic of Ireland. That a considerable proportion of that state's population possessed irredentist tendencies goes some way towards explaining this phenomenon. Certainly, while not always being so strong a tendency as to induce active involvement in the IRA, it could lead to other manifestations of support such as safe houses, financial contributions or simply funeral solidarity.

Major blunders by state actors, such as Bloody Sunday and responses to various hunger strikes, ensured that the Provisionals' campaign would be like no other before it in maintaining this republican sympathy or ambiguity.

Nearly 50,000 pounds of explosives were detonated in Northern Ireland in the first six months of 1973, the majority of which came from IRA bombs.[17] This study has provided numerous examples to support the contention that nearly all the explosives – commercial or homemade – used by the Provisionals during the 1970s originated in the Republic of Ireland. The Provisional IRA would not have been able to materially sustain a campaign for more than a year or so without the guns, training and finance which that state provided, willingly or not. Longevity derived from many factors. For example, it is the contention here that the introduction of juryless courts in 1972 to deal with IRA suspects was not driven by jury intimidation, as has long been maintained.[18] Cases of juries congratulating acquitted republicans and a remarkable leniency on the part of district and circuit court judges in the preceding years worried British and Irish politicians, as well as enraging the Garda establishment. This is but one aspect of the conflict which demands re-evaluation. Republicans long understood the benefits of implicit tolerance in the South. Decades of harassment and repression had impressed upon them the need for most of their active supporters to be 'lily-whites', that is, IRA volunteers who were completely unknown to the Gardai or other security forces – men and women who were ordered to avoid socialising with known republicans, attending republican fundraisers etc.[19] Tied to this, of course, was the imperative of having a public face to the movement. As one interviewee remarked:

> You'd have what we would call the 'known republicans', who'd have their few pints every weekend, and if the cops wanted to watch them, they'd watch them; and they'd go out selling papers, and that was grand. That suited us, everyone at the time, that people would drink their few pints and, if the cops can focus on them, let them focus on them, and keep the people who were unknown totally away from them, totally trained and totally focused on whatever area they were involved in.[20]

Numerous claims that Fine Gael, Fianna Fáil or Labour party members and supporters aided the Provisional movement is indicative of a level of cooperation hitherto downplayed. To paraphrase one expert, all insurgencies need the passivity and implicit support of local communities to safeguard, keep quiet, or actively support their activities: activities such as the storage of weapons and protection of personnel.[21] The nature of republicanism in the South doubtless contributed significantly to this conclusion being reached. The British Army leadership had long maintained internally that the IRA would never be militarily defeated.[22] Southern Irish republicanism, if perhaps less aggressive and confrontational than in the North, arguably was more ubiquitous. Ultimately, its nature and experience appear to be as individualistic as those who abided by its tenets and participated in its struggle.

ACKNOWLEDGEMENTS

I wish to first acknowledge the support and guidance of Dr Ruán O'Donnell. Faculty, staff and postgraduate students at the University of Limerick and Mary Immaculate College, Limerick, provided assistance and advice during preliminary research. Similarly, with staff at the National Archives and National Library, Ireland, the British Library and the National Archives of the UK. *An Phoblacht* and online blogs – notably Cedar Lounge Revolution and An Sionnach Fionn – were valuable sources of information, with generous hosts. My current employer, Frontiers, graciously allowed me a reduced-hours contract to focus on the book in 2016–17.

I want to express sincerest gratitude to those who consented to be interviewed for this study and my earlier undergraduate dissertation. Some requested anonymity, for a variety of reasons. I can only regret that this prevents my thanking them in print more personally. The generosity of all interviewees with regards their free time as well as the sharing of their experiences was truly humbling.

Finally, I want to thank my family: Blaise, Agnes, Michelle, Caoimhghin, Vanessa and the little men as well as cousins, aunts and uncles, all of whom in different ways supported me through the years. The experiences of my maternal grandparents encouraged my interest in this period and subject. My partner, Sara, was patient and supporting in equal measure, always renewing my self-belief when it faltered. Thank you.

BIBLIOGRAPHY

Archives and Libraries

The National Archives of Ireland, Dublin (NAI)
Department of Justice
Roinn an Taoisigh

The National Archives (UK), Kew (TNA)
Criminal Justice
Foreign & Commonwealth Office
Home Office
Ministry of Defence

National Library of Ireland, Dublin (NLI)
Seán O'Mahony Papers
Dáil Éireann parliamentary minutes

Glucksman Library, University of Limerick
'The Fight Goes On': tape-recorded memoir of Gearóid MacCárthaigh

Hardiman Library, National University of Galway
Ruairí Ó Brádaigh Papers

Official Publications

Disturbances in Northern Ireland, report of the commission (under the chairmanship of Lord Cameron) appointed by the Governor of Northern Ireland (Belfast, 1969).
Violence and civil disturbances in Northern Ireland in 1969, report of the tribunal of inquiry by the honorary Mr Justice Scarman (Belfast, 1972).

House of the Oireachtas, joint committee on justice, equality, defence and women's rights: final report on the report of the independent commission of inquiry into the Dublin and Monaghan Bombings (Dublin, 2004).
Operation Banner: an analysis of military operations in Northern Ireland (London, 2006).

Interviews and Correspondence

Email correspondence between the author and Anthony McIntyre (former Provisional IRA volunteer, Long Kesh prisoner and Blanketman), 5 April 2011.

Interview with 'interviewee C' (former Provisional republican activist; left the movement during the 1990s), Limerick, 25 March 2011.

Interview with 'Claire' (former resident of Northern Ireland; fled south with her family during communal violence, 1971), Clare, 18 August 2008.

Interview with Des Ellis (Sinn Féin TD and former Provisional IRA volunteer; imprisoned in Portlaoise prison, 1983–90), Dublin, 30 September 2010.

Interview with 'interviewee E' (former Provisional IRA volunteer and Sinn Féin official), Limerick, 16 March 2011.

Interview with 'interviewee A' (former Provisional IRA volunteer; imprisoned in England), Limerick, 11 August 2010.

Interview with 'interviewee B' (former Provisional IRA volunteer; imprisoned in England), Limerick, 1 August 2010.

Interview with 'Joe' (former resident of Northern Ireland; fled south with his family during communal violence, 1972), Clare, 17 September 2008.

Interview with Labhras Ó Donnghaile (former IRA volunteer, 1950s; Sinn Féin member), Clare, 6 March 2010.

Interview with 'Limerick Republican' (former Provisional republican activist; left the movement in 1986), Limerick, 17 September 2010.

Interview with Martin Ferris (Sinn Féin TD and former Provisional IRA volunteer; imprisoned in Portlaoise prison, 1975, 1977, 1984–94), Kerry, 22 June 2010.

Interview with Maurice Quinlivan (Sinn Féin TD), Limerick, 10 May 2010.

Interview with 'interviewee D' (former Provisional republican activist; left the movement during the 1980s), Clare, 27 March 2010.

Interview with NGA (National Graves Association) committee member, Dublin, 10 September 2010.

Interview with Pat Magee (former Provisional IRA volunteer and internee; imprisoned in England, 1985–99), Limerick, 11 October 2010.

Interview with Seán O'Neill (former Official IRA volunteer; member of Republican Sinn Féin), Limerick, 30 March 2011.

Interview with Tommy McKearney (former Provisional IRA volunteer; imprisoned in H-Block, 1977–93), Monaghan, 30 July 2013.

Newspapers

An Phoblacht
An Phoblacht-Republican News
Belfast Telegraph
Bottom Dog
Chicago Tribune
Clare Champion
Connaught Telegraph
Derry Journal
Donegal News
Evening Echo
Evening Herald
Hibernia
Irish Examiner
Irish Independent
Irish Press
Irish Times
Kerryman
Leitrim Observer
Londonderry Sentinel
Munster Express
Nenagh Guardian
New York Times
News Letter
Republican News
Saoirse

Sunday Independent
Sunday Times
The Guardian
Westmeath Examiner

Pamphlets, Magazines and Other Publications

Belfast Graves
Brian Keenan, 1941–2008: A Republican Legend
Fortnight
Freedom Struggle
Green River: In Honour of Our Dead
History Ireland
Ireland Today
Magill
New Left Review
Phoenix
Portlaoise Prison, For Security Reasons
Where Sinn Féin Stands

Articles Cited in Periodicals

Gill, Paul and John Horgan, 'Who were the Volunteers? The Shifting Sociological and Operational Profile of 1240 Provisional Irish Republican Army Members' in *Terrorism and Political Violence*, 25 (3), pp. 435–56.

Hanley, Brian, '"I ran away"? The IRA and 1969' in *History Ireland*, 17 (4), July/August 2009.

Janke, Peter, 'Ulster: Consensus and Coercion' in *Conflict Studies*, no. 50 (October 1974).

Lemieux, Simon, 'Britain and Ireland 1798–1921: changing the question or altering the answers?' in *History Today* (52), pp. 37–41.

Van Voris, W.H., 'The Provisional IRA and the Limits of Terrorism' in *The Massachusetts Review*,16 (3), pp. 413–28.

White, R.W., 'From Peaceful Protest to Guerrilla War: Micromobilisation of the Provisional Irish Republican Army' in *American Journal of Sociology: Comparative Studies in Society and History*, 94 (6), pp. 1277–302.

White, R.W., 'The 1975 British–Provisional IRA Truce in Perspective' in *Eire-Ireland*, 45 (3), pp. 211–44.
Yeates, P., 'Obituary of Tomás MacGiolla' in *Saothar*, 36 (2011).

Secondary Sources

Allen, K., *Fianna Fáil and Irish Labour: 1926 to the Present* (London: Pluto Press, 1997).
Anderson, B., *Joe Cahill, A Life in the IRA* (Dublin: O'Brien Press, 2003).
Aretxaga, B., *Shattering Silence: Women, Nationalism and Political Subjectivity in Northern Ireland* (New Jersey: Princeton University Press, 1997).
Barrett, J.J., *Martin Ferris, Man of Kerry* (Dingle: Mount Eagle Publications, 2005).
Bean, K. and M. Hayes, *Republican Voices* (Monaghan: Unrast Verlag, 2001).
Bell, J.B., *The Secret Army: A History of the I.R.A., 1916–1970* (London: Routledge, 1972).
Bell, J.B., *A Time of Terror* (New York: Basic Books, 1978).
Bell, J.B., *The Gun in Irish Politics: An Analysis of the Irish Political Conflict, 1916–1986* (New Jersey: Routledge, 1987).
Bell, J.B., *The Irish Troubles: A Generation of Violence, 1967–1992* (Dublin: St Martin's Press, 1992).
Bell, J.B., *IRA: Tactics & Targets* (Dublin: Poolbeg Press, 1993).
Beresford, D., *Ten Men Dead: The Story of the 1981 Hunger-Strike* (London: Hunter Publishing, 1987).
Bernard, M., *Daughter of Derry: The Story of Brigid Sheils Makowski* (London: iUniverse, 1989).
Bishop, P. and E. Mallie, *The Provisional IRA* (London: Corgi, 1988).
Boland, K., *The Rise and Decline of Fianna Fáil* (Cork: Mercier Press, 1982).
Boyne, S., *Gunrunners: The Covert Arms Trail to Ireland* (Dublin: O'Brien Press, 2006).
Brady, E., Patterson, E., McKinney, K., Hamill, R. and P. Jackson (compilers), *In the Footsteps of Anne: Stories of Republican ex-Prisoners* (Belfast: Shanway, 2011).
Brendon, P., *The Decline and Fall of the British Empire, 1781–1997* (London: Vintage Press, 2008).

Burton, F., *The Politics of Legitimacy: Struggles in a Belfast Community* (London: Routledge, 1978).

Cadwallader, A., *Lethal Allies: British Collusion in Ireland* (Cork: Mercier Press, 2013).

Clarke, G., *Border Crossing: True Stories of the RUC Special Branch, the Garda Special Branch and the IRA Moles* (Dublin: Gill Books, 2009).

Collins, E., *Killing Rage* (London: Granta Books, 1998).

Coogan, T.P., *Disillusioned Decades: Ireland 1966–87* (Dublin: Gill Books, 1987).

Coogan, T.P., *The Troubles* (London: Zeus, 1996).

Cronin, S., *Irish Nationalism: A History of its Roots and Ideology* (Dublin: Continuum, 1980).

Davis, F.F., *The History and Development of the Special Criminal Court, 1922–2005* (Dublin: Bloomsbury, 2007).

Devine, F., F. Lane and N. Puirséil (eds), *Essays in Irish Labour History* (Dublin: Irish Academic Press, 2008).

de Baróid, C., *Ballymurphy and the Irish War* (Padstow: Pluto Press, 2000; second edition).

Dillon, M., *Killer in Clowntown: Joe Doherty, the IRA and the Special Relationship* (London: Cornerstone, 1992).

Dooley, T., *'The land for the people': The Land Question in Independent Ireland* (Dublin: UCD Press, 2004).

Durney, J., *On the One Road: Political Unrest in Kildare, 1913–1994* (Naas: James Durney, 2001).

English, R., *Armed Struggle: A History of the IRA* (Oxford: Picador, 2003).

Faligot, R., *Britain's Military Strategy in Ireland* (Dingle: Zed Books, 1983).

Fennell, D., *Heresy: Battle of Ideas in Modern Ireland* (Belfast: Blackstaff Press, 1993).

Fitzgerald, G., *All in a Life: An Autobiography* (Dublin: Gill and Macmillan, 1991).

Flynn, B., *Soldiers of Folly: The IRA Border Campaign, 1956–1962* (Cork: Collins Press, 2009).

Flynn, S. and P. Yeates, *Smack: The Criminal Drugs Racket in Ireland* (Dublin: Gill Books, 1985).

Gallagher, M., *The Irish Labour Party in Transition, 1957–82* (Manchester: Manchester University Press, 1982).

Green, A. and M. Hutching (eds), *Remembering: Writing Oral History* (London: Auckland University Press, 2004).

Hanley, B. and S. Millar, *The Lost Revolution: The Story of the Official IRA and the Workers Party* (Dublin: Penguin, 2009).

Hederman, M.P. and R. Kearney (eds), *The Crane Bag Book of Irish Studies* (Dublin: Blackwater Press, 1981).

Hennessey, T., *Northern Ireland: The Origins of the Troubles* (Dublin: Gill and Macmillan, 2005).

Hennessey, T., *The Evolution of the Troubles, 1970–72* (Dublin: Irish Academic Press, 2007).

Holland, J., *The American Connection: Guns, Money and Influence in Northern Ireland* (Dublin: Viking Press, 1999).

Holland, J. and H. McDonald, *INLA: Deadly Divisions* (Dublin: Poolbeg Press, 1994).

Holland, J. and S. Phoenix, *Phoenix, Policing the Shadows* (London: Hodder & Stoughton, 1996).

Holroyd, F. and N. Burbridge, *War Without Honour* (Hull: Medium, 1989).

Joyce, J. and P. Murtagh, *Blind Justice* (Dublin: Littlehampton, 1984).

Kautt, W.H., *Ambushes and Armour: the Irish Rebellion, 1919–21* (Dublin: Irish Academic Press, 2010).

Kelley, K.J., *The Longest War: Northern Ireland and the I.R.A.* (London: Zed Books, 1990).

Kennedy-Pipe, C., *The Origins of the Present Troubles in Northern Ireland* (London: Routledge, 1997).

Larkin, P., *A Very British Jihad: Collusion, Conspiracy and Cover Up in Northern Ireland* (Belfast: Beyond the Pale Publications, 2004).

MacEoin, U., *Survivors* (Dublin: Argenta, 1983).

MacEoin, U., *The IRA in the Twilight Years, 1923–48* (Dublin: Argenta, 1997).

MacGréil, M., *Prejudice and Tolerance in Ireland* (Dublin: National College of Ireland Press, 1977).

MacStiofáin, S., *Memoirs of a Revolutionary* (Edinburgh: Gordon and Cremonesi, 1975).

Magee, G., *Tyrone's Struggle* (Omagh, 2012).

Magee, P., *Gangsters or Guerrillas? Representations of Irish Republicans in 'Troubles Fiction'* (Belfast: Beyond the Pale Publications, 2001).

Magrath, M., *The Comic History of Irish Politics* (Cork: Mercier Press, 1977).

Maguire, J., *Internment and the IRA, 1939–62* (unpublished PhD thesis, University of Limerick, 2006).

McArdle, E., *The Secret War* (Cork: Mercier Press, 1984).

McCann, E., *War and an Irish Town* (Harmondsworth: Haymarket Books, 1974).

McCarthy, K., *Republican Cobh and the East Cork Volunteers Since 1913* (Dublin: Nonsuch, 2008).

McGarry, F. (ed.), *Republicanism in Modern Ireland* (Dublin: UCD Press, 2003).

McGladdery, G., *The Provisional IRA in England: The Bombing Campaign, 1973–1997* (Dublin: Irish Academic Press, 2006).

McKittrick, D., B. Feeney, S. Kelters and C. Thornton, *Lost Lives: The Stories of the Men, Women and Children Who Died as a Result of the Northern Ireland Troubles* (Edinburgh: Mainstream Publishing, 2001).

Mitchell, A., *Northern Ireland: Soldiers Talking, 1969 to Today* (London: Sidgwick and Jackson, 1987).

Moloney, E., *A Secret History of the IRA* (London: Penguin, 2003).

Moloney, E., *Voices from the Grave, Two Men's War in Ireland* (London: Faber and Faber, 2010).

Morrison, D. (ed.), *Hunger-Strike, Reflections on the 1981 Hunger-Strike* (Dingle: Mount Eagle Publications, 2006).

Mulroe, P., *Bombs, Bullets and the Border: Policing Ireland's Frontier: Irish Security Policy, 1969–1978* (Dublin: Irish Academic Press, 2017).

Murphy, D., *A Place Apart: Northern Ireland in the 1970s* (Harmondsworth; Eland Publishing, 1978).

Murray, R., *Hard Time: Armagh Gaol, 1971–1986* (Cork: Mercier Press, 1998).

O'Brien, C.C., *States of Ireland* (London, 1972).

O'Brien, C.C., *Herod: Reflections on Political Violence* (London: Faber and Faber, 1978).

O'Brien, C.C., *Passion and Cunning and Other Essays* (London: Paladin, 1990).

O'Brien, C.C., *Memoir: My Life and Themes* (Dublin: Profile Books, 1999).

O'Callaghan, S., *The Informer* (Reading: Corgi, 1999).

Ó Dochartaigh, N., *From Civil Rights to Armalites: Derry and the Birth of the Irish Troubles* (Cork: Palgrave Macmillan, 1997).

O'Doherty, M., *The Trouble with Guns* (Belfast: Blackstaff Press, 1998).

O'Doherty, M., *The Telling Year: Belfast, 1972* (Dublin: Gill Books, 2007).

O'Doherty, S., *The Volunteer: A Former IRA Man's True Story* (London: Strategic Book Publishing, 1993).

O'Donnell, C. *Fianna Fáil, Irish Republicanism and the Northern Ireland Troubles, 1968–2005* (Dublin: Irish Academic Press, 2007).

O'Donnell, R., *From Vinegar Hill to Edentubber: the Wexford IRA and the Border Campaign* (Loch Garman: Cairde na Laochra, 2007).

O'Donnell, R., *Special Category, The IRA in English Prisons, Vol. 1: 1968–1978* (Dublin: Irish Academic Press, 2012).

O'Donoghue, D., *The Devil's Deal: The IRA, Nazi Germany and the Double Life of Jim O'Donovan* (Dublin: New Island Books, 2011).

O'Halpin, E., *Defending Ireland: The Irish State and its Enemies since 1922* (Oxford: Oxford University Press: 1999).

O'Hearn, D., *Bobby Sands, Nothing but an Unfinished Song* (London: Pluto Press, 2006).

O'Malley, P., *The Uncivil Wars: Ireland Today* (Boston: Beacon Press, 1997).

Oppenheimer, A.R., *IRA, The Bombs and Bullets: A History of Deadly Ingenuity* (Dublin: Irish Academic Press, 2010).

O'Rawe, R., *Blanketmen: An Untold Story of the H-Block Hunger Strike* (Dublin: New Island Books, 2005).

Ó Suilleabháin, C., *Leitrim's Republican Story, 1900–2000* (Cumann Cabhrach Liaotrama, 2014).

O'Sullivan, P.M., *Patriot Graves: Resistance in Ireland* (Chicago: Follett, 1972).

Parkinson, A.F. and É. Phoenix (eds), *Conflicts in the North of Ireland, 1900–2000* (Dublin: Four Courts Press, 2010).

Parkinson, A.F., *1972 and the Ulster Troubles* (Dublin: Four Courts Press, 2010).

Parkman, T., *Countering Terrorist Finances: A Training Handbook for Financial Services* (Aldershot: Routledge, 2007).

Patterson, H., *The Politics of Illusion: A Political History of the IRA* (London: Serif Publishers, 1997).

Penniman, H.R. (ed.), *Ireland at the Polls – The Dáil Elections of 1977* (Washington DC: AEI Press, 1978).

Perks, R. and A. Thompson (eds), *The Oral History Reader* (London: Routledge, 1998).

Prince, S. and G. Warner, *Belfast and Derry in Revolt: A New History of the Start of the Troubles* (Dublin: Irish Academic Press, 2012).

Purkiss, D., *The English Civil War, A People's History* (London: Harper Press, 2006).

Rafter, K., *Sinn Féin, 1905–2005* (Dublin: Gill Books, 2005).

Ruane, J. and J. Todd, *The Dynamics of Conflict in Northern Ireland: Power, Conflict and Emancipation* (Cambridge: Cambridge University Press, 1996).

Rumpf, E. and A.C. Hepburn, *Nationalism and Socialism in Twentieth-Century Ireland* (Liverpool: Liverpool University Press, 1977).

Ryan, M., *Tom Barry: IRA Freedom Fighter* (Cork: Mercier Press, 2003).

Sheehan, W. and M. Cronin (eds), *Riotous Assemblies: Rebels, Riots and Revolts in Ireland* (Cork: Mercier Press, 2011).

Smith, R., *Garret, The Enigma: Dr. Garret FitzGerald* (Dublin: Aherlow Publishers, 1985).

Staunton, E., *The Nationalists of Northern Ireland, 1918–73* (Dublin: Columba Press, 2001).

Swan, S., *Official Irish Republicanism, 1962 to 1972* (Lulu, 2007).

Sweeney, E., *Down, Down, Deeper and Down: Ireland in the 70s & 80s* (Dublin: Gill and Macmillan, 2010).

Sweetman, R., *On Our Knees, Ireland 1972* (London: Macmillan, 1972).

Taylor, P., *Provos: The IRA and Sinn Féin* (London: Bloomsbury, 1998).

Townshend, C., *Political Violence in Ireland: Government and Resistance since 1848* (Oxford: Oxford University Press, 1983).

Treacy, M., *The IRA, 1956–62: Rethinking the Republic* (Manchester: Manchester University Press, 2011).

Treacy, M., *A Tunnel to the Moon: The End of the Irish Republican Army* (Lulu, 2017).

Walsh, P., *Irish Republicanism and Socialism: The Politics of the Republican Movement 1905–1994* (Belfast: Repsol, 1994).

Waters, J., *Jiving at the Crossroads* (Belfast: Transworld, 1991).

Wharton, K., *Wasted Years, Wasted Lives: Vol II: The British Army in Northern Ireland, 1978–79* (Warwick: Helion and Co., 2014).

White, R.W., *Provisional Irish Republicans, an Oral and Interpretative History* (London: Praeger Publishers, 1993).

White, R.W., *Ruairí Ó Brádaigh: The Life and Politics of an Irish Revolutionary* (Indiana: Indiana University Press, 2006).

Wilson, A.J., *Irish America and the Ulster Conflict, 1968–1995* (Washington DC: The Catholic University of America Press, 1995).

Wilson, D., *Democracy Denied* (Dublin: Mercier Press, 1997).

Television Programmes/Documentaries

Bombings (produced by RTÉ; broadcast on RTÉ One, 2009).

Bráthadóirí (produced by ScunScan productions; broadcast on TG4, 2008).

Garda ar Lár (produced by RTÉ; broadcast on RTÉ One, 2008–9).

Mná an IRA (produced by Loopline Film; broadcast on TG4, 2011).

The Irish Behind Bars (produced by TV3; broadcast on TV3, 2012).

TV50: Battle Stations (produced by RTÉ; broadcast on RTÉ One, 2012).

Online Sources

CAIN (Conflict Archive Northern Ireland). URL: http://cain.ulst.ac.uk/

Cedar Lounge Revolution. URL: http://cedarlounge.wordpress.com/

Cork Sinn Féin website. URL: http://www.corksf.20m.com/

Derry-Londonderry city of culture. URL: http://www.cityofculture2013.com/

Ed Moloney's blog. URL: http://thebrokenelbow.com/

Irish statute book. URL: http://www.irishstatutebook.ie/

Justice for the Forgotten. URL: http://www.dublinmonaghanbombings.org/

Mixcloud (online clouding source for interviews). URL: http://www.mixcloud.com/

Oireachtas website and debates. URL: http://www.oireachtas.ie/ and http://historical-debates.oireachtas.ie/plweb-cgi/fastweb?Template Name=search.tmpl&view=oho-view

PBS, Frontline documentaries. URL: http://www.pbs.org/

Ring, County Waterford. URL: http://ringcowaterford.blogspot.com/

Roy Johnston's online memoir. URL: http://www.iol.ie/~rjtechne/

RTÉ official website. URL: http://www.rte.ie/

The Irish Story (historical articles): The Court Martial of Captain Joe
    Keohane.   URL: http://www.theirishstory.com/2013/06/30/the-court-
    martial-of-captain-joe-keohane/#.Ue6B9awWA_Y
War of Independence. URL: http://www.warofindependence.info
YouTube:
Bodenstown parade 1969 and 1970. URL: http://www.youtube.com/
    watch?v=ttAWEE-wj1Q
Civil right march in Derry. URL: http://www.youtube.com/watch?v=3H11Ce
    8mmWM

ENDNOTES

Introduction

1   John Darby, 'Northern Ireland: the background to the peace process' (http://cain. ulst.ac.uk/events/peace/darby03.htm) (10 May 2013).

2   David McKittrick, Brian Feeney, Seamus Kelters and Chris Thornton, *Lost Lives: The Stories of the Men, Women and Children Who Died as a Result of the Northern Ireland Troubles* (Edinburgh: Mainstream Publishing, 2001), pp. 143–9 and 1141–2.

3   *News Letter*, 15 May 2013; BBC News, 1 July 2009; 'Oireachtas committee chairman welcomes moves on peace walls', 10 May 2013 (http://www.oireachtas. ie/parliament/mediazone/pressreleases/name-16573-en.html) (13 May 2013).

4   *Irish Times*, 30 January 2013; *News Letter*, 15 May 2013; *Belfast Telegraph*, 1 September 2012.

5   *Irish Times*, 27 February 2012.

6   Begoña Aretxaga, *Shattering Silence: Women, Nationalism and Political Subjectivity in Northern Ireland* (New Jersey: Princeton University Press, 1997), p. 115.

7   Ruán O'Donnell, *Special Category, The IRA in English Prisons, Vol. 1: 1968–1978* (Dublin: Irish Academic Press, 2012), p. 55; Gary McGladdery, *The Provisional IRA in England: The Bombing Campaign, 1973–1997* (Dublin: Irish Academic Press, 2006), p. 134; Jack Holland and Susan Phoenix, *Phoenix, Policing the Shadows* (London: Hodder & Stoughton, 1996), p. 125; David O'Donoghue, *The Devil's Deal: The IRA, Nazi Germany and the Double Life of Jim O'Donovan* (Dublin: New Island Books, 2011), p. 91.

8   Eamonn Sweeney, *Down, Down, Deeper and Down: Ireland in the 70s & 80s* (Dublin: Gill and Macmillan, 2010), pp. 34–5.

9   *House of the Oireachtas, joint committee on justice, equality, defence and women's rights: final report on the report of the independent commission of inquiry into the Dublin and Monaghan Bombings* (March 2004), pp. 24–5, 27–9 and 55–8. J.B. Bell stated: 'On Saturday 18 May men with Northern accents had left a car together at Connolly Station, bought tickets separately, and sat on the Belfast train in different carriages; and despite a telephone call by a concerned citizen from the station nothing was done.' J.B. Bell, *In Dubious Battle: The Dublin and Monaghan Bombings, 1972–74* (Dublin: Poolbeg Press, 1996), p. 88.

10   'Justice for the forgotten' (http://www.dublinmonaghanbombings.org/index2.html) (10 May 2013).

11   *Irish Times*, 15 June 1996; Ed Moloney, *A Secret History of the IRA* (London: Penguin, 2003), pp. 3–33; Peter Taylor, *Provos: The IRA and Sinn Féin* (London: Bloomsbury, 1998), p. 227.

12   Department of Justice, 2005/155/6, National Archives of Ireland (NAI).

13   Patrick Magee, *Gangsters or Guerrillas? Representations of Irish Republicans in 'Troubles Fiction'* (Belfast: Beyond the Pale Publications, 2001), p. 5.

14   See McGladdery, *The Provisional IRA in England*; Jack Holland, *The American Connection: Guns, Money and Influence in Northern Ireland* (Dublin: Viking Press, 1999).

15   J.J. Barrett, *Martin Ferris, Man of Kerry* (Dingle: Mount Eagle Publications, 2005).

16   Sean O'Callaghan, *The Informer* (Reading: Corgi, 1999).

17   *Irish Times*, 18 December 1996, 8 January, 15 January and 17 December 1997. See also 'IRA killer tells of his £175,000 book advance' in *Irish Independent*, 7 May 1998.

18   Cormac Ó Suilleabháin, *Leitrim's Republican Story, 1900–2000* (Cumann Cabhrach Liaotrama, 2014); Kieran McCarthy, *Republican Cobh and the East Cork Volunteers since 1913* (Dublin: Nonsuch, 2008); James Durney, *On the One Road: Political Unrest in Kildare, 1913–1994* (Naas: James Durney, 2001).

19   John Maguire, 'Internment and the IRA, 1939–62' (PhD thesis, University of Limerick, 2006), p. 15.

20   Interview with 'interviewee C', Limerick, 25 March 2011; *Irish Times*, 17 December 1973 and 2 February 1974; Denis O'Hearn, *Bobby Sands, Nothing but an Unfinished Song* (London: Pluto Press, 2006), p. 72.

21   Diane Purkiss, *The English Civil War, A People's History* (London: Harper Press, 2006), p. 161.

22   Samuel Schrager, 'What is social in oral history?' in Robert Perks and Alistair Thompson (eds), *The Oral History Reader* (London: Routledge, 1998), p. 294; Peter Burke, 'History of events and the revival of narrative' in Peter Burke (ed.), *New Perspectives on Historical Writing* (Oxford: Polity, 2001), p. 284.

23   Alessandro Portelli, 'What makes oral history different?' in Perks and Thompson, *The Oral History Reader*, p. 69.

24   Section 31 was implemented incrementally.

25   *Irish Independent*, 20 December 1983.

26   Portelli, 'What makes oral history different?', p. 70.

27   Ibid.

28   See *History Ireland*, March–April, May–June, June–July and August–September 2005.

29   Lesley Hall, 'Confidentially speaking: ethics in interviewing' in Anna Green and Megan Hutching (eds), *Remembering: Writing Oral History* (London: Auckland University Press, 2004), p. 156.

30 *History Ireland* has given this issue much coverage. See, for example, articles in the March–April 2012 and May–June 2013 issues.

31 White's work is an honourable exception where Southerners are concerned; R.W. White, *Provisional Irish Republicans, an Oral and Interpretative History* (London: Praeger Publishers, 1993).

32 J.B. Bell, *The Gun in Irish Politics: An Analysis of the Irish Political Conflict, 1916–1986* (New Jersey: Routledge, 1987), p. 263.

33 David Beresford, *Ten Men Dead: The Story of the 1981 Hunger-Strike* (London: Hunter Publishing, 1987), p. 7.

34 'Derry-Londonderry city of culture 2013' (http://www.cityofculture2013.com/) (15 May 2013).

Chapter 1

1 See Taylor, *Provos*, p. 21; Richard English, *Armed Struggle: A History of the IRA* (Oxford: Picador, 2003), p. 81; Brian Hanley and Scott Millar, *The Lost Revolution: The Story of the Official IRA and the Workers Party* (Dublin: Penguin, 2009), pp. 20–1.

2 Barry Flynn, *Soldiers of Folly: The IRA Border Campaign, 1956–1962* (Cork: Collins Press, 2009), p. 200.

3 See, for example: Paul Larkin, *A Very British Jihad: Collusion, Conspiracy and Cover Up in Northern Ireland* (Belfast: Beyond the Pale Publications, 2004), p. 81 and Hanley and Millar, *The Lost Revolution*, p. 205.

4 'Where Sinn Féin stands' (17 January 1970), pp. 1–4.

5 A 1973 Provisional IRA booklet provides the same justifications with a minor shift in emphasis. *Freedom Struggle* (Dublin, 1973), p. 10.

6 See Padraig Yeates' obituary on Tomás MacGiolla, *Saothar*, 36 (2011), p. 127; Rosita Sweetman, *On Our Knees, Ireland 1972* (London: Macmillan, 1972), p. 16.

7 Sean Swan, *Official Irish Republicanism, 1962 to 1972* (Lulu, 2007), pp. 224–34.

8 'Ireland today' (March 1969), p. 11.

9 'Ireland today', p. 15.

10 'Where Sinn Féin stands', pp. 2–3.

11 Interview with 'Limerick Republican', Limerick, 17 September 2010.

12 'Where Sinn Féin stands', p. 2.

13 Interview with Seán O'Neill, Limerick, 30 March 2011. See also Swan, *Official Irish Republicanism* and Hanley and Millar *The Lost Revolution* for a more in-depth analysis of their involvement and influence. Coughlan was only officially active in the Wolfe Tone societies and was never an IRA volunteer.

14 'Where Sinn Féin stands', p. 2.

15 '(…) observing with detachment some war-gaming, but basically attempting to foster the primacy of the political role. I remember helping to upgrade the diet

with dried apricots, and sleeping somewhat uncomfortably on the floor. To convey ideas to activists effectively it is necessary to share their hardships'. Roy Johnston, 'Century of endeavour: the 60s republican movement (1), 1959–1966' (http://www.iol.ie/~rjtechne/century130703/1960s/index60.htm) (14 January 2013).

16   Roy Johnston, 'Century of endeavour' (webpage, cited above).

17   Gearóid MacCárthaigh's tape-recorded memoir, 'The fight goes on', 08tape_sideA01_T005, Special Collections, Glucksman Library, University of Limerick.

18   Costello was temporarily IRA Chief-of-Staff while Goulding served a short prison sentence. Swan, *Official Irish Republicanism*, p. 167; Matt Treacy, *The IRA, 1956–62: Rethinking the Republic* (Manchester: Manchester University Press, 2011), p. 91.

19   MacCárthaigh, 'The fight goes on', 08tape_sideA01_T005. It should be noted that Johnston has rejected this account, stating: 'The meeting took place in a car (…) The level of hostility was such that I sat in the back with Mac Stiofain and Gerry sat in the front, looking out the front. He avoided face to face contact. I was uncomfortable but did not feel threatened. We went on eventually to set up the Cork Wolfe Tone Society (…)' (http://cedarlounge.wordpress.com/2013/08/25/desmond-swanton-commemoration-cork-1964/) (3 September 2013).

20   Henry Patterson, *The Politics of Illusion: A Political History of the IRA* (London: Serif Publishers, 1997), p. 109.

21   Brian Hanley, 'The IRA and trade unionism, 1922–72' in Francis Devine, Fintan Lane and Niamh Puirséil, *Essays in Irish Labour History* (Dublin: Irish Academic Press, 2008), p. 169.

22   O'Callaghan, *The Informer*, p. 39.

23   Swan, *Official Irish Republicanism*, p. 142.

24   *Irish Times*, 31 March 1964.

25   Ibid., 2 August 1968.

26   Ibid., 30 May 1968; interview with Seán O'Neill, Limerick, 30 March 2011. See also Kieran Allen, *Fianna Fáil and Irish Labour: 1926 to the Present* (London: Pluto Press, 1997), p. 130.

27   Interview with Labhras Ó Donnghaile, Clare, 6 March 2010.

28   *Irish Times*, 5 August 1968.

29   *Sunday Independent*, 2 January 1966.

30   Interview with 'interviewee D', Clare, 27 March 2010.

31   See Patterson, *The Politics of Illusion*, p. 107; J.B. Bell, *The Secret Army: A History of the I.R.A., 1916–1970* (London: Routledge, 1972), p. 403. Both operations were unsanctioned.

32   Jim Lane, 'Miscellaneous notes' (Appendix 1: Statement from Gerry Madden, the survivor of the St Patrick's Day 1963 explosion at Cork's republican plot), p. 25.

33   Terence Dooley, 'IRA veterans and land division in independent Ireland, 1925–48' in Fearghal McGarry (ed.), *Republicanism in Modern Ireland* (Dublin: UCD Press, 2003), p. 95; interview with Frank MacNamara, Clare, 12 September 2010.

34   Interview with 'interviewee D', Clare, 27 March 2010.

35   'Ireland – split in Sinn Féin' in *New Left Review* (March/April, 1970).

36   *New Left Review* (March/April, 1970).

37   Terence Dooley, *'The land for the people': The Land Question in Independent Ireland* (Dublin: UCD Press, 2004), p. 187.

38   Interview with 'interviewee E', Limerick, 16 March 2011; O'Donnell, *Special Category*, p. 41; Treacy, *The IRA*, p. 135.

39   For example, Paddy Mulcahy in Limerick was chairperson and a founding member of his local credit union. See his obituary in *Saoirse*, June 1990.

40   Treacy, *The IRA*, p. 126; P.M. O'Sullivan, *Patriot Graves: Resistance in Ireland* (Chicago: Follett, 1972), p. 162; *Brian Keenan, 1941 – 2008: A Republican Legend* (Dublin, 2008), p. 9.

41   Swan, *Official Irish Republicanism*, p. 188.

42   R.W. White, *Ruairí Ó Brádaigh: The Life and Politics of an Irish Revolutionary* (Indiana: Indiana University Press, 2006), p. 132. The practice remained a feature of many rural Official IRA meetings for years after the split. 'Talking about a lost revolution'.

43   Interview with Labhras Ó Donnghaile, Clare, 6 March 2010 [italics added for emphasis].

44   Patrick Bishop and Eamonn Mallie, *The Provisional IRA* (London: Corgi, 1988), p. 58. Johnston declared at a meeting in January 1966 that 'force as a means of winning freedom is out (…)'. See Gearóid MacCárthaigh's letter to representatives of the republican movement in *Evening Echo*, 25 June 1968. Quoted in Lane, 'Miscellaneous notes', p. 30.

45   Interview with NGA committee member, Dublin, 10 September 2010.

46   Interview with Labhras Ó Donnghaile, Clare, 6 March 2010.

47   'The split was personality driven. It wasn't solely ideological. It was also ego-driven.' *Brian Keenan*, p. 9.

48   Patterson, *The Politics of Illusion*, p. 116.

49   Johnston, 'Century of endeavour'.

50   Hanley and Millar, *The Lost Revolution*, p. 93.

51   Swan, *Official Irish Republicanism*, p. 219.

52   Interview with 'Limerick Republican', Limerick, 17 September 2010.

53   Taylor, *Provos*, pp. 64–7.

54   Seán MacStiofáin, *Memoirs of a Revolutionary* (Edinburgh: Gordon and Cremonesi, 1975), p. 133.

55   Interview with 'Limerick Republican', Limerick, 17 September 2010. Ironically, similar tactics would later be used by the Official leadership on Costello himself when they sought to expel him from their ranks in 1974. Interview with Seán O'Neill, Limerick, 30 March 2011; Hanley and Millar, *The Lost Revolution*, p. 272.

56   Johnston, 'Century of endeavour'.

57   Lane, 'Miscellaneous notes', p. 11.

58   'Where Sinn Féin stands', pp. 3–5. Connolly Youth was the youth wing of the Communist Party of Ireland.

59   MacCárthaigh, 'The fight goes on', 08tape_sideA01_T005.

60   'Bodenstown parade 1969 and 1970' (http://www.youtube.com/watch?v=ttAWEE-wj1Q) (16 January 2013).

61   Swan, *Official Irish Republicanism*, p. 187. White maintains that this latter expulsion was due to their refusal to distribute anti-de Valera leaflets during the 1966 presidential election; Sinn Féin members in Kerry argued against this tactic's impracticality in a rural area as everybody would know who was responsible. White, *Ruairí Ó Brádaigh*, pp. 134–5.

62   White, *Ruairí Ó Brádaigh*, p. 162.

63   MacCárthaigh, 'The fight goes on', 08tape_sideA01_T005.

64   'Where Sinn Féin stands', p. 4.

65   Ibid. [italics added for emphasis].

66   *Freedom Struggle*, p. 11.

67   Thomas Hennessey, *Northern Ireland: The Origins of the Troubles* (Dublin: Gill and Macmillan, 2005), p. 359.

68   Ibid., p. 359.

69   *Irish Times*, 25 July 1963.

70   Ministry of Defence, 69/730 (TNA).

71   Interview with 'interviewee E', Limerick, 16 March 2011.

72   Interview with 'Limerick Republican', Limerick, 17 September 2010.

73   Interview with 'interviewee D', Clare, 27 March 2010.

74   Swan, *Official Irish Republicanism*, p. 162.

75   *Irish Times*, 20 August 1969.

76   Treacy, *The IRA*, pp. 52–3 [italics added for emphasis].

77   Interview with 'interviewee E', Limerick, 16 March 2011.

78   Treacy, *The IRA*, pp. 52–3.

79   'Recording of talk on 1960s republicanism by Brian Hanley and Matt Treacy' (http://www.mixcloud.com/dublincommunitytv/recording-of-talk-on-1960s-republicanism-by-brian-hanley-and-matt-treacy-26-06-12/?utm_source=widgetandutm_medium=webandutm_campaign=base_linksandutm_term=resource_link) (18 January 2013).

80   Ibid.

81   Brian Hanley, '"I ran away"? The IRA and 1969' in *History Ireland*, vol. 17, no. 4 (July/August, 2009), pp. 24–7.

82   Hanley and Millar, *The Lost Revolution*, p. 125, 'Where Sinn Féin stands'; Simon Prince and Geoffrey Warner, *Belfast and Derry in Revolt: A New History of the Start of the Troubles* (Dublin: Irish Academic Press, 2012), p. 151.

83   'Talking about a lost revolution'.
84   [Official Republican Movement booklet] *Liam McMillen: Separatist, Socialist, Republican* (Dublin, 1976), p. 11.
85   Ibid., p. 10.
86   K.J. Kelley, *The Longest War: Northern Ireland and the I.R.A.* (London: Zed Books, 1990), p. 122 and O'Brien, *The Arms Trial*, p. 22. This latter statement in itself may not adequately represent IRA numbers.
87   Bishop and Mallie, *The Provisional IRA*, p. 108.
88   Treacy, *The IRA*, pp. 91 and 95; Sean Cronin, *Irish Nationalism: A History of its Roots and Ideology* (Dublin: Continuum, 1980), p. 108.
89   Interview with 'interviewee D', Clare, 27 March 2010.
90   Ó Suilleabháin, *Leitrim's Republican Story*, p. 307.
91   Interview with 'Limerick Republican', Limerick, 17 September 2010.
92   Bishop and Mallie, *The Provisional IRA*, p. 94. Another account has it that Goulding refused such requests from Derry prior to 12 August 1969, telling the Derry Citizens Defence Association 'I haven't the men nor the guns to do it'. Niall Ó Dochartaigh, *From Civil Rights to Armalites: Derry and the Birth of the Irish Troubles* (Cork: Palgrave Macmillan, 1997), p. 117.
93   Interview with 'interviewee E', Limerick, 16 March 2011; Patterson, *The Politics of Illusion*, p. 126.
94   MacStiofáin, *Memoirs*, pp. 148 and 190. For example, following the burnings, the Ballymurphy IRA unit's arms dump 'took six or seven big vans to cart it all away'. Ciarán de Baróid, *Ballymurphy and the Irish War* (Padstow: Pluto Press, 2000; second edition), p. 39.
95   Swan, *Official Irish Republicanism*, p. 297.
96   Lane, 'Miscellaneous notes', p. 22.
97   Hanley and Millar, *The Lost Revolution*, pp. 40–1.
98   Interview with Labhras Ó Donnghaile, Clare, 6 March 2010. Interestingly, MacGiolla's oration at the 1966 Easter commemoration in Cork city also contained a denunciation of communism. See Lane, 'Miscellaneous notes', p. 13.
99   *Kerryman*, 17 January 1970.
100   *New Left Review* (March/April, 1970); *Irish Times*, 12 January 1970 [italics added for emphasis].
101   *Irish Times*, 12 January 1970.
102   Ernst Rumpf and A.C. Hepburn, *Nationalism and Socialism in Twentieth-Century Ireland* (Liverpool: Liverpool University Press, 1977), p. 187.
103   Bell, *The Secret Army*, p. 123.
104   O'Sullivan, *Patriot Graves*, pp. 222–4.
105   Kelley, *The Longest War*, p. 126.
106   White, *Provisional Irish Republicans*, p. 54.

107   'Talking about a lost revolution'.
108   Interview with Labhras Ó Donnghaile, Clare, 6 March 2010 (former IRA volunteer involved in Operation Harvest).
109   Interview with 'interviewee B', Limerick, 1 August 2010.
110   Interview with Seán O'Neill, Limerick, 30 March 2011.
111   Interview with 'interviewee A', Limerick, 11 August 2010.
112   Interview with Martin Ferris, Kerry, 22 June 2010.
113   Interview with 'interviewee E', Limerick, 16 March 2011.
114   *Hibernia*, 19 January 1973.
115   Lane, 'Miscellaneous notes', p. 21.
116   Prince and Warner, *Belfast and Derry in Revolt*, p. 211; Gerard Magee, *Tyrone's Struggle* (Omagh, 2012), p. 117; A.F. Parkinson and Éamon Phoenix (eds), *Conflicts in the North of Ireland, 1900–2000* (Dublin: Four Courts Press, 2010), p. 251. Gerry Bradley recalled that in north Belfast, where twelve Catholic civilians were shot, the IRA leadership could only provide residents with 'pick-axe handles' as defensive weapons. Gerry Bradley, *Insider: Gerry Bradley's Life in the IRA* (Dublin: O'Brien Press, 2012) p. 37; *Violence and Civil Disturbances in Northern Ireland in 1969, Report of the Tribunal of Inquiry by the Honorary Mr Justice Scarman* (Belfast, 1972), p. 189.
117   Parkinson and Phoenix, *Conflicts in the North of Ireland*, p. 251; Liam Kelly, 'Belfast, August 1969: the limited and localised pattern(s) of violence' in William Sheehan and Maura Cronin (eds), *Riotous Assemblies: Rebels, Riots and Revolts in Ireland* (Cork: Mercier Press, 2011), p. 232.
118   Frank Burton, *The Politics of Legitimacy: Struggles in a Belfast Community* (London: Routledge, 1978), p. 77.
119   Bishop and Mallie, *The Provisional IRA*, p. 125.
120   Cronin, *Irish Nationalism*, p. 108; O'Donnell, *Special Category*, p. 41.
121   O'Sullivan, *Patriot Graves*, p. 162; *Brian Keenan*, p. 9. Pat Ward, for example, who sided with the Provisionals in 1970 and with Republican Sinn Féin following the 1986 split, was a staunch trade unionist and a former member of the Communist Party. See his obituary in *Saoirse*, April 1988.
122   *Irish Times*, 12 January 1970. Jack McCabe, for example; Treacy, *The IRA*, p. 108.
123   Sweetman, *On Our Knees*, p. 212; *Brian Keenan*, p. 9.
124   'Recording of talk on 1960s republicanism' (see fn. 94).
125   O'Brien, *The Arms Trial*, p. 21.

Chapter 2

1   A civil rights march in Derry City on 5 October 1968 was violently broken up by the RUC. The attack was captured on film by an RTÉ news crew. See *Munster Express*, 11 October 1968; *Kerryman*, 12 October 1968; Eamonn McCann, *War*

and an Irish Town (Harmondsworth: Haymarket Books, 1974), pp. 43–8; 'Civil rights march in Derry'

(http://www.youtube.com/watch?v=3H11Ce8mmWM) (7 June 2013).

2   Cronin, *Irish Nationalism*, p. 33.

3   See, for example: Pat Walsh, *Irish Republicanism and Socialism: The Politics of the Republican Movement 1905–1994* (Belfast: Repsol, 1994), p. 146.

4   *Hibernia*, 19 January 1973.

5   Des Wilson and Enda Staunton, between them, note that such attacks erupted every ten to twelve years in Belfast. Des Wilson, *Democracy Denied* (Dublin: Mercier Press, 1997), p. 36; Enda Staunton, *The Nationalists of Northern Ireland, 1918–73* (Dublin: Columba Press, 2001), p. 8.

6   Interview with Tommy McKearney, Monaghan, 30 July 2013.

7   Sweetman, *On Our Knees*, p. 16.

8   Charles Townshend, *Political Violence in Ireland: Government and Resistance since 1848* (Oxford: Oxford University Press, 1983), p. 371.

9   One former internee, speaking of the Curragh during the 1940s, remarked 'It eventually grew to a large section who did not go to mass.' Uinseann MacEoin, *The IRA in the Twilight Years, 1923–48* (Dublin: Argenta, 1997), p. 583.

10   Sweetman, *On Our Knees*, p. 212. Both Ivor Bell and Brian Keenan were hard-line Marxists.

11   Simon Lemieux, 'Britain and Ireland 1798–1921: changing the question or altering the answers?' in *History Today* (52).

12   Piers Brendon, *The Decline and Fall of the British Empire, 1781–1997* (London: Vintage Press, 2008), p. 290.

13   Interview with 'interviewee D', Clare, 27 March 2010. Martin Ferris noted this, the 'emotions of the last atrocity', stating that it took more than events such as Bloody Sunday to maintain commitment to republicanism. To term it 'irredentism' is somewhat accurate but risks distorting the issue – through terminology – by linking it with nationalism in the Europe of the twentieth century. Interview with Martin Ferris, Kerry, 22 June 2010.

14   Pádraig O'Malley, *The Uncivil Wars: Ireland Today* (Boston: Beacon Press, 1997), p. 258.

15   Interview with 'interviewee C', Limerick, 25 March 2011.

16   Meda Ryan, *Tom Barry: IRA Freedom Fighter* (Cork: Mercier Press, 2003), p. 273.

17   Hanley and Millar, *The Lost Revolution*, p. 145. Attendance at the Officials' Easter commemoration in Derry City in 1971 was apparently twice that of the Provisionals. Ó Dochartaigh, *From Civil Rights to Armalites*, pp. 241 and 238.

18   Quoted in Kevin Bean and Mark Hayes, *Republican Voices* (Monaghan: Unrast Verlag, 2001), p. 36.

19   Compare Dooley, 'IRA veterans and land division' in McGarry, *Republicanism in*

Modern Ireland, p. 91 and Malachi O'Doherty, *The Trouble with Guns* (Belfast: Blackstaff Press, 1998), p. 131.

20   Magee, *Tyrone's Struggle*, pp. 124–5 and 590.

21   Rumpf and Hepburn, *Nationalism and Socialism*, pp. 104 and 146.

22   Arthur Mitchell, *Revolutionary Government in Ireland: Dáil Éireann 1919–22* (Dublin: Gill and Macmillan, 1995), p. 138. See also Joost Augusteijn, *From Public Defiance to Guerrilla Warfare: The Experience of Ordinary Volunteers in the Irish War of Independence, 1916–21* (Dublin: Irish Academic Press, 1996), p. 284; Michael Hopkinson, *The Irish War of Independence* (Dublin: Gill Books, 2002), pp. 20–44.

23   See Mitchell, *Revolutionary Government*, p.130; Rumpf and Hepburn, *Nationalism and Socialism*, pp. 104–6; White, *Ruairí Ó Brádaigh*, pp. 152 and 158.

24   White, *Ruairí Ó Brádaigh*, p. 152.

25   Martyn Frampton, *Legion of the Rearguard, Dissident Irish Republicanism* (Dublin: Irish Academic Press, 2011), p. 25; Hanley, *The IRA, 1926–36*, p. 80; Uinseann MacEoin, *Survivors* (Dublin: Argenta Press, 1987), p. 4.

26   Bell described the situation in Kerry, for example, as a vast network involving many personal relations. Bell, *The Gun in Irish Politics*, p. 111.

27   Interview with Dessie Ellis, Dublin, 30 September 2010. Hanley and Millar, *The Lost Revolution*, p. 1.

28   Interview with 'interviewee E', Limerick, 16 March 2011. White, *Ruairí Ó Brádaigh*, p. 5.

29   Interview with Labhras Ó Donnghaile, Clare, 6 March 2010.

30   Interview with 'Limerick Republican', Limerick, 17 September 2010.

31   J.B. Bell, *The IRA 1968–2000: Analysis of a Secret Army* (London: Routledge, 2000), p. 100.

32   White, *Provisional Irish Republicans*, p. 137.

33   Interviews with 'interviewee D', Clare, 27 March 2010 and 'interviewee B', Limerick, 1 August 2010; Maria McGuire, *To Take Arms: A Year in the Provisional IRA* (London: Quartet Books, 1973), p. 8.

34   Interview with 'interviewee D', Clare, 27 March 2010.

35   A British report that examined the disturbance of 1968–9 in Northern Ireland explicitly linked the emergence of the civil rights campaign there with similar movements in Europe and the USA, adding: 'The psychological effect of this example in other countries and other circumstances cannot be discounted.' Paragraph 55 of *Disturbances in Northern Ireland, report of the commission (under the chairmanship of Lord Cameron) appointed by the Governor of Northern Ireland* (Belfast, 1969), p. 55.

36   Interview with Pat Magee, Limerick, 11 October 2010.

37   Interview with 'interviewee D', Clare, 27 March 2010.

38   Ibid.

39   Interview with 'interviewee A', Limerick, 11 August 2010.

40   Interview with 'interviewee B', Limerick, 1 August 2010.

41   Bean and Hayes, *Republican Voices*, p. 52; email correspondence between the author and Anthony McIntyre, 5 April 2011.

42   The term has erroneously gone down in history as 'no longer stand idly by'.

43   Footage shown on '*Bombings*', RTÉ One. Broadcast on 6 July 2010.

44   Moloney, *A Secret History*, pp. 87–92.

45   *Irish Times*, 9 August 1971.

46   McCann, *War and an Irish Town*, p. 102.

47   Interview with 'Joe', Clare, 17 September 2008.

48   Interview with Martin Ferris, Kerry, 22 June 2010 [italics added for emphasis].

49   Over one thousand Catholic families were forced to flee their homes between July and September 1969 alone. *Violence and civil disturbances in Northern Ireland in 1969 (Scarman)*, p. 248. Geraghty estimated that there were 60,000 displaced northerners living in the South by 1975. Tony Geraghty, *The Irish War: The Hidden Conflict Between the IRA and British Intelligence* (Baltimore: Harper Collins, 1998), p. 70.

50   *Irish Times*, 25 August 1969 and 14 July 1970; *Irish Press*, 11 August 1971 and 14 August 1972. Usage of the term was not confined to republicans and was used quite commonly by Irish and international newspapers. See, for example: *Irish Times*, 22 August 1969; *Irish Independent*, 21 August 1969; *Chicago Tribune*, 13 August 1971.

51   Interview with 'Claire', Clare, 18 August 2008.

52   Interviews with 'interviewee B', Limerick, 1 August 2010 and 'interviewee A', Limerick, 8 August 2010.

53   P.B. Ellis, *A History of the Irish Working Class* (London: Pluto Press, 1989), p. 252; Mary Kotsonouris, *Retreat from Revolution: the Dáil Courts, 1920–24* (Dublin: Irish Academic Press, 1994), p. 20; Brian Hanley, *The IRA, 1926–1936* (Dublin: Four Courts Press, 2002), p. 80.

54   *Republican News*, March 1971.

55   Hanley, *The IRA, 1926–1936*, p. 26; Tim Pat Coogan, *The I.R.A.* (London: RR Press, 1995), p. 40.

56   MacEoin, *Survivors*, p. 341.

57   MacCárthaigh, 'The fight goes on', 08tape_sideB01_T005.

58   Interview with Maurice Quinlivan, Limerick, 10 May 2010.

59   Michael Hopkinson, *Green against Green: The Irish Civil War* (Dublin: Gill Books, 1988), p. 228; interview with Labhras Ó Donnghaile, Clare, 6 March 2010.

60   *Republican News*, April 1971.

61   *Sunday Times*, 8 October 2017. Six IRA volunteers were shot in that county after surrendering to Free State soldiers in September 1922.

62   Ibid., 23 December 2012.

63   MacEoin, *The IRA in the Twilight Years*, p. 475.

64   Interview with Kieran Conway, Dun Laoghaire, 25 September 2016.

65   Ibid. [italics added for emphasis].

66   Bell, *The Gun in Irish Politics*, p. 111.

67   Kieran Conway, *Southside Provisional: From Freedom Fighter to the Four Courts* (Dublin: Orpen Press, 2017), p. 99.

68   *Irish Times*, 28 June 1972; *Irish Press*, 13 August 1973; *Saoirse*, November 1988. Durney, *On the One Road*, pp. 183–4.

69   Interview with 'interviewee A', Limerick, 11 August 2010.

70   Interview with 'interviewee B', Limerick, 1 August 2010.

71   Interview with 'interviewee D', Clare, 27 March 2010.

72   Interview with 'interviewee A', Limerick, 11 August 2010.

73   Interview with Martin Ferris, Kerry, 22 June 2010.

74   Jack McCabe was just one of the more notable veteran republicans who had re-joined the IRA following the August 1969 burnings. *Freedom Struggle*, p. 48.

75   Eoin Ó Broin, *Sinn Féin and the Politics of Left Republicanism* (London: Pluto Press, 2009), pp. 152 and 202.

76   Interview with 'interviewee E', Limerick, 16 March 2011.

77   Hanley and Millar, *The Lost Revolution*, p. 145.

78   White, *Ruairí Ó Brádaigh*, pp. 152 and 158.

79   *Irish Press*, 19 January 1970.

80   Swan, *Official Irish Republicanism*, p. 187.

81   Ibid., p. 183.

82   MacCárthaigh, 'The fight goes on', 08tape_sideB01_T005.

83   See John O'Callaghan, *The Battle for Kilmallock* (Cork: Mercier Press, 2011), p. 22; Peter Hart, *The I.R.A. & its Enemies: Violence and Community in Cork, 1916–1923* (Oxford: Oxford University Press, 1999), p. 256; Brendan O'Brien, *The Long War: The IRA and Sinn Féin* (Dublin: O'Brien Press, 1999), p. 122; P.M. Currie and Max Taylor, *Dissident Irish Republicanism* (London: Continuum, 2011), p. 30.

84   Treacy, *The IRA, 1956–69*, p. 178. The author cites Dublin as one example of an area where decisions were made less on a left–right ideological basis as on personal loyalty.

85   Interview with 'Limerick Republican', Limerick, 17 September 2010.

86   Treacy, *The IRA*, p. 169; Jim Lane, 'Miscellaneous notes', p. 22. Liz Walsh erroneously attributes this Leitrim meeting to the actual establishment of the Provisional IRA. See Liz Walsh, *The Final Beat, Gardaí Killed in the Line of Duty* (Dublin: Gill and Macmillan, 2001), p. 137.

87   Bell, *The Gun in Irish Politics*, p. 120.

88   Tommy McKearney, *The Provisional IRA: From Insurrection to Parliament* (London: Pluto Press, 2011), pp. 78 and 97.

89 Interview with 'Limerick Republican', Limerick, 17 September 2010. As to why this was the case, there are no simple answers. Likely it was a combination of MacStiofáin rewarding loyal friends, an acknowledgement that the province was in safe hands in terms of the presence of veteran but active republicans as well as the early recognition that Munster would act as the logistical key for the Provisionals.

90 Interviews with 'Limerick Republican', Limerick, 17 September 2010 and Seán O'Neill, Limerick, 30 March 2011.

91 Interview with Seán O'Neill, Limerick, 30 March 2011. That the Officials' newspaper was being sold by young Corkonians indicates the numerical weakness of that organisation in Limerick city. It must be noted that subsequent recruitment did lead to the establishment of a sizeable Official unit in the city.

92 O'Donnell, *Special Category*, p. 110.

93 Interviews with Seán O'Neill, Limerick, 30 March 2011 and 'Limerick Republican', Limerick, 17 September 2010. The Ennis assault occurred during a period of heightened tension between the Officials and Provisionals in Belfast; Charlie Hughes, a senior Provisional volunteer, had been shot dead by Officials the previous week. For clashes between the two factions, see 'Counter allegations by Goulding wing' in *Irish Times*, 18 March 1971.

94 Foreign & Commonwealth Office, 33/1593 (TNA).

95 Interview with 'interviewee E', Limerick, 16 March 2011.

96 *Irish Times*, 5 March 1970.

97 Interview with 'interviewee E', Limerick, 16 March 2011.

98 Lane, 'Miscellaneous notes', pp. 18–19.

99 Ibid., p. 19.

100 Interview with 'interviewee E', Limerick, 16 March 2011.

101 MacCárthaigh, 'The fight goes on', 08tape_sideA01_T005.

102 Ibid.; interview with 'interviewee E', Limerick, 16 March 2011. These latter two units may be one and the same, though distinctions are made in the locations by the two sources quoted.

103 Interview with 'interviewee E', Limerick, 16 March 2011.

104 *Irish Times*, 15 October 1971.

105 Interview with 'interviewee E', Limerick, 16 March 2011.

106 'Armies of the South' in *Fortnight*, no. 28 (12 November 1971).

107 Ibid.

108 *Irish Independent*, 5 January 1972.

109 Interview with 'interviewee A', Limerick, 11 August 2010.

110 Interviews with 'interviewee C', Limerick, 25 March 2011.

111 *Irish Times*, 1 April 1972 and 29 April 1972.

112 *Magill*, August 1986.

113   Interview with Seán O'Neill, Limerick, 30 March 2011 (former member of the Official republican movement). The Provisional IRA rescinded their ban on court recognition in 1976.

114   See *Irish Press*, 14 April and 18 October 1973; *Irish Times*, 20 February 1973. This was in adherence to the IRA's General Standing Order Number Eight.

115   Shevlin's obituary in *Saoirse* stated that he was Adjutant-General of the IRA in 1958–9, while Ó Brádaigh noted at his funeral: 'For the last 20 years he remained on call to visit prisons, police barracks and holding centres (…)', *Saoirse*, December 1990. *Irish Independent*, 7 April 1973.

116   Jack Holland and Henry McDonald, *INLA: Deadly Divisions* (Dublin: Poolbeg Press, 1994), p. 80. For Official IRA criticism of the Provisional's bombing campaign, see Hanley and Millar, *The Lost Revolution*, pp. 171 and 180; Patterson, *The Politics of Illusion*, pp. 151–2.

117   Dataset compiled by the author.

118   Paul Gill and John Horgan, 'Who were the Volunteers? The shifting Sociological and Operational Profile of 1240 Provisional Irish Republican Army Members' in *Terrorism and Political Violence* (25:3), p. 439.

119   'Extracts from "Brits speak out"', compiled by John Lindsay (http://cain.ulst.ac.uk/othelem/people/accounts/lindsay.htm#colin)   (10 December 2012).

120   Some activists graduated to full military while still members of Na Fianna: Tobias Molloy was the oldest Fianna member to be killed on active service, at eighteen, in 1972. *An Phoblacht*, 24 July 2008 (Molloy is claimed for the Official republican movement by Hanley and Millar. See *The Lost Revolution*, p. 183). Cumann na gCáilíní was open to females between the ages of seven and eighteen years. *Saoirse*, June 1987.

121   Gearóid Ó Danachair, *Provos: Patriots or Terrorists?* (Dublin, 1974), p. 36.

122   Magee, *Tyrone's Struggle*, p. 233. Conflict Archive Northern Ireland erroneously gives his age as eighteen.

123   MacCárthaigh, 'The fight goes on', 08tape_sideB01_T005; 'Volunteer Dermot Crowley' (http://www.corksf.20m.com/photo.html) (10 December 2012).

124   See, for example: 'In the ghettoes – where the IRA "godfathers" rule' in *Irish Independent*, 9 July 1979.

125   *Irish Independent*, 9 August 1974 and MacCárthaigh, 'The fight goes on', 08tape_sideA01_T005.

126   MacCárthaigh, 'The fight goes on', 08tape_sideB01_T005.

127   J.M. Glover, 'Northern Ireland, future terrorist trends', p. 4. Document reproduced in appendix of Cronin, *Irish Nationalism*.

128   MacCárthaigh, 'The fight goes on', 08tape_sideB01_T005.

129   *Irish Independent*, 13 September 1974.

130 Interview with Kieran Conway, Dun Laoghaire, 25 September 2016.

131 Dessie Ellis, TD for Dublin North-West and a former IRA volunteer, has spoken of how Finglas played a crucial role during the Provisionals' campaign. *Sunday Times*, 23 December 2012. As recently as May 2013 a commemoration for volunteer Martin Doherty of Finglas, killed by pro-British paramilitaries in Dublin city centre in 1994, was attended by a large crowd of locals. See *An Phoblacht*, 26 May 2013. For the turnout for his funeral, see *Irish Press*, 26 May 1994.

132 Indeed, sections of Tralee were put under virtual 'siege' by the Irish Defence Forces in August 1974 ostensibly for the delivery of cash to post offices. All cars in the vicinity were checked and hoteliers requested to produce lists of their guests. *Irish Independent*, 14 August 1974.

133 Gill and Horgan, 'Who were the Volunteers?', p. 446.

134 Three autograph books containing signatures of Republican prisoners, 1974', MS 42,000 (NLI).

135 Ibid., p. 449.

136 Sweeney, *Down, Down, Deeper and Down*, p. 77.

137 Peter Taylor, 'Britain's Irish problem' in M.P. Hederman and Richard Kearney (eds), *The Crane Bag Book of Irish Studies* (Dublin: Blackwater Press, 1981), p. 681.

138 Interview with Pat Magee, Limerick, 11 October 2010.

139 The deaths of IRA volunteers were always the exception. The aftermath of such occasions always witnessed overt displays of sympathy. Tens of thousands of people attended the funeral of Seán Sabhat in Limerick in 1957, while Ruán O'Donnell's book on Operation Harvest noted Paddy Parle's funeral in Wexford as having similar attendance. See *From Vinegar Hill to Edentubber: the Wexford IRA and the Border Campaign* (Loch Garman: Cairde na Laochra, 2007), p. 43 and *Irish Independent*, 5 January 1957.

140 Interview with 'interviewee B', Limerick, 1 August 2010 [italics added].

141 *Hibernia*, 17 January 1980.

Chapter 3

1 Kelley, *The Longest War*, p. 150. British military commanders referred to the conflict during this period as a 'shooting war'. *Irish Times*, 10 February 1971; *Irish Press*, 8 February 1971.

2 Coogan, *The IRA*, p. 375.

3 *Irish Times*, 27 August 1969. A Garda-issued license was necessary for public collections, so all republican collections were illegal as they refused to recognise the state and apply for a license (which would likely be denied anyway).

4 Interview with Labhras Ó Donnghaile, Clare, 6 March 2010.

5   *Fortnight*, 12 November 1971.

6   *Irish Times*, 14 August 1971.

7   *Fortnight*, 12 November 1971.

8   Interview with Seán O'Neill, Limerick, 30 March 2011 (interviewee was a former member of the Official republican movement); *Irish Press*, 30 October 1971.

9   *Fortnight*, 12 November 1971. The article does not mention that the Provisionals had two papers, *Republican News* in the North and *An Phoblacht* in the South.

10   Interview with 'interviewee B', Limerick, 1 August 2010.

11   Interview with Labhras Ó Donnghaile, Clare, 6 March 2010.

12   Ibid.; 'The Easter lily' (http://www.anphoblacht.com/contents/16643) (07 March 2011).

13   *Irish Times*, 31 January 1992.

14   Ibid., 18 May 1963.

15   Ibid., 13 March and 17 August 1964.

16   *Irish Independent*, 15 November 1963.

17   *Irish Times*, 12 April 1965 and 11 April 1966.

18   Ibid., 17 May 1966.

19   *Irish Independent*, 19 April 1965.

20   O'Donnell, *Special Category*, p. 112.

21   *Irish Times*, 12 April 1971.

22   Interview with Labhras Ó Donnghaile, Clare, 6 March 2010.

23   *Fortnight*,12 November 1971.

24   Interview with 'interviewee B', Limerick, 1 August 2010.

25   *Irish Times*, 8 April 1971; interview with 'Limerick Republican', Limerick, 17 September 2010. The NGA publication, *Belfast Graves*, recorded that Henderson 'died as a result of an accidental shooting at a training camp near Portlaoise on April 4th 1971'. *Belfast Graves* (Dublin, 1985), p. 73.

26   *Irish Times*, 6 April 1971.

27   Interview with Kieran Conway, Dun Laoghaire, 25 September 2016.

28   Bean and Hayes, *Republican Voices*, p. 52; McKearney, *The Provisional IRA*, p. 75.

29   *Irish Times*, 1 December 1971.

30   Ibid., 9 November 1970.

31   Ibid., 9 November 1970. This incident is also mentioned in *Freedom Struggle*, p. 22.

32   Foreign & Commonwealth Office, 87/43 (TNA).

33   Hanley and Millar, *The Lost Revolution*, p. 167. During his time with the Official IRA, 'interviewee A' had attended this camp. Interview with 'interviewee A', Limerick, 11 August 2010.

34   'Ulster: consensus and coercion' in *Conflict Studies*, no. 50 (Oct. 1974), p. 22.

35   O'Donnell, *Special Category*, p. 104.

36   Interview with ['Limerick Republican'], Limerick, 17 September 2010.

37   White, *Ruairí Ó Brádaigh*, pp. 152 and 158.

38   Interview with 'Limerick Republican', Limerick, 17 September 2010.

39   Interview with 'interviewee D', Clare, 27 March 2010.

40   *Irish Times*, 20 March 1972.

41   Interview with 'interviewee D', Clare, 27 March 2010.

42   *Irish Times*, 8 April 1971.

43   See *Irish Times*, 30 March 1970, 8 November 1971 and 22 December 1972.

44   Interview with 'Limerick Republican', Limerick, 17 September 2010.

45   Ibid.

46   Interviews with Labhras Ó Donnghaile, Clare, 6 March 2010 and 'interviewee E', Limerick, 16 March 2011.

47   McKearney, *The Provisional IRA*, p. 78.

48   Interview with 'Limerick Republican', Limerick, 17 September 2010; Bell, *The IRA, 1968–2000*, p. 123. Bell and Moloney give different dates for the tenure of this chief-of-staff. Moloney, *A Secret History*, p. 513.

49   *Derry Journal*, 28 December 2012.

50   Bishop and Mallie, *The Provisional IRA*, p. 170. This can largely be determined by the relative dearth of loyalist bombings at this time and the fact that the Official IRA were ideologically opposed to commercial bombings. See Kelley, *The Longest War*, p. 140.

51   Taylor, *Provos*, p. 70.

52   *Irish Times*, 11 March 1970.

53   Ibid.

54   *Irish Independent*, 11 March 1970.

55   Foreign & Commonwealth Office, 33/1199 (TNA).

56   *Irish Times*, 25 July 1970.

57   Ibid., 25 July 1970 and 24 November 1970. The Provisional IRA did not have a monopoly on access to or knowledge of easily acquired commercial explosives, however. Reportedly, the Official IRA and later the INLA had limited access 'thanks to a [Seamus] Costello supporter who worked in Tara silver mines at Nenagh, County Tipperary'. Holland and McDonald, *INLA*, p. 80. The identification of this mine is incorrect. The mines close to Nenagh were the Canadian-controlled Mogul Mines at Silvermines, County Tipperary.

58   *Irish Times*, 19 July and 17 December 1971.

59   Ibid., 14 September 1971.

60   Ibid., 14 April 1970.

61   *Irish Press*, 16 December 1971; *Irish Times*, 16 December 1971. A fortnight earlier, fellow Ulster Unionist MP, Herbert Whitten, stated that 'terrorists can find safe sanctuary in Southern Ireland'. Ibid., 1 December 1971. Such accusations were a recurring theme on the part of unionists during the conflict. For example, in the aftermath of a premature explosion at Castlederg, County Tyrone, in 1976 in

which several IRA volunteers were killed, the head of the Orange Order in Belfast declared that the incident proved 'beyond doubt that an Irish Ho Chi Minh trail exists in spite of the much talked about co-operation between security forces on both sides'. *Irish Independent*, 19 July 1976. One of the IRA volunteers killed at Castlederg was a member of the IRA's Dublin Brigade.

62 'Living with bombs', *Fortnight*, no. 25 (1 October 1971).
63 Ceisteanna – questions. Oral answers – gelignite raids, 1972 (258/1972) (17 February 1972).
64 Ceisteanna – questions. Oral answers – thefts of gelignite, 1971 (256/1971) (4 November 1971).
65 Ibid.
66 *Irish Independent*, 11 January 1972.
67 Department of Justice, 2005/34/194 (NAI).
68 *Irish Times*, 18 October 1971.
69 *Irish Press*, 28 September and 5 October 1971.
70 *Irish Times*, 18 October 1971.
71 There is a quantity of correspondence in this regard in the Department of Justice files, 2005/34/194 (NAI).
72 *Irish Times*, 13 January 1972.
73 Ibid.
74 Ibid., 22 January 1972.
75 *Irish Independent*, 7 February 1972.
76 Department of Justice, 2005/34/194 (NAI).
77 *Irish Times*, 12 June 1972.
78 'A chronology of the conflict: 1972' (http://cain.ulst.ac.uk/othelem/chron/ch72.htm) (2 February 2011).
79 Department of Justice, 2005/34/15 (NAI).
80 Ibid.
81 Taylor, *Provos*, p. 133.
82 MacStiofáin, *Memoirs*, pp. 220 and 242.
83 *Irish Times*, 12 June 1972 and 23 August 1972.
84 Eight Provisional IRA volunteers were killed that month due to premature explosions, most commonly when the bomb was in transit. There were also several IRA deaths due to premature explosions in February and March of that year; 'An index of deaths from the conflict in Ireland' (CAIN).
85 *Irish Times*, 8 August 1973.
86 Shane O'Doherty, *The Volunteer: A Former IRA Man's True Story* (London: Strategic Book Publishing, 1993), p. 69.
87 Magee, *Tyrone's Struggle*, p. 162.
88 *Magill*, September 1980; Fred Holroyd with Nick Burbridge, *War Without Honour* (Hull: Medium, 1989), p. 92.

89 Moloney, *A Secret History*, p. 159; Sean Boyne, *Gunrunners: The Covert Arms Trail to Ireland* (Dublin: O'Brien Press, 2006), p. 245.

90 Roinn an Taoisigh, 2003/16/109 (NAI).

91 Interview with 'Limerick Republican', Limerick, 17 September 2010.

92 Bradley, *Insider*, p. 95.

93 Ibid., O'Doherty, *The Volunteer*, p. 134.

94 W.H. Kautt, *Ambushes and Armour: the Irish Rebellion, 1919–21* (Dublin: Irish Academic Press, 2010), p. 161.

95 *Hibernia*, 24 August 1973.

96 MacStiofáin, *Memoirs*, p. 148.

97 Ibid., p. 190.

98 D Company – 2nd Battalion, Annual Commemorative Function (Irish Republican Felons Club, *c*.1980).

99 Bishop and Mallie, *The Provisional IRA*, p. 168.

100 Interview with Shannon Republican, Clare, 18 August 2008; *Irish Times*, 30 November 1987.

101 *Irish Times*, 23 October 1971.

102 'The IRA & Sinn Fein' (http://www.pbs.org/wgbh/pages/frontline/shows/ira/readings/america.html) (4 March 2011).

103 Ó Conaill had a number of useful contacts for such endeavours, including several freelance or mercenary pilots. See Seán O'Mahony Collection, MS 44, 162/9 (NLI).

104 *Irish Times*, 27 February 1970.

105 *Irish Times*, 11 July 1970. These Dungarvan arms were later recovered when Gardaí raided a house in Mogeely, County Cork.

106 *Irish Times*, 1 April 1970.

107 *Irish Independent*, 3 January 1971.

108 *Irish Times*, 9 March 1972.

109 MacEoin, *The IRA in the Twilight Years*, p. 550.

110 Interview with 'interviewee E', Limerick, 16 March 2011.

111 See *Irish Times*, 3 June 1971 and 19 February 1973.

112 *Irish Times*, 26 May 1970

113 Ibid., 9 December 1971.

114 Ibid.

115 Ibid., 8 October 1971.

116 Ibid., 1 December 1971.

117 Ibid., 10 September 1939 and 10 March 1972.

118 Ibid., 10 September 1971.

119 *Irish Independent*, 3 December 1971.

120 Ibid. this was subsequently further extended.

121 *Irish Press*, 8 March 1972.

122   Ibid.

123   Ibid.

124   *Irish Times*, 10 March 1972.

125   Aontacht Éireann was a short-lived nationalist party formed by Kevin Boland following the 1970 arms trial. See Catherine O'Donnell, *Fianna Fáil, Irish Republicanism and the Northern Ireland Troubles, 1968–2005* (Dublin: Irish Academic Press, 2007).

126   *Irish Times*, 10 March 1972. Keohane stood unsuccessfully for Aontacht Éireann during the 1973 General Election for the Kerry North constituency.

127   Ibid.

128   Ibid., 20 November 1971.

129   'Births, marriages and deaths', *Irish Press*, 13 August 1973.

130   *Hibernia*, 20 October 1972. See also McGuire, *To Take Arms*, p. 128.

131   *Irish Times*, 9 October 1972.

132   Kelley, *The Longest War*, p. 294.

133   'Brian Moore RIP'
(http://thebrokenelbow.com/category/cormac/) (18 February 2013).

134   Hanley, 'The IRA and trade unionism' in Devine, Lane and Puirséil, *Essays in Irish Labour History*, p. 174.

135   Email correspondence between the author and Anthony McIntyre, 5 April 2011.

136   In early 1973, a prominent article in *Republican News* called for the establishment of a 'socialist republic'; this was during a period when that newspaper was still supposedly reflective of a more conservative readership. *Hibernia*, 16 March 1973.

137   Figures taken from *Irish Times*, 26 October 1970, 25 October 1971 and 30 October 1972, respectively.

138   *Irish Times*, 14 June 1971.

139   Interview with 'interviewee E', Limerick, 16 March 2011.

140   *Hibernia*, 20 October 1972.

141   MacCárthaigh, 'The fight goes on', 08tape_sideB01_T005.

142   Bradley, *Insider*, p. 16. In an interview in 1971, Liam Hannaway stated: 'most Sinn Féin members are outside the Army. They have the same principles as volunteers, but there are very few who actually hold dual membership.' O'Sullivan, *Patriot Graves*, p. 63.

143   *Hibernia*, 30 March 1973. Eamon Collins used the term 'draft-dodgers'; Eamon Collins, *Killing Rage* (London: Granta Books, 1998), p. 205.

144   Interview with 'interviewee E', Limerick, 16 March 2011.

145   *Republican News*, 13 July 1974.

146   Patrick Mulroe, *Bombs, Bullets and the Border: Policing Ireland's Frontier: Irish Security Policy, 1969–1978* (Dublin: Irish Academic Press, 2017).

147   O'Malley, *The Uncivil Wars*, p. 80; Michael Gallagher, *The Irish Labour Party in Transition, 1957–82* (Manchester: Manchester University Press, 1982), p. 142.

148   Micheál MacGréil, *Prejudice and Tolerance in Ireland* (Dublin: National College of Ireland Press, 1977), p. 127.

149   Ibid.

150   Ibid., p. 247.

151   Bell, *The Irish Troubles*, p. 168.

152   Bernard, *Daughter of Derry*, p. 67.

153   *Irish Independent*, 21 September 2003.

154   Interview with 'interviewee A', Limerick, 11 August 2010.

155   Interview with 'Limerick Republican', Limerick, 17 September 2010.

156   Matt Treacy, *A Tunnel to the Moon: The End of the Irish Republican Army* (Lulu, 2017), p. 44.

157   Brendan Anderson, *Joe Cahill, A Life in the IRA* (Dublin: O'Brien Press, 2003), pp. 177 and 235.

158   Conway, *Southside Provisional*, p. 65.

159   MacCárthaigh, 'The fight goes on', 08tape_sideB01_T005.

160   Hanley and Millar, *The Lost Revolution*, p. 212; Barrett, *Man of Kerry*, p. 56; O'Sullivan, *Patriot Graves*, p. 230. The latter source actually provides photographic evidence and was subsequently banned in the Republic.

161   O'Sullivan, *Patriot Graves*, p. 229.

162   Interview with Labhras Ó Donnghaile, Clare, 6 March 2010.

163   Whether such action (or inaction) comes under the definition of collusion is difficult to determine. Although some of those incidents would certainly be considered individual collusion, it bears little resemblance to collusion as understood in the context of that which occurred between loyalist paramilitaries and the security forces of the northern state. See Anne Cadwallader, *Lethal Allies: British Collusion in Ireland* (Cork: Mercier Press, 2013), pp. 15–16 and 374–6. Patrick Mulroe's book – *Bombs, Bullets and the Border* – contains useful discussions on the multi-faceted relationship between Gardaí and republicans in border areas.

164   Interview with 'Limerick Republican', Limerick, 17 September 2010.

165   See, for example, CJ 4/3730, Security co-operation with the Republic of Ireland (TNA).

166   McCarthy, *Republican Cobh*, pp. 357–8.

167   MacEoin, *The IRA in the Twilight Years*, p. 550.

168   *Irish Times*, 8 October 1971.

169   Kevin Boland, *The Rise and Decline of Fianna Fáil* (Cork: Mercier Press, 1982), p. 40.

170   Interview with 'interviewee B', Limerick, 1 August 2010.

171 *Irish Independent*, 11 August 1971.

172 Bernard, *Daughter of Derry*, p. 89.

173 Interview with 'interviewee A', Limerick, 11 August 2010.

174 McGuire, *To Take Arms*, p. 23.

175 Ibid., p. 35; J.B. Bell, *The Irish Troubles: A Generation of Violence, 1967–1992* (Dublin: St Martin's Press, 1992), p. 165.

176 *Irish Times*, 13 August 1971.

177 Interview with 'interviewee E', Limerick, 16 March 2011.

178 MacCárthaigh, 'The fight goes on', 08tape_sideB01_T005. Crowley was later killed on active service in Northern Ireland. McCarthy had been working in England when the civil rights movement was attacked in Derry in October 1968. He travelled to that city to provide assistance, later returning to Cork to join the IRA there.

179 Interview with 'interviewee E', Limerick, 16 March 2011.

180 Interview with 'interviewee C', Limerick, 25 March 2011.

181 *Irish Times*, 14 August 1971.

182 Ibid., 11 August 1971.

183 *Irish Independent*, 16 August 1971. Parallels can perhaps be drawn with earlier periods where bigoted locals took advantage of turmoil to attack Protestant churches; as with county Clare in 1920–1. See 'Clare 1919–21, a sectarian conflict?' (http://www.warofindependence.info/?page_id=225) (6 June 2013).

184 Foreign & Commonwealth Office, 33/1600 (TNA). Local Official IRA members were suspected of carrying out this attack.

185 Ibid.

186 Ibid.

187 *Irish Times*, 15 October 1971. This attack led to a minor diplomatic dispute as the Irish government refused to pay compensation for what was an Isle of Man-registered vessel. See FCO 33/1600, Acts of Sabotage carried out by Political Extremists in Republic of Ireland.

188 *Irish Times*, 15 October 1971.

189 Interview with 'interviewee E', Limerick, 16 March 2011.

190 Foreign & Commonwealth Office, 87/1 (TNA).

191 McKearney, *The Provisional IRA*, p. 78.

Chapter 4

1   Caroline Kennedy-Pipe, *The Origins of the Present Troubles in Northern Ireland* (London: Routledge, 1997), pp. 54–5.

2   For local reporting, see, for example, *Leitrim Observer*, 5 February 1972; *Connaught Telegraph*, 3 February 1972; *Westmeath Examiner*, 5 February 1972; *Nenagh Guardian*, 5 February 1972.

3   J.B. Bell, *A Time of Terror* (New York: Basic Books, 1978), p. 217. This was a
     legitimate concern for the government; up to 2,000 republican supporters
     clashed with Gardaí and the Irish Defence Forces following the arrest of several
     republicans in Monaghan Town several weeks after Bloody Sunday. *Irish Times*,
     20 March 1972.

4   *Irish Times*, 31 January 1972.

5   *Irish Independent*, 1 February 1972.

6   Ibid.

7   *Irish Times*, 1 February 1972.

8   Ibid.

9   Ibid., 2 February 1972.

10   *Irish Press*, 2 February 1972.

11   *Irish Times*, 2 and 3 February 1972.

12   Ibid., 2 February 1972.

13   *Irish Independent*, 2 February 1972.

14   Ibid; Hanley and Millar, *The Lost Revolution*, p. 174.

15   *Irish Independent*, 3 February 1972.

16   Ibid; *Irish Times*, 3 February 1972.

17   *Irish Times*, 3 February 1972.

18   *Irish Independent*, 1 February 1972.

19   Ibid., 2 February 1972.

20   *Irish Times*, 1 February 1972.

21   Interview with 'Limerick Republican', Limerick, 17 September 2010.

22   *Irish Times*, 4 February 1972.

23   *Irish Independent*, 16 August 1971. Parallels can perhaps be drawn with earlier
     periods where bigoted locals took advantage of turmoil to attack Protestant
     churches; as with county Clare in 1920-1. See 'Clare 1919-21, a sectarian
     conflict?' (http://www.warofindependence.info/?page_id=225) (6 June 2013).

24   *Irish Independent*, 17 February 1972. The victim's brother was serving with the
     RAF: *Irish Times*, 15 February 1972.

25   Interview with 'interviewee B', Limerick, 1 August 2010.

26   MacStiofáin, *Memoirs*, p. 222.

27   *Irish Times*, 1 February and 2 February 1972.

28   *Irish Independent*, 2 February 1972.

29   Interview with Martin Ferris, Kerry, 22 June 2010.

30   Conway, *Southside Provisional*, p. 174.

31   R.W. White, 'From Peaceful Protest to Guerrilla War: Micromobilisation of the
     Provisional Irish Republican Army' in *The American Journal of Sociology*, vol. 94,
     no. 6 (May, 1989), p. 1292.

32   Interview with 'interviewee C', Limerick, 25 March 2011.

33   Bell, *The Gun in Irish Politics*, p. 187.

34   The US government used FARA to try to conclusively prove the NORAID–IRA connection. For a summation of these federal activities, see A.J. Wilson, *Irish America and the Ulster Conflict, 1968–1995* (Washington DC: The Catholic University of America Press, 1995), pp. 85–6.

35   Tim Parkman, *Countering Terrorist Finances: A Training Handbook for Financial Services* (Aldershot: Routledge, 2007), p. 58.

36   *Irish Times*, 20 February 1985.

37   Interview with 'interviewee C', Limerick, 25 March 2011. Early IRA atrocities such as the 'Bloody Friday' bombings in July 1972 were also said to have had a massively negative impact on support from Irish-America. Wilson, *Irish America*, p. 82.

38   Interview with 'interviewee C', Limerick, 25 March 2011.

39   Ibid; Horgan and Taylor, 'Playing the "green card", part 2'.

40   It is generally accepted that the Official IRA was responsible for the majority of the armed robberies in the early part of the conflict. *Hibernia*, 3 August 1973; *Irish Times*, 23 March 1972; George Clarke, *Border Crossing: True Stories of the RUC Special Branch, the Garda Special Branch and the IRA Moles* (Dublin: Gill Books, 2009), p. 88; Hanley and Millar, *The Lost Revolution*, p. 167.

41   *Irish Independent*, 1 January 1972.

42   Foreign & Commonwealth Office, 33/1199 (TNA).

43   Interview with 'Limerick Republican', Limerick, 17 September 2010.

44   Foreign & Commonwealth Office, 33/1593 (TNA).

45   Foreign & Commonwealth Office, 87/165 (TNA).

46   Ibid.

47   Interview with 'Limerick Republican', Limerick, 17 September 2010; A.R. Oppenheimer, *IRA, The Bombs and Bullets: A History of Deadly Ingenuity* (Dublin: Irish Academic Press, 2010), p. 240.

48   One rocket attack on a British army post struck a primary school in Ballymurphy (*Irish Times*, 30 May 1973); another aimed at a police station in Fermanagh hit the roof of a house 200 feet away (*Irish Times*, 14 July 1973). Daithi Ó Conaill subsequently admitted that there had been 'deficiencies' in the IRA's use of rockets (*Irish Times*, 24 August 1973).

49   Interview with 'Limerick Republican', Limerick, 17 September 2010.

50   Cited in Holland, *The American Connection*, p. 89. An internal British Army log of rocket attacks in early 1973 report a number of misfires, rockets striking walls, etc. See Foreign & Commonwealth Office, 87/252 (TNA).

51   Foreign & Commonwealth Office, 87/252 (TNA).

52   'Ulster: consensus and coercion' in *Conflict Studies* (October 1974), p. 9.

53   Bell, *The IRA*, p. 154 (the exception to this would be within the England/overseas dept.).

54   Bradley, *Insider*, p. 108.

55 O'Callaghan, *The Informer*, p. 92; A.F. Parkinson, *1972 and the Ulster Troubles* (Dublin: Four Courts Press, 2010), p. 174.

56 Ed Moloney, *Voices from the Grave, Two Men's War in Ireland* (London: Faber and Faber, 2010), p. 148.

57 McGuire, *To Take Arms*, p. 140.

58 Clarke, *Border Crossing*, p. 185.

59 Moloney, *Voices from the Grave*, p. 150 [italics added for emphasis].

60 Ibid., p. 264.

61 Interview with 'interviewee C', Limerick, 25 March 2011.

62 O'Hearn, *Bobby Sands*, pp. 56 and 72.

63 Interview with Tommy McKearney, Monaghan, 30 July 2013.

64 Interview with 'interviewee D', Clare, 27 March 2010.

65 Ibid.

66 Bell, *The Gun in Irish Politics*, p. 253.

67 Beresford, *Ten Men Dead*, p. 154.

68 *Irish Times*, 15 October 1971.

69 O'Donnell, *Fianna Fáil, Irish Republicanism and the Northern Ireland Troubles*, p. 33.

70 'Political censorship, Section 31' (http://www.rte.ie/archives/exhibitions/681-history-of-rte/705-rte-1970s/139350-broadcasting-section-31/) (6 October 2012).

71 'History' (http://www.rte.ie/about/literature/history.pdf) (14 November 2011).

72 Peter Feeney, 'Censorship and RTÉ' in *The Crane Bag*, vol. 8, no. 2 (1984).

73 Foreign & Commonwealth Office, 87/15 (TNA).

74 Hanley and Millar, *The Lost Revolution*, p. 212. Factional segregation was in place in Portlaoise Prison; interview with Tommy McKearney, Monaghan, 30 July 2013.

75 Hanley and Millar, *The Lost Revolution*, p. 212.

76 Criminal Justice, 4/850 (TNA).

77 Ibid.

78 *Hibernia*, 29 April 1977.

79 Criminal Justice, 4/850 (TNA).

80 *Irish Times*, 22/23 September 1972.

81 Ibid., 26 September 1972.

82 *Fortnight*, 12 November 1971.

83 *Irish Times*, 15 July 1971. That twelve sleeping bags as well as other camping paraphernalia were also discovered on the farmer's land would indicate that this was an IRA training camp rather than just an arms dump.

84 Foreign & Commonwealth Office, 33/1593 (TNA).

85 *Irish Independent*, 28 September 1972.

86 Foreign & Commonwealth Office, 33/1593 (TNA).

87 Department of Justice, 2005/34/194 (NAI).

88 Foreign & Commonwealth Office, 33/1619 (TNA).

89   Department of Justice, 2003/26/7 (NAI).
90   Foreign & Commonwealth Office, 87/43 (TNA).
91   Foreign & Commonwealth Office, 87/1 (TNA).
92   Foreign & Commonwealth Office, 87/43 (TNA).
93   The Special Criminal Court was in place from November 1961–October 1962, during the Border Campaign; introduced following the fatal IRA shooting of an RUC officer. That court was different, however, being presided over by five senior army officers. During that period, twenty-nine men received sentences ranging from four months to eight years. *Irish Times*, 3 October 1962.
94   C.C. O'Brien, *States of Ireland* (London: Faber and Faber, 1972), p. 293.
95   F.F. Davis, *The History and Development of the Special Criminal Court, 1922–2005* (Dublin: Bloomsbury, 2007), p. 139.
96   Foreign & Commonwealth Office, 87/43 (TNA).
97   http://www.irishstatutebook.ie/eli/1972/act/26/enacted/en/html   (31   December 2018)
98   *Final Report on the Report of the Independent Commission of Inquiry into the Dublin Bombings of 1972 and 1973* (February 2005).
99   Foreign & Commonwealth Office, 87/45 (TNA).

Chapter 5

1   Home Office, 4/1762 (TNA).
2   O'Doherty mentions rocket-launchers or a rocket-launcher being available in Derry city in 1971. O'Doherty, *The Volunteer*, p. 106.
3   The initial contact with the Libyans had come about through former QMG, Jack McCabe. *An Phoblacht*, 21 July 2005.
4   Taylor, *Provos*, p. 156.
5   Foreign & Commonwealth Office, 87/263 (TNA).
6   'The Claudia affair' (http://ringcowaterford.blogspot.com/2009_05_17_archive.html) (1 March 2011).
7   *An Phoblacht*, 21 July 2005.
8   *Irish Times*, 15 April 1974.
9   Ibid., 15 April 1974.
10   Department of Justice, 2004//24/4 (NAI).
11   *Irish Examiner*, 16 May 1973.
12   *Irish Independent*, 22 May 1973.
13   Ibid.
14   *Irish Press*, 30 May 1973.
15   *Irish Times*, 18 February 1974.
16   Ceisteanna – questions. Oral answers – Submarine sighting, 1974 (272/1974) (25 April 1974). See also *Irish Times*, 25 April 1974; *Irish Independent*, 14 May 1974; *Irish Examiner*, 14 May 1973.

17   *Belfast Telegraph*, 26 April 1973 and *Evening Herald*, 26 April 1973.

18   *Irish Times*, 1 October 1974; Moloney, *A Secret History*, p. 10. The Mayo-based former-Fianna Fáil TD cited above claimed to have seen the unloading of arms shipments on the west coast.

19   Foreign & Commonwealth Office, 87/263 (TNA).

20   Foreign & Commonwealth Office, 87/392 (TNA).

21   *Irish Independent*, 3 October 1974.

22   Ibid.

23   O'Doherty, *The Volunteer*, p. 167.

24   Foreign & Commonwealth Office, 87/2 (TNA).

25   Ibid.

26   Home Office, 4/821 (TNA).

27   Interview with Kieran Conway, Dun Laoghaire, 25 September 2016.

28   Ó Suilleabháin, *Leitrim's Republican Story*, p. 401.

29   MacCárthaigh, 'The fight goes on', 08tape_sideB01_T005.

30   *Irish Independent*, 11 May 1973.

31   *An Phoblacht*, 3 July 2003 and *Irish Times*, 14 May 1973.

32   *Irish Times*, 30 June 1973 and *Irish Press*, 28 June 1973.

33   *Irish Times*, 2 February 1974.

34   MacCárthaigh, 'The fight goes on', 08tape_sideB01_T005.

35   *Hibernia*, 29 September 1972.

36   MacCárthaigh, 'The fight goes on', 08tape_sideB01_T005. For another example, see 'Engineering firm was front for arms factory, court told' in *Irish Times*, 13 July 1976; *Irish Independent*, 5 January 1976.

37   Foreign & Commonwealth Office, 87/434 (TNA).

38   Ibid.

39   *An Phoblacht*, 6 July 1973.

40   MacCárthaigh, 'The fight goes on', 08tape_sideB01_ T005; *Hibernia*, 24 August 1973; Magee, *Tyrone's struggle*, p. 207.

41   *Hibernia*, 30 November 1973; Max Arthur, *Northern Ireland: Soldiers Talking, 1969 to Today* (London: Sidgwick and Jackson, 1987), p. 200.

42   *Irish Times*, 4 June 1974.

43   MacCárthaigh, 'The fight goes on', 08tape_sideB01_ T005.

44   Home Office, 4/1762 (TNA).

45   Evelyn Brady, Eva Patterson, Kate McKinney, Rosie Hamill and Pauline Jackson (compilers), *In the Footsteps of Anne: Stories of Republican ex-Prisoners* (Belfast: Shanway, 2011), p. 172.

46   J.B. Bell, *IRA: Tactics & Targets* (Dublin: Poolbeg Press, 1993), p. 40. Whether this is the robbery in which James Farrell was killed is not clear.

47   O'Callaghan, *The Informer*, p. 71.

48   *Fortnight*, 12 November 1971.

49   Hanley and Millar, *The Lost Revolution*, p. 118 (the money was later recovered).
50   Sean Flynn and Padraig Yeates, *Smack: The Criminal Drugs Racket in Ireland* (Dublin: Gill Books, 1985), p. 25.
51   *Hibernia*, 3 August 1973; *Irish Times*, 23 March 1972; Clarke, *Border Crossing*, p. 88; Hanley and Millar, *The Lost Revolution*, p. 167.
52   *Irish Times*, 9 August 1974.
53   MacCárthaigh, 'The fight goes on', 08tape_Sideb01_T005; Boyne, *Gunrunners*, p. 245.
54   *Irish Times*, 20 December 1974; interview with 'Claire', Clare, 18 August 2008.
55   *Irish Independent*, 7 May 1974.
56   Ibid., 18 December 1974.
57   Joe Joyce and Peter Murtagh, *Blind Justice* (Dublin: Littlehampton, 1984), p. 26.
58   Bell, *The Gun in Irish Politics*, p. 188.
59   Bell, *The IRA 1968–2000*, p. 189.
60   Ibid., p. 187; interview with 'Limerick Republican', Limerick, 17 September 2010.
61   Interview with 'interviewee C', Limerick, 25 March 2011.
62   *Irish Times*, 21 June 1986.
63   Ibid., 24 February 1978.
64   Ibid., 11 July 1977.
65   Ibid.
66   *An Phoblacht*, 22 June 1973 and 28 June 1974.
67   Ibid., 3 May 1974.
68   *Western People*, 15 June 1974.
69   *An Phoblacht*, 11 October 1974. RTÉ had previously refused to play Barleycorn's song about internment, *The Men Behind the Wire*, on the basis that it was 'not considered a pop song'. *Irish Independent*, 8 January 1972.
70   Taylor, *Provos*, p. 158.
71   MacGréil, *Prejudice and Tolerance*, p. 247.
72   Bell, *The IRA, 1968–2000*, p. 38.
73   Department of Justice, 2004/27/7 (NAI).
74   *Irish Examiner*, 4 December 1973.
75   C.C. O'Brien, *Herod: Reflections on Political Violence* (London: Faber and Faber, 1978), p. 137.
76   Interview with 'Limerick Republican', Limerick, 17 September 2010.
77   Interview with 'interviewee D', Clare, 27 March 2010.
78   Roinn an Taoisigh, 2004/21/105 (NAI).
79   John Waters, *Jiving at the Crossroads* (Belfast: Transworld, 1991), pp. 73–4.
80   T.P. Coogan, *Disillusioned Decades: Ireland 1966–87* (Dublin: Gill Books, 1987), p. 68.
81   No more so than in Northern Ireland where IRA volunteers allegedly stayed in the homes of SDLP supporters while 'on the run'. *Londonderry Sentinel*, 18 November 2012.

82   Interview with Labhras Ó Donnghaile, Clare, 6 March 2010.

83   Ó Suilleabháin, *Leitrim's Fighting Story*, pp. 397–9.

84   *Irish Independent*, 14 October 1974.

85   *Irish Times*, 28 January 1975.

86   Ibid., 5 February 1975.

87   Ibid., 10 July 1973.

88   Ibid., 15 October 1974.

89   Ó Suilleabháin, *Leitrim's Fighting Story*, pp. 397–9.

90   *Irish Times*, 30 July 1974.

91   Ibid., 17 January 1973.

92   Ibid., 9 October 1974; Coogan, *The I.R.A.*, p. 422.

93   *Irish Times*, 16 November 1972; *Irish Press*, 23 November 1972.

94   *Irish Times*, 19 September 1974.

95   *An Phoblacht*, 14 September 1973; *Hibernia*, 5 October 1973.

96   Interview with 'Limerick Republican', Limerick, 17 September 2010. *Irish Times*, 4 February 1975.

97   Bowyer Bell, *A Time of Terror*, p. 224.

98   *Hibernia*, 1 February 1974.

99   Ibid., 12 April 1974.

100   'TV50: battle stations', RTÉ One. Broadcast on 27 July 2012.

101   Ibid.

102   Foreign & Commonwealth Office, 87/626 (TNA). A number of addresses – now redacted – were provided in the letter. It is not recorded whether the Gardaí acted on this information.

103   '*Bráthadóirí*', TG4. Broadcast on 19 August 2010.

104   *Hibernia*, 24 May 1974.

105   *Lost Lives*, pp. 426–7.

106   See, for example, Kevin Myers in *Irish Times*, 24 March 1996.

107   RTÉ   documentary   (http://www.rte.ie/radio1/doconone/2009/0609/646016-rumours/) (31 December 2018).

108   *An Phoblacht*, 10 May 1974.

109   Coogan, *The I.R.A.*, p. 404.

110   Interview with 'interviewee D', Clare, 27 March 2010.

111   MacCárthaigh, 'The fight goes on', 08tape_sideB01_ T005.

112   *Irish Times*, 20 May 1972.

113   *An Phoblacht*, March 1973. Hoban was a Mayo man and, prior to his imprisonment, was responsible for organising and overseeing the numerous training camps that took place in the Newport area. The prison statement noted that there were forty-two prisoners in the 'Glasshouse', over one-third of whom were married and thirty of whom were from Northern Ireland.

114   *An Phoblacht*, May 1973.

115   Coogan, *The I.R.A.*, p. 426.

116   Interview with Martin Ferris, Kerry, 22 June 2010.

117   *Hibernia*, 22 October 1976.

118   *Irish Times*, 1 July 1974.

119   *Irish Independent*, 19 August 1974.

120   Durney, *On the One Road*, p. 189.

121   'The Irish Behind Bars', TV3. Broadcast on 19 April 2012.

122   *An Phoblacht*, 11 October 1974.

123   Bell, *The Secret Army*, p. 411. Ten of the nineteen escapees were from the South. *An Phoblacht*, 23 August 1974.

124   *Irish Independent*, 2 January 1975; *Irish Times*, 1 January 1975.

125   MacCarthaigh, 'The fight goes on', 09tape_sideB01_T005.

126   Barrett, *Martin Ferris*, p. 59.

127   See Taylor, *Provos*, p. 199; Bishop and Mallie, *The Provisional IRA*, p. 310; McKearney, *The Provisional IRA*, pp. 138–41.

128   R.W. White, 'The 1975 British–Provisional IRA truce in perspective' in *Eire-Ireland*, 45 no. 3/4 (autumn/winter, 2010), p. 227.

129   *Irish Independent*, 24 August 1974.

130   Richard O'Rawe, *Blanketmen: An Untold Story of the H-Block Hunger Strike* (Dublin: New Island Books, 2005), pp. 72–3.

131   *Hibernia*, 9 April 1976.

132   *Clare Champion*, 10 December 2010.

133   White, *Provisional Irish Republicans*, p. 134.

134   Ruairí Ó Brádaigh Papers, POL 28/22, James Hardiman Library (National University of Galway). It should be noted that the first Provisional Sinn Féin meeting largely comprised cumainn from Dublin, Dun Laoghaire, Clare, Donegal, Leitrim, Meath, Monaghan, Roscommon and Galway. The first executive including men and women from Limerick, Leitrim, Louth, Roscommon, Galway, Westmeath, Fermanagh, Dublin and Clare. *Irish Independent*, 12 January 1970.

135   *Clare People*, 9 December 2014.

Chapter 6

1   *An Phoblacht*, 6 January 2000.

2   McKittrick et al., *Lost Lives*, p. 512.

3   Ó Suilleabháin, *Leitrim's Republican Story*, p. 334.

4   *Irish Times*, 15 December 1972. All five young men were active service IRA volunteers at the time of their arrest. Ó Suilleabháin, *Leitrim's Fighting Story*, p. 334.

5   *Irish Times*, 24 January 1975.

6   Ibid., 28 June 1973.

7   Ibid.

8   *Irish Times*, 19 January 1976.

9   Ibid., 22 July 1975.

10   Ibid., 15 March 1976.

11   *Irish Independent*, 15 February 1977.

12   Indeed, by the latter part of the decade, the British Army concluded that there was a noticeable 'evolutionary improvement' in their explosives' capabilities. Glover, 'Future terrorist trends', p. 12.

13   Bell, *IRA: Tactics & Targets*, p. 50; Oppenheimer, *IRA, The Bombs and Bullets*, p. 42; W.H. Van Voris, 'The Provisional IRA and the limits of terrorism' in *The Massachusetts Review*, vol. 16, no. 3 (summer, 1975), p. 421.

14   Ibid., p. 99.

15   Coogan, *The I.R.A.*, p. 257.

16   *Irish Times*, 24 February 1978.

17   Interview with 'Limerick Republican', Limerick, 17 September 2010.

18   *Irish Times*, 28 September 1974 and 11 July 1977.

19   *Irish Times*, 11 July 1977; interview with 'Limerick Republican', Limerick, 17 September 2010.

20   *Hibernia*, 16 December 1977.

21   Interview with Tommy McKearney, Monaghan, 30 July 2013.

22   Kevin Rafter, *Sinn Féin, 1905–2005* (Dublin: Gill Books, 2005), p. 202.

23   Coogan, *The I.R.A.*, p. 412. This operation was a local initiative, unsanctioned by the leadership. See 'Mná an IRA', episode one (Rose Dugdale), TG4. Broadcast on 5 January 2012.

24   *Irish Times*, 10 June 1974.

25   That this was not a sanctioned IRA operation was accepted by the Dutch government from the beginning. Foreign and Commonwealth Office, 87/437 (TNA). It should be noted, however, that some of the kidnappers had previously been Provisional IRA activists.

26   *Irish Times*, 6 October 1975.

27   Interview with Kieran Conway, Dun Laoghaire, 25 September 2016.

28   Foreign and Commonwealth Office, 87/437 (TNA). The British Embassy in Dublin also notified their government that a member of the Garda Special Branch had warned them to be extra vigilant as the area between Tullamore and Monasterevin was full of IRA sympathisers.

29   Ibid.

30   Joyce and Murtagh, *Blind Justice*, p. 329

31   For instances of strike actions at the plant, see *Irish Press*, 24 and 25 September 1971; *Irish Independent*, 29 February 1972; *Irish Times* 3 January 1973.

32   Conflict Archive Northern Ireland (cain.ulst.ac.uk) lists more than thirty IRA killings of British security forces in 1975.

33   For example, a seven-county command had operated during the S-campaign of 1939–40. Bell, *The Secret Army*, p. 169.

34   According to one interviewee, MacStiofáin had forbade members of the Dublin-based GHQ from travelling over the border for some time during the early 1970s. This undoubtedly caused resentment among Northern volunteers. The establishment of separate commands allowed for or even necessitated the creation of a parallel GHQ of sorts, with a distinctive Northern Command Quartermaster General, for example. Interview with 'Limerick Republican', Limerick, 17 September 2010.

35   *Phoenix*, 21 November 1986.

36   The last Southern Chief-of-Staff was Tipperary man, Eamonn Doherty, in the summer of 1974. Moloney, *A Secret History*, p. 513.

37   Brendan Hughes complained that Daithi Ó Conaill had 'not visited Belfast except during the [1972] ceasefire'; Moloney, *Voices from the Grave*, p. 150. Ó Conaill delivered the Easter oration at Belfast's Milltown cemetery the following year; *Irish Press*, 1 May 1973.

38   Interview with Tommy McKearney, Monaghan, 30 July 2013.

39   O'Callaghan, *The Informer*, p. 73; 'Ulster: consensus and coercion' in *Conflict Studies* (October 1974), p. 9.

40   Bell, *The IRA*, p. 154 (the exception to this would be within the England/overseas dept.).

41   Percentage collated from 'Republican roll of honour, 1969–2012' (http://www.anphoblacht.com/contents/1420) (13 February 2013).

42   Interview with 'Limerick Republican', Limerick, 17 September 2010.

43   Interview with 'interviewee D', Clare, 27 March 2010.

44   This is based on prison records. See Raymond Murray, *Hard Time: Armagh Gaol, 1971–1986* (Cork: Mercier Press, 1998), p. 79.

45   Interview with 'Limerick Republican', Limerick, 17 September 2010.

46   Ibid.

47   Hanley and Millar, *The Lost Revolution*, p. 219.

48   Holland and McDonald, *INLA*, p. 52.

49   Interview with Seán O'Neill, Limerick, 30 March 2011.

50   Department of Justice, 2006/933/770 (NAI).

51   Frank Stagg's father was a lifelong republican who had fought in the War of Independence and Civil War as part of the Second Western Division. *Irish Independent*, 13 February 1976.

52   *Irish Independent*, 13 February 1976.

53   *An Phoblacht*, 1 February 2016.

54   Coogan, *The I.R.A.*, p. 417. Several years earlier, a priest from County Mayo declared that any 'person, group or organisation' had the right to use controlled force as a means of achieving legitimate aspirations. *Irish Independent*, 2 January 1972.

55   Roinn an Taoiseach, 2003/26/7 (NAI).

56   *Irish Press*, 28 April and 24 June 1976.

57   Foreign and Commonwealth Office, 87/513 (TNA). Thornley had previously refused to condemn the burning of the British Embassy following Bloody Sunday. This was reported at the time and was likely not forgotten by the British. *Irish Times*, 4 February 1972.

58   *Irish Times*, 26 April 1976.

59   Foreign and Commonwealth Office, 87/513 (TNA)

60   Myler Magrath, *The Comic History of Irish Politics* (Cork: Mercier Press, 1977), p. 52.

61   Tim Pat Coogan, *The Troubles* (London: Zeus, 1996), p. 381.

62   *Irish Times*, 7 February 1977.

63   Ibid., 5 February 1977.

64   For *The Irish Times*' three-part investigation, see 14, 15 and 16 February, 1977.

65   Interview with 'interviewee D', Clare, 27 March 2010.

66   *Hibernia*, 4 November 1977.

67   Interview with Seán O'Neill, Limerick, 30 March 2011.

68   *Bottom Dog*, 6 August 1976.

69   Interview with Seán O'Neill, Limerick, 30 March 2011.

70   Interview with Martin Ferris, Kerry, 22 June 2010.

71   Ibid.

72   Patsy McArdle, *The Secret War* (Cork: Mercier Press, 1984), p. 39.

73   Raymond Smith, *Garret, The Enigma: Dr. Garret FitzGerald* (Dublin: Aherlow Publishers, 1985), p. 317; Garret FitzGerald, *All in a Life: An Autobiography* (Dublin: Gill and Macmillan, 1991), pp. 314–15.

74   O'Brien, *Herod*, p. 77.

75   C.C. O'Brien, *Memoir: My Life and Themes* (Dublin: Profile Books, 1999), p. 355.

76   *Magill*, June 1978.

77   *Irish Times*, 18 March 1975.

78   *An Phoblacht*, 15 March 2017 and *Irish Times*, 27 September 1975. The jury at the inquest expressed concerns that not all evidence and testimony were made available to them and that they were willing to continue the inquest. The coroner, Mr Philip Meagher, stated that this was unnecessary.

79   Department of Justice, 2003/26/7 (NAI). The latter included the destruction of buildings or particular crimes that could lead to loss of life.

80   *Irish Times*, 24 March 1975.

81   Ibid. See also *Irish Times*, 25 February 1975 and 26 May 1975 for a continuation of such searches.

82   'Portlaoise Prison, for security reasons' (Portlaoise Prisoners' Relatives Action Committee, no date).

83   Gallagher, *The Irish Labour Party*, p. 205; *Irish Times*, 6 February 1975.

84   *Irish Times*, 7 February 1975. The publicity bureau was linked to the Provisional republican movement.

85   MacCarthaigh, 'The fight goes on', 09tape_sideB01_T006. See also *Irish Times*, 2 May 1975.

86   'Statements by prisoners and prisoners' relatives relating to conditions in Portlaoise prison, solitary confinement, strip searching, visiting etc.', MS 44, 183 /6, O'Mahony Papers (NLI).

87   *Irish Press*, 16 July 1976.

88   O'Mahony Papers, MS 44, 183/6 (NLI).

89   Ibid.

90   White, *Ruairí Ó Brádaigh*, p. 387.

91   *Irish Times*, 24 July 1976.

92   Ibid., 23 July 1976.

93   Home Office, 325/276 (TNA).

94   *Irish Times*, 1 March 1977. For more on this fiasco, see *Magill*, November 1977 and March 1979.

95   *Magill*, November 1977, February 1978 and March 1979.

96   Home Office, 4/1753 (TNA).

97   Roger Faligot, *Britain's Military Strategy in Ireland* (Dingle: Zed Books, 1983), p. 108. Cleary, an IRA volunteer from South Armagh, was captured and killed by the SAS allegedly while trying to grab one of his captors' rifles. This account is disputed by republicans. McKittrick et al., *Lost Lives*, p. 640.

98   Interview with Kieran Conway, Dun Laoghaire, 25 September 2016.

99   Joyce and Murtagh, *Blind Justice*, p. 121; Walsh, *The Final Beat*, p. 61

100   Foreign and Commonwealth Office, 87/513 (TNA).

101   Paul Larkin identified *The Irish Times* as being particularly 'heavily populated' with journalists of such a political persuasion (Larkin, *A Very British Jihad*, p. 81). Indeed, its political reporter Dick Walsh socialised with and advised members of the Official republican leadership (Hanley and Millar, *The Lost Revolution*, p. 205). Hanley and Millar's book details many Official-linked journalists, as well as pillars of academia such as John A. Murphy, who provided a character reference for Official IRA Chief-of-Staff, Cathal Goulding, when he appeared in court on charges of 'incitement to cause explosions' in 1971 (Ibid., p. 244). Television broadcast staff were no less likely to have a preponderance of Workers Party devotees (Ibid., pp. 271–3 and 280).

102   Ó Danachair, *Provos*, p. 62. The British keenly followed the editorial lines of various Irish media, noting any journalist who was potentially sympathetic or not overtly hostile to the IRA. Following an interview conducted by Vincent Browne with Seamus Twomey in 1977, the British Embassy noted, 'It is unlikely that any of the Irish dailies – even the *Irish Press* – would carry an interview of this kind. Vincent Browne, who did the *Sunday Independent* interview, has since been

demoted to a less influential role. The *Hibernia*, on the other hand, seems to be becoming more and more overtly sympathetic to the IRA ... It includes none of the aggressive questioning which would have been directed against any politician in the Republic.' Foreign and Commonwealth Office, 87/626 (TNA).

103 C.C. O'Brien, *Passion and Cunning and Other Essays* (London: Paladin, 1990), p. 321.

104 Coogan, *The I.R.A.*; p. 422; FitzGerald, *All in a Life*, p. 318.

105 O'Brien, *Passion and Cunning*, p. 315.

106 Danny Morrison (ed.), *Hunger-Strike, Reflections on the 1981 Hunger-Strike* (Dingle: Mount Eagle Publications, 2006), p. 77.

107 Foreign and Commonwealth Office, 87/439 (TNA).

108 *Irish Independent*, 29 December 2006.

109 MacEoin, *Survivors*, p. 368.

110 Foreign and Commonwealth Office, 87/490 (TNA).

111 Ibid.

112 Ibid. and Home Office, 4/3730 (TNA).

113 *Irish Independent*, 5 October 1976. See *Irish Independent*, 31 July 1976 for the first stirrings of IRA policy change.

114 The Cork-based *An Phoblacht* publication of the mid-1960s (unrelated to the later Provisional newspaper) noted that permission had been given by the IRA leadership for three volunteers to recognise the courts, potentially as a Trojan horse for policy change. *An Phoblacht*, September 1965.

115 MacEoin, *The IRA in the Twilight Years*, p. 853.

116 Bell, *The Secret Army*, p. 247; Patterson, *The Politics of Illusion*, p. 88; Brendan Lynn, 'Republicanism and the abstentionist tradition, 1970–98' (http://cain.ulst.ac.uk/issues/politics/docs/lynn01.htm) (13 March 2013).

117 Malachi O'Doherty, *The Telling Year: Belfast, 1972* (Dublin: Gill Books, 2007), p. 132. O'Doherty believes that court recognition was merely the ostensible reason for Dutch's expulsion, being linked to internal power struggles or personality clashes.

118 See *Irish Press*, 8 March 1972 and 10 February 1973; *Irish Independent*, 6 June and 18 October 1973; *Irish Times*, 28 June 1973 and 30 October 1974.

119 Interview with Lawrence Murray, Clare, 20 August 2008. Brady et al., *In the Footsteps of Anne*, pp. 49, 115 and 308–10.

120 O'Doherty, *The Volunteer*, p. 194.

121 O'Rawe, *Blanketmen*, pp. 16–17.

122 *Irish Independent*, 12 April 1972.

123 Eunan O'Halpin, *Defending Ireland: The Irish State and its Enemies since 1922* (Oxford: Oxford University Press: 1999), p. 325.

124 O'Rawe, *Blanketmen*, p. 16.

125 Interview with 'interviewee C', Limerick, 25 March 2011.

126 Interview with Labhras Ó Donnghaile, Clare, 6 March 2010.

127   O'Malley, *The Uncivil Wars*, p. 305.

128   *Irish Independent*, 18 October 1976.

129   *Irish Independent*, 5 October 1976; *Irish Press*, 16 October 1976.

130   *Irish Independent*, 6 October 1976.

131   Bradley claims the directive was introduced simultaneously on both sides of the border. Bradley, *Insider*, p. 187.

132   Coogan, *The I.R.A.*, p. 424.

133   Foreign and Commonwealth Office, 87/725 (TNA)

134   Extract collated from 'A day in the life of a prison Provisional', *Irish Times*, 25 April 1977 and *Hibernia*, 3 December 1976.

135   Interview with Martin Ferris, Kerry, 22 June 2010. Indeed, *Hibernia* questioned the government's failure to transfer prisoners to the Curragh where £200,000 had been spent on maintenance and upgrade since 1972. Common perceptions of the Curragh as a POW camp very likely made the government reticent. *Hibernia*, 29 April 1977.

136   O'Mahony Papers, MS 44, 183/7 (NLI).

137   Coogan, *The I.R.A.*, p. 427.

138   O'Mahony Papers, MS 44, 183/7 (NLI).

139   O'Mahony Papers, MS 44, 183/6 (NLI).

140   Ibid. and MS 44, 183/7 (NLI).

141   *Irish Press*, 5 September 1984.

142   O'Mahony Papers, MS 44, 183/7 (NLI).

143   Ibid.

144   O'Mahony Papers, MS 44, 183/6 (NLI).

145   Ibid.

146   Ibid.

147   Barrett, *Martin Ferris*, p. 79.

148   O'Mahony Papers, MS 44, 183/6 (NLI).

149   *Irish Press*, 5 September 1984.

150   O'Mahony Papers, MS 44, 183/6 (NLI).

151   '*Garda ar Lár*' (Garda Michael Clerkin), RTÉ One. Broadcast on 9 February 2009.

152   Foreign and Commonwealth Office, 87/513 (TNA).

153   *Irish Independent*, 31 December 1974.

154   Ibid., 17 October 1976.

155   Walsh, *The Final Beat*, p. 69.

156   '*Garda ar Lár*' (Garda Michael Clerkin).

157   *Irish Press*, 10 November and 13 November 1976.

158   Foreign and Commonwealth Office, 87/626 (TNA).

159   Home Office, 4/1753 (TNA).

160   Ibid.

161   Ibid.

162 Ibid.
163 Foreign and Commonwealth Office, 87/626 (TNA).
164 *An Phoblacht*, 13 October 2005.
165 Coogan, *The I.R.A.*, p. 418.
166 *Irish Times*, 20 April 1977. See also Gallagher, *The Irish Labour Party*, p. 205.
167 *Irish Times*, 18 April 1977.
168 *Hibernia*, 29 April 1977.
169 MacCarthaigh, 'The fight goes on', 09tape_sideB01_T006 and Barrett, *Martin Ferris*, p. 102.
170 Sweeney, *Down, Down, Deeper and Down*, p. 126.
171 H.R. Penniman (ed.), *Ireland at the Polls – The Dáil Elections of 1977* (Washington DC: AEI Press, 1978), p. 58.
172 *Hibernia*, 24 June 1977 [italics added for emphasis].
173 Interview with Martin Ferris, Kerry, 22 June 2010; Coogan, *The I.R.A.*, p. 428.

Chapter 7

1 These calls were ultimately rebuffed by NI Secretary Roy Mason in the House of Commons on 22 September.
2 *An Phoblacht*, 1 February 1978.
3 The British Embassy in Dublin issued a particularly cautionary note as Irish newspapers were covering Mason's comments prominently. Foreign & Commonwealth Office, 87/808 (TNA).
4 Martin Dillon, *Killer in Clowntown: Joe Doherty, The IRA and the Special Relationship* (London: Cornerstone, 1992), p. 63.
5 Interview with 'Limerick Republican', Limerick, 17 September 2010. That the Portuguese offer – or allegations of one – predate the arrest of Seamus Twomey in Dublin in 1977 is perhaps significant. If there is any veracity in the claims, it might show a mellowing of Twomey's stance or an example of Northern Command overriding GHQ.
6 *Irish Times*, 26 April 1977.
7 *Magill*, 1 August 1978.
8 *Irish Times*, 30 April 1981. Several years later, Republican Sinn Féin condemned the arrest of Otelo Saraiva de Carvalho, one of the leading leftist generals behind the 1974 revolution in Portugal. See *Saoirse*, August 1988.
9 *Newsletter*, 19 January 2015.
10 'An index of deaths from the conflict in Ireland' (http://cain.ulst.ac.uk/sutton/chron/1978.html) (17 May 2012).
11 Roinn an Taoisigh, 2008/148/702 (NAI).
12 McCann, *War and an Irish Town*, p. 106. See also *Irish Times*, 8 August 1973 for their use.

13   Dervla Murphy, *A Place Apart: Northern Ireland in the 1970s* (Harmondsworth: Eland Publishing, 1978), p. 261.

14   *Irish Times*, 13 October 1975. For further examples, see Magee, *Tyrone's Struggle*, pp. 169–70.

15   *Irish Times*, 15 October 1977.

16   Indeed, according to a former member of the Royal Army Ordnance Corps, 1976 was statistically one of the busiest years of the conflict. Arthur, *Northern Ireland: Soldiers Talking*, p. 112.

17   Despite this ban, 'box bombs' saw occasional use in subsequent months. See, for example, *Irish Times*, 19 July 1978.

18   Hansard, House of Commons Debates, vol 942, c755W (26 January 1978).

19   Ken Wharton, *Wasted Years, Wasted Lives: Vol II: The British Army in Northern Ireland, 1978–79* (Warwick: Helion and Co., 2014), p. 161.

20   'Letters to the editor' in *Irish Times*, 1, 3 and 4 September 1979.

21   *Irish Independent*, 4 April 2005.

22   *New York Times*, 3 October 1979.

23   Glover, 'Northern Ireland, Future Terrorist Trends', p. 4.

24   Foreign & Commonwealth Office, 87/976 (TNA).

25   Ibid.

26   *Magill*, June 1979.

27   Home Office, 4/3730 (TNA).

28   Ibid.

29   Ibid.

30   *An Phoblacht*, 15 June 2000.

31   *Westmeath Examiner*, 5 February 1977.

32   Foreign & Commonwealth Office, 87/490 (TNA).

33   *Irish Times*, 10 December 1977.

34   Ibid., 24 March 1979.

35   Foreign & Commonwealth Office, 87/906 (TNA).

36   Foreign & Commonwealth Office, 87/490 (TNA).

37   Home Office, 4/2316 (TNA).

38   Durney, *On the One Road*, p. 192.

39   *Irish Times*, 15 February 1979.

40   Ibid., 29 August 1978.

41   Ibid., 20 February 1979.

42   Ibid., 9 February 1979.

43   Ibid., 24 December 1979 and McKittrick et al., *Lost Lives*, p. 811.

44   *Irish Press*, 22 February and 10 December 1977 and 13 July 1978.

45   Glover, 'Northern Ireland, Future Terrorist Trends', p. 6.

46   *Irish Times*, 20 February 1985.

47   Ibid., 24 February 1978.

48   Ibid., 28 June 1978. It should be noted that subversive organisations were consistently regarded as being responsible for about one-third of armed robberies in the state, albeit the more lucrative ones. See *Irish Times*, 29 November 1977 and 4 September 1978.

49   Ibid., 9 August 1979.

50   *Hibernia*, 4 November 1977.

51   Ibid., 8 July 1978.

52   Ibid., 5 September 1978.

53   *Irish Independent*, 8 and 9 June, 1978. Interview with Seán O'Neill, Limerick, 30 March 2011; Coogan, *The I.R.A.*, p. 429.

54   Interview with 'interviewee D', Clare, 27 March 2010.

55   *Wexford People*, 29 January 2013.

56   *Irish Times*, 19 June 1980.

57   Ibid., 5 January 1981.

58   *Magill*, September 1980.

59   *Irish Times*, 19 June 1980.

60   Information collated from *Irish Times*, 8, 9 and 13 August 1979 & McKittrick et al., *Lost Lives*, p. 793.

61   *Donegal News*, 11 February 1978.

62   McKittrick et al., *Lost Lives*, p. 743.

63   Foreign & Commonwealth Office, 87/626 (TNA).

64   Foreign & Commonwealth Office, 87/725 (TNA).

65   Ibid.

66   Interview with 'interviewee C', Limerick, 25 March 2011.

67   'Brian Moore RIP'; *Green River: In Honour of Our Dead* (Beechmount, 1998), p. 38. Morrison's friendship with Proinsias MacAirt was said to have secured him the position of editor. See White, *Provisional Irish Republicans*, p. 155.

68   *Hibernia*, 19 September 1975; 'Brian Moore RIP'.

69   *Hibernia*, 8 February 1978.

70   Ibid.

71   Ibid., 17 January 1980.

72   Foreign & Commonwealth Office, 87/626 (TNA).

73   Ibid.

74   *Republican News*, 17 September 1977.

75   Roinn an Taoisigh, 2007/116/743 (NAI).

76   The IRA killed three prison officers in 1976 and 1977, respectively. Two were killed in 1978. Information collated from Conflict Archive Northern Ireland (cain.ulst.ac.uk).

77   *An Phoblacht*, 2 September 1978.

78   Foreign & Commonwealth Office, 87/626 (TNA).

79 For example, relatives of prisoners claimed that violent strip-searching continued in 1978 and onwards. 'Portlaoise Prison, for security reasons'.

80 Home Office, 4/3302 (TNA).

81 Ibid.

82 Ibid.

83 *An Phoblacht*, 22 April 1978.

84 Home Office, 4/4640 (TNA).

85 Protestor numbers began to breach the 1,000-mark again. See, for example, *Irish Times*, 3 March 1980.

86 Foreign & Commonwealth Office, 87/725 (TNA).

87 Interview with 'interviewee D', Clare, 27 March 2010.

88 Mitchell, *Northern Ireland: Soldiers Talking*, pp. 136–8.

Overview

1 See 'B Specials and UVF stormed in' in *Irish Press*, 19 August 1969. The British tribunal which was established to investigate the cause and course of this violence rejected claims that the RUC or B Specials aided loyalist mobs. Feeney and Bradley, however, have highlighted how selective was the inclusion of testimonies to this tribunal. See *Violence and civil disturbances in Northern Ireland in 1969, report of the tribunal of inquiry by the honorary Mr Justice Scarman* (Belfast, 1972), pp. 14–19 and Bradley, *Insider*, pp. 30–5.

2 Interview with 'interviewee D', Clare, 27 March 2010.

3 O'Donnell, *From Vinegar Hill to Edentubber*, pp. 51–5; Flynn, *Soldiers of Folly*, p. 155.

4 Sinn Féin had remained proscribed in Northern Ireland until shortly before the collapse of the Sunningdale executive. Taylor, *Provos*, p. 165.

5 See, for example, Bean and Hayes, *Republican Voices*.

6 *Irish Press*, 4 April 1973; Coogan, *The I.R.A.*, p. 351.

7 Thomas Hennessey, *The Evolution of the Troubles, 1970–72* (Dublin: Irish Academic Press, 2007), p. 194; Maguire, *IRA Internments and the IRA*, pp. 4–5 and 208.

8 Taoiseach Jack Lynch's threats to introduce internment in December 1970 met with a wave of protests across the state, for example. See *Irish Times*, 14 December 1970, 12 January and 18 January 1971.

9 Roinn an Taoisigh, 2004/21/105 (NAI).

10 O'Malley, *The Uncivil Wars*, p. 75.

11 MacGréil, *Prejudice and Tolerance*, 305; Joseph Ruane and Jennifer Todd, *The Dynamics of Conflict in Northern Ireland: Power, Conflict and Emancipation* (Cambridge: Cambridge University Press, 1996), pp. 252–3; Desmond Fennell, *Heresy: Battle of Ideas in Modern Ireland* (Belfast: Blackstaff Press, 1993), p. 198.

12   *Irish Press*, 18 and 23 August 1976; *Irish Times*, 13 October 1976; Faligot, *Britain's Military Strategy*, p. 208.

13   Interviews with 'interviewee D', Clare, 27 March 2010 and 'Limerick Republican', Limerick, 17 September 2010.

14   White, *Provisional Irish Republicans*, p. 133.

15   A 1984 interview of Danny Morrison by Gene Kerrigan is one such example. The questions asked by Kerrigan seem predicated upon acceptance of their being an internal struggle along left–right, North–South divisions. See *Magill*, September 1984.

16   See Chapter 2 for a discussion of prisoner numbers in the Republic.

17   *Hibernia*, 24 August 1973.

18   O'Brien noted one case of jury intimidation but made no concession to the notion of popular support for militant republicanism; O'Brien, *States of Ireland*, p. 293.

19   Edward O'Brien was an example in a later period. For local reaction to news of his death and IRA involvement, see *Irish Times*, 22 February 1996.

20   Interview with 'interviewee C', Limerick, 25 March 2011.

21   Oppenheimer, *IRA, The Bombs and Bullets*, p. 151.

22   A 2006 report prepared under the direction of the British Chief-of-General-Staff for the Ministry of Defence stated: 'It should be recognised that the Army did not "win" in any recognisable way.' See *Operation Banner*, paragraph 855. Some years previously, former British Head of Armed Forces in Northern Ireland, James Glover stated in an interview: 'In no way can, or will, the Provisional IRA ever be defeated militarily.' *The Guardian*, 16 June 2000.

INDEX

abstentionism 8–9, 15–17, 20

Adams, Gerry 28, 162, 165–166

Ahern, Anthony 39–40, 97–98

Aiken, Frank 135

Amnesty International 164

An Phoblacht 103, 111, 113, 148, 155, 165

    establishment of 64

    merge with *Republican News* 161–162

    raids of Dublin offices 108

    report on H-Block protest 164

    sales of 48

An Phoblacht-Republican News (*AP/RN*) 162

Andrews, Todd 109

Anglo-Irish Treaty (1921) 23, 25

Anglo-Irish War 25, 59

Antwerp arms seizure 155, 158

Aontacht Éireann 105

armed robberies 78, 101–103, 117–118, 158–160

arms acquisitions 59–63

arms dumps 14, 31, 53, 59–60

arms factories 99

arms importation 79, 92–100, 103, 155

arms possession 86–87, 135, 169

arms shipments see arms importation

Army Council 3, 50, 115, 122, 137, 171

    allegiance to 33

    ban on use of box bombs 151

    decision to recognise the courts 38

    expansion of 8, 9

    organisation of 34

Atkins, Robert 154

bank robberies 102, 120, 159

Barron Report 89

Barry, Tom 24, 63, 75

Belfast

    Falls Curfew 43

    Provisional IRA bombing of 91

    Provisional IRA volunteers from 123

Belfast Brigade 13–14, 22, 60, 85, 114–115

Bell, Geoffrey 36

Bell, Ivor 162

Benbulbin mountain, County Sligo 163

Birmingham pub bombings 114

Bloody Sunday 74–77, 101

    1978 commemoration 148

    response of Official IRA to 75–76

Bodenstown, County Kildare 4, 10, 65, 103

Boland, Kevin 63, 69

bombs see weapons

border counties 30

Bradley, Gerry 65

Brendon, Piers 23

British Army 28, 73, 143

    Falls Curfew 43

    Operation Motorman 91

British–Irish Security Cooperation 142–144, 156

'Brits Out – Peace In' slogan 162–163

Broadcasting Authority Act (1960), Section 31 of the 83, 127, 132

Browne, Bernard 160–161

Browne, Noel 88

Burke, Christy 113

Cabhair Uladh 47, 84
Cahill, Joe 67, 120, 149, 165
   on abstentionism 17
   arms importation 92, 94
Carrigtwohill, County Cork 53
Carty, Patrick 98
Castleconnell, County Limerick 37
Catholic Church 22
Section 31 (of the Broadcasting Act 83, 132
civil rights campaign 22, 26–27
Civil War 25, 26, 30, 31, 52
Clan na Gael 11–12
Clann na Poblachta 25
Clare, County 25, 30, 32, 35, 52
Claudia 92–95, 105
Cleary, Peter 132
Clerkin, Michael 141
Coen, Kevin 116–117
Collins, Gerry 154, 159
Comic History of Irish Politics, The 126
communism 4–5
Connacht 31, 43
Connolly Youth movement 10
Conway, Kieran 41, 67, 77, 97, 98, 132
Coogan, Tim Pat 132
Cook, Judith 130–132
Cooney, Patrick 112, 114, 129, 133, 142,
   146
   on lawlessness 102
   on prisoners and their rights 113
   on support for the Provisionals in
      Portlaoise 145
Cooper, Frank 153
Corish, Brendan 84
Cork city, republican politics in 9–10
Cork, County 35–36
Cosgrave, Liam 106, 125, 170
Costello, Seamus 4, 8, 9, 15, 36
Coughlan, Anthony 3
courts, non-recognition of 135–137
credit union movement 7

Criminal Law Act 132
Cronin, Seán 22
Crowley, Dermot 39, 40, 70, 97, 98, 117
Cruise O'Brien, Conor 105, 128, 132–133,
   146
Crumlin Road Gaol 84
Cubbon, Brian 130–131
Cumann na gCáilíní 38
Cumann na mBan 10, 98
Curragh Camp 84–85, 112
Currie, Austin 158

Dáil Éireann 15, 16, 89, 94
Dáil Uladh 64
Dálaigh, Mai 134
de Valera, Éamon 6
defence groups 13
demilitarisation 11, 19
Derry 15, 24
Devlin, Bernadette 17
Doherty, Anthony 'Dutch' 136
Doherty, Joe 149
Doherty, Pat 82
Donegan, Patrick 92, 134
Donoughmore, Lord and Lady 119–120
Drumm, Jimmy 161
Drumm, Máire 18, 22, 115
Dublin, 1974 bombing 110
Dugdale, Rose 112

Easter lilies 49–50
Ei Electronics factory, Shannon, County
   Clare 5
Éire Nua 64
Ellis, Dessie 25, 31
Emergency Powers Bill 132, 134, 135, 142
England, IRA bombs in 91
European Convention on Human Right 169
European Court of Human Rights 135, 147
European Economic Community (EEC) 65
Ewart-Biggs, Christopher 130–133, 134

Explosives Act (1875) 59
explosives 53–59, 172
    arrests for manufacture of 96
    fertiliser-boiling 58–59, 96–97, 117
    gelignite 107
    homemade 57–58, 117

Falls Curfew, July 1970 43
Farrell, James 101
Faul, Fr Denis 158
Feakle, County Clare 115
Ferris, Martin 32, 67, 76, 127, 140
    on conditions in Portlaoise prison 112
    on incarceration policies of coalition
        government 138
Fianna Fáil 25, 73, 89, 91, 105, 106, 145
    clamping down on militant
        republicanism 107–111
    on collection of 'defence' funds 47
    control of possession of gelignite 55
    media censorship 83
Fine Gael–Labour coalition 91, 144
Finglas, County Dublin 31
firearms 99
FitzGerald, Garret 127–128, 156
Fitzpatrick, Seán 8
Flynn, Phil 120
Foreign Agents Registration Act (FARA) 78
Forsa Cosanta Aitiuil (FCA) 61, 69
Fortnight 50, 54
Fox, Billy 110–111
Freedom Struggle 105
funding 47–50, 77–80, 100–103, 158–161

GAA 107
Gallagher, Eddie 120
Gardaí
    abuse of suspects 164
    discovery of IRA bomb factories 154
    'heavy gang' 126–128, 164, 165
Garland, Seán 13

Garvey, Ned 131
Garvey, Seán 93, 94
Gaughan, Michael 104, 124, 125
General Army Convention 8, 9, 10, 13, 19,
    34
Gladstone, W.E. 23
Glover, James 153
Glover Report 158
Goulding, Cathal 8–9, 13, 15, 17, 25, 36,
    171
    and the 1968 Bodenstown
        commemoration 10
    leadership of the IRA 1, 6
    support for 33
Green, John Francis 116, 134
Guildford attacks 114

H-Blocks 140, 148, 163, 164, 165
Harris, Lord William 133, 134
Harrison, George 60
Haughey, Charles 49
Hazelton, Stanley 158
Hehir, Hugh 99
Henderson, Tony 51
Herrema, Tiede 120
Hibernia 59, 65, 109, 110, 145, 146, 162
    description of Dáil Uladh conference
        64
    and police brutality 126
Higgins, Gerry 9
Hillery, Patrick 134
HMS Maidstone 159
Hoban, Dan 112, 145
Holland, Mary 133
housing committees and co-ops 7
Hughes, Brendan 28, 51, 53, 81–82, 162
hunger strikes 49, 84, 106, 129, 144, 152,
    167
    in the Curragh 85
    by Michael Gaughan 104
    in Portlaoise prison 145, 164

incident centres 121–122
internment 47, 69–72, 147, 169
IRA
    1975 truce 114, 116
    1978–1980 147–167
    activity in the South 117–121
    border campaigns 1, 143
    clashes with the State 124–125
    decline in activity in late 1970s 154–158
    post-ceasefire restructure of 121–124
    role in the 'Troubles' 169
    tolerance for the 84
    volunteers 170
Irish Civil Rights Association 165
Irish Defence Forces 61, 69, 83, 107, 124, 154
Irish Independent 55, 74, 76, 102, 142
Irish Industrial Explosives factory, Enfield
    107, 117
Irish National Liberation Army (INLA) 36,
    37, 38, 124, 157
Irish Press 132
Irish question 23–24
Irish Republican Publicity Bureau 129
Irish Republican Socialist Party (IRSP) 127
Irish Times, The 5, 16, 48, 51, 149, 158
    on arms importation attempts 103
    on disturbances after Bloody Sunday 74
    on Garda 'heavy gang' 126
    on IRA training camps 50
Irish Transport and General Workers'
    Union (ITGWU) 75
Irish Workers' Party 3

John Paul II, Pope 152
Johnston, Roy 3–5, 7, 8, 9
judges, sentences issued by 86–88
juryless courts 172

Kelly, Gerry 67
Kelly, Liam 16
Keohane, Joe 62–63

Kerry, County 30, 33
Kerryman 63
kidnappings 119–121

La Mon hotel attack, County Down 150
land issues 24–25
Lane, Jim 9, 15, 34
Lawlor, John 156–157
Leinster 41
Limerick city 34
London bombings, 1973 81
Loughran, Seamus 115
Loughran, Seán 98
Lynch, Conor 36
Lynch, Jack 7, 13, 35, 71, 88, 144, 147
    August 1969 speech 28
    and Bloody Sunday 76
    and the INLA 36

MacBride, Seán 62, 112
McCabe, Jack 58
MacCárthaigh, Gearóid 10–11, 36, 39, 59,
    97–98, 114, 129
    arrest of 41
    on conditions in Portlaoise prison 113
    and Gardaí visit to Light Machine
        Services factory 101
    on mortar training camps 100
    on republican movement in north
        Kerry 30, 37
    resignation from the IRA 3–4
    unlicensed collection after internment
        67
McCarthy, Donal 70
McCaughey, Seán 112
McElvenna, Peadar 157
MacEoin, Uinseann 30
McGahon, Hugh 85
MacGiolla, Tomás 15, 20
McGirl, John Joe 136
MacGréil, Fr Mícháel 66

McGuinness, Martin 112, 123
McGuire, Maria 70, 81
McInerney, Denis 92, 94
McIntyre, Anthony 28
McKearney, Tommy 24, 113
McKee, Billy 19, 84, 114, 115, 162
McKenna, Sean 134
McMahon, Thomas 152
McMillen, Billy 13, 18, 19
McNamara, Michael 140
MacStiofáin, Seán 3, 4, 9, 70, 76, 81, 171
    on arms acquisitions 59–60
    as Chief-of-Staff of the Provisional IRA
        10
    on developing supplies of explosives 58
    distribution of rosary edition of *United
        Irishman* 7–8
MacTomáis, Éamonn 108
Magee, Pat 26
Magee, Paul 149
Magill 149, 160
Maguire, Tom 34
Makowski, Brigid 66
Mallon, Kevin 16, 67–68, 111, 113, 115
Maloney, Oliver 109
Marita Ann arms importation attempt 103
Martin, Eva 100
Martin, Leo 113, 145
Meehan, Martin 81
membership of the IRA 62, 94, 132
    denial of 137–138
    in the South 32–37
Mise Éire (film) 26
Moloney, Ed 28, 78
Monaghan, 1974 bombing 110
Monaghan, Jim 33–34
Morrison, Danny 162
Mountbatten, Louis 152
Mountjoy Prison 83–84, 128
Mulcahy, Susie 10
Mullaghmore, County Sligo 152

Munster 42
Murphy, Dervla 150

Na Fianna Éireann 38, 39
National Graves Association 8
National Liberation Front (NLF) 2, 3
Nationalist Party 16
Neave, Airey 148
Nelis, Mary 133
Nelson's Pillar, Dublin 6
New Left Review 16
NORAID 78, 101
North America 78
Northern Command 122
Northern Ireland Office 101

Ó Brádaigh, Ruairí 7, 13, 25, 51, 65, 101,
    115
Ó Brádaigh, Seán 10, 64
O Briain, Justice Barra 164
Ó Conaill, Daithí 60, 65, 81, 100, 115, 137,
    145
Ó Dálaigh, Cearbhall 134
Ó Duill, Father Piaras 128, 129
Ó Muimhneacháin, Colman 108
Observer 133
O'Callaghan, Seán 4, 100, 101
O'Doherty, Shane Paul 58, 136
O'Donnell, Phil 52
O'Duffy, Eoin 30
Offences against the State Act, Section 30 of
    the 37, 136
Official IRA 1, 13, 32
    and bank robberies 102
    court recognition 37
    Derry city 24
    disapproval of bombing campaigns 38
    membership in 1970 36
    statement following Bloody Sunday
        75–76
    training camps 51, 70

O'Grady, John 157
O'Hagan, J.B. 98, 111, 113, 115
O'Hare, Desmond 157
O'Hare, Gerry 120
O'Leary, Martin 13
O'Leary, Michael 88
O'Malley, Des 55
O'Malley, Padraig 170
O'Neill, Joe 140
Operation Harvest 1, 12, 40, 49, 50, 52
O'Rawe, Richard 136

peace attempts 114–115
Peace People 150, 171
People's Democracy 84
police brutality 126–128
Portlaoise prison 111–114, 127, 128–130,
    144–145, 165
    conditions of prisoners at 138–142
    Provisional IRA prisoners in 44
    treatment of visitors by prison staff 139
Portuguese Communist Party 149
Prison Officers Association 139, 141
prison sentencing 108
prisons, republicans in 37
Progressive Democrats 67
propaganda 162
Provisional Army Council 34
Provisional IRA
    bombing campaign in N. Ireland 53
    clashes with the Southern state 83–89
    composition in the South 37–45
    early politics of 63–65
    feuds between Official IRA and 34–35
    formal establishment of 9
    Freedom Struggle 11
    identification with Catholicism 22
    North–South divisions 80–82
    in the Republic, 1970 21–45
    split and emergence of, 1962–9 1–20
    support for 21, 29–31

Provisional republican movement see
    Provisional IRA
Provisional Sinn Féin 2, 9, 11

QE2 60
Quaid, Seamus 159
Quinn, Patrick 39

Republic of Ireland
    deaths and casualties during the
        'Troubles' 168
    IRA membership levels in 32–37
    republican prisoners in 111–114
    support for militant republicanism in
        the 66–69, 103–107
Republican News 30, 31, 64, 65, 161, 162
republicanism, in rural Ireland 6
Rogers, Peter 159
Rossiter, Bernard 133
Royal Ulster Constabulary (RUC) 12, 143,
    151
RTÉ 28, 29
Ryan, Eamon 160

Sallins train robbery 127, 159
Sands, Bobby 149
Saoirse (film) 26
Saor Éire 71–72, 88, 101, 127
Saor Uladh 16
sectarianism 22
Shevlin, Myles 38
Sinclair, Betty 4
Sinn Féin
    1978 ardfheis 165
    'Ireland today' 2–3
    relationship between IRA and 65
    split in January 1970 9
Smith, Thomas 128
Socialist Republican Alliance 120
solitary confinement 138
South, the see Republic of Ireland

Special Branch 109, 126
Special Category status, for prisoners in
    Northern Ireland 122, 144
Special Criminal Court 37, 88, 135
Stack, Brian 140–141
Stagg, Emmet 124–125
Stagg, Frank 51, 124–125
Stagg, Joe 165
Steele, Jimmy 18
Stormont 16
Stratton Mills, W. 54
Sullivan, Tom 140
Sunday Independent 5, 132
Survivors (MacEoin) 30
Sykes, Richard 155, 156

Thornley, David 125
training camps 12, 50–52, 91, 148
Treacy, Sean 67
'Troubles'
    British soldiers killed on active service
        46
    deaths up to 1972 89
    origin of the 11
    toleration and sympathy in Republic
        during 66–69

Twomey, Seamus 19, 112, 115, 123, 124,
    149, 161
    capture of 155
    escape from Mountjoy prison 111
Tyrone, County 24–25

Ulster Defence Regiment (UDR) 100
Ulster Volunteer Force (UVF) 28–29, 116
unionist marching season 29
United Irishman 7

Walsh, Gerard 93, 94
Warrenpoint ambush 151
Washington Post 133
Waters, John 106
weapons 11–15
    box bombs 150–151
    machine guns 148–149
    manufacture of 99
    mortars 96, 99–100, 151
Wexford, County 31
Whelan, Donal 93, 94
Where Sinn Féin Stands 2, 3, 9, 10, 11, 64
White, Larry 127
Whitten, Herbert 51